Urban Space and Representation

Edited by Maria Balshaw
and Liam Kennedy

Urban Space and Representation

Pluto Press
LONDON • STERLING, VIRGINIA

First published 2000 by Pluto Press
345 Archway Road, London N6 5AA
and 22883 Quicksilver Drive,
Sterling, VA 21066–2012, USA

British Library Cataloguing in Publication Data
A catalogue record for this book is available from
the British Library

ISBN 0 7453 1349 3 hbk

Library of Congress Cataloging in Publication Data
Urban space and representation / edited by Maria Balshaw and Liam
    Kennedy.
        p.   cm.
    ISBN 0–7453–1349–3 (hbk.)
    1. Open spaces—United States. 2. City and town life in
literature. 3. Arts, Modern—20th century—United States—Themes,
motives. 4. Arts, American—Themes, motives. I. Balshaw, Maria.
II. Kennedy, Liam, 1946–   .
HT167.U7534 2000
307.76'0973—dc21   99–37925
                                                       CIP

Designed and produced for Pluto Press by
Chase Production Services, Chadlington, OX7 3LN
Typeset from disk by Stanford DTP Services, Northampton
Printed in the EU by TJ International, Padstow

Contents

Acknowledgements

The editors would like to thank the Arts and Humanities Research Board for their generous support of Dr Balshaw's research during the writing of this project. We would also like to thank the AHRB for their continued support of the *Three Cities* project, based at the University of Birmingham and the University of Nottingham. The collaborative work we have engaged in as part of the *Three Cities* project has been very important to the collection; particular thanks go to Professor Douglas Tallack and Dr Anna Notaro.

We also gratefully acknowledge the support of the University of Birmingham in providing for Dr Kennedy's research leave, and Dr Kennedy would like to thank the University of Iowa's IFUSS programme for generously hosting his three-month research sabbatical in the USA. We would like to thank Anne Beech at Pluto Press for her enthusiastic support of this project, and for the patience Pluto have shown in awaiting its completion.

We extend our gratitude to the colleagues and friends whose work, support and criticism have shaped the intellectual framework of the collection. We would particularly like to thank all the members of the Birmingham Urban Cultures group – notably Peter Brooker, Jude Davies, Danielle Fuller, Matthew Hilton, Michael Green, Helen Laville, Carol Smith – whose lively discussion and enthusiastic commitment to urban studies have helped provide a focus for this collection. Great thanks are also due to all the contributors to this volume, whose excellent work and commitment to the collection have made the editorial task much easier.

Finally, as academics who have shared personal as well as intellectual commitments we would like to thank all those whose childcare and domestic assistance made writing and editing this book possible: without Colette and Walter Balshaw, Cath Wood, Helen Laville and Scott and Ryan Lucas this book would never have reached its end. This book is dedicated to Nathan and Jake Kennedy who remind us that intellectual work is not the only pursuit we are involved in.

Photographs

George Bellows, *New York*, 1911, collection of Mr and Mrs Paul Mellon, photograph copyright of Board of Trustees, National Gallery of Art, Washington.

George Bellows, *Blue Morning*, 1909, Chester Dale collection, photograph copyright of Board of Trustees, National Gallery of Art, Washington.

Maria Balshaw and Liam Kennedy,
University of Birmingham

Introduction: Urban Space and Representation

The city, long a subject for cross-disciplinary study in the humanities and social sciences, has in recent years become the focus of a great deal of new theoretical work by scholars in the increasingly distended fields of urban studies. This current thinking highlights the spatial formations of urban identity and calls into question commonplace conceptions of the city as a synthetic totality, pointing to a loss of coherence or legibility in the category of 'the city'. An important result is that the city, as a universal object or category of analysis, has been demythologised and positioned as a site of spatial formations produced across diverse discursive regimes and everyday practices. This thinking – aided by common perceptions of the heightened semiology of urban experience at the end of the twentieth century – has helped spur the dissemination of fresh theoretical interest in urban studies across many disciplines. This collection of essays brings together new work which reflects and expands upon this theorising while focusing upon cultural productions and textual representations of urban space.

Space and Representation

Space has become an increasingly irrepressible metaphor in contemporary cultural and critical theorising and a point of convergence for the work emerging from the disciplinary meltdown of the humanities and, to a lesser extent, of the social sciences. This is already apparent, for example, with geographers' attraction to the spatial models of Michel Foucault, Giles Deleuze and Felix Guattari and the literary theoretical discourses of bell hooks, Homi Bhabha and Fredric Jameson among others. David Harvey observes that literary theory has 'permeate[d] social theory' in analysis of urban space while others point to the emergence of a new 'cultural geography' embracing aesthetics and cultural critique.[1] There has been a generation of new vocabularies which are reframing questions of identity, location, positionality, territoriality, diaspora and interstitiality. These disciplinary and theoretical convergences and intersections (which, to continue our use of spatial metaphors, still require some form of critical mapping) have not provided a unitary method or agreed-upon lexicon of terms and issues. However, as theory itself travels from one locus to another, we can detect the emergence of a common interest: the making of space as a social product.

Our common understanding of space is that it is simply there, intangible but given. Attempts to fix it in language can quickly tumble into tautologies and negations – not surprisingly, as we can no more think outside of metaphorisations of space than we can live outside its representations. To approach space as a social product, though, prompts fresh consideration of the instrumentality of space as a register not only of built forms but also of embedded ideologies. This entails a demystifying of space as natural and transparent so that it is understood as a social entity with particular, localised meanings. Such demystification has already been well advanced by the work of Foucault, Henri Lefebvre, Edward Soja and others who have tapped the critical potentials of spatiality as a positive response to the decline of historicism (the waning sense of history and grand narratives) in the postmodern era. For Foucault, space can no longer be treated as 'the dead, the fixed, the undialectical, the immobile'; it is to be understood as intricately operative in the constructions of social power and knowledge.[2] While Foucault's explicit commentary on space is dispersed in fragments of prose and interviews, Lefebvre has produced voluminous mediations on 'the production of space', advancing schematic and typological analyses which have had a major impact on contemporary studies of urban space and spatiality.) Soja has built on the ideas of these French theorists in Anglo-American contexts through his analysis of how space becomes 'filled with politics and ideology', both inscribing and concealing the contradictions of global capitalism.[3]

Questions of representation figure centrally in the work of these theorists on the production of urban space, though often in a querulous or anxious form. Lefebvre wants us to see that space is not simply the parameter or stage of social relations and actions, rather it is operative in the 'assembly' of these. He argues that traditional dualities of physical space and mental space are bridged by the processes of the production of space, especially as these are enacted through 'spatial practice' which he founds not on political economy (the more obvious Marxist focus), but on the material experience of social relations in 'everyday life'. While stressing the complexities of interconnections between physical and mental space, he has reservations about what he sees as the 'predominance of the readable and the visible' in interpretations of space. Interpretation, he argues, always 'comes later, almost as an afterthought' to the production of social space; '"reading" follows production in all cases except those in which space is produced especially in order to be read'.[5] Soja too has worries about the 'illusion of transparency' in conceptions of space, though his complaint is both more acute and more sweeping: 'Social space folds into mental space, into diaphanous concepts of spatiality which all too often take us away from materialized social realities.' In their critiques of transparency Lefebvre and Soja are concerned that images or textual representations of reality may be attributed a false 'epistemological precedence' over the realities of lived social space.[7] This seems a legitimate concern given their interests in how space can conceal relations of power. 'Nothing can be taken for granted in space' Lefebvre writes, 'because what are involved are real or possible acts, and not mental states or more or less well-told stories'.[8] However, statements such as these, while well-founded in political terms, also delimit the role of representation (and more particularly its cultural forms – ideational, narratological and imagistic) in the production of space.

While not ignoring issues of transparency we need also to consider the formations and functions of the illusory power of representation. The city is inseparable from its representations, but it is neither identical with nor reducible to them – and so it poses complex questions about how representations traffic between physical and mental space. Rob Shields recognises a key aspect of this complexity: '"The City" is a slippery notion. It slides back and forth between an abstract idea and concrete material.'[9] While this is a useful reminder of the basic instability of perception, sliding back and forth between the subject and object of attention, it also suggests that critical analysis needs to be attentive to this slipperiness and its spatialisation in cognitive (and less conscious) apprehension of 'the city'. To put this once again in terms of representation: the relationship between material and imaginary spaces is one that is rendered opaque as well as transparent by the force of representation. We need to understand not only the will to transparency in representations of urban space but also its necessary correlate, the production of opacity – this correlation is ever active in the illusory power of representation to render space 'legible'.[10] To focus exclusively upon transparency as a veil of power leaves us contesting 'false' representations – a useful enough practice and one that can have political effect – but may blind us to the ambiguous, overlapping and disjunctive relations, the slippage, between transparency and opacity in the production of space. It may also blind us to the fresh transparencies of our critical analyses, the forms and products of which cannot simply be cut free from systems of representation. We do not propose that the generative relations between space, ideology and representation can readily be typologised or simply 'interpreted', but they can be brought under analysis, with the under-standing that representation provides us with an illusory – partial and provisional – framing of the city as a legible space.

In this volume the (il)legibility of urban space is the focus of much critical attention. Analysis of the formations and functions of the illusory power of representation is one of the ways in which scholars from literary, film and cultural studies can contribute to the new under-standings of space and spatiality. They bring particular disciplinary perspectives and interpretative practices, which both illuminate the workings of and question assumptions about representation. The making of urban space invites theoretical consideration of the conditions and effects of the signifying practices, discourses and images that give it legible form. Representation does powerful cultural work in a wide variety of forms to produce and maintain (but also to challenge and question) common notions of urban existence. Literature, film, architecture, painting, tourist guides, postcards, photography, city plans – all provide selective representations of the city and shape the metaphors, narratives and syntax which are widely used to describe the experience of urban living. Analysis of visual and textual representations of urban space is not simply a study of images of place or narratives of urban consciousness. Rather it responds to the cultural work of repre-sentations of urban space, which offer us specific readings and visual practices for approaching the spatiality of the city.

While it should be clear that we do not want to subsume urban space into analytical formations of textuality and visuality, this must be iterated more directly as these are common enough approaches in forms of literary and visual studies. The elucidation of the 'city as text', for example, has long been favoured by literary critics, stimulated in part by modernist and postmodernist literary representations of the city, though perhaps also signifying a will to interpretative power on the part of those schooled in techniques of textual interpretation. At any rate, we are wary of models that posit the city as analogous to language as these all too often decontextualise and relativise their object – as in William Sharpe's and Leonard Wallock's view that 'like a literary text, the city has as many interpretations as it has readers'.[11] While there can be no doubt that language plays an important part in shaping our comprehension of the city, representation also involves material, visual and psychic forms and practices that cannot be reduced to textuality.

Having disclaimed, as most urban theorists will, the errors of abstraction and relativism, we still have to pause to consider Soja's worry that when '[s]ocial space folds into mental space' the urban real is displaced by the urban imaginary. We pause, in order to submit that it is this very enfolding of these spaces that characterises the meanings of urban space in fields of representation. The production of urban space is simultaneously real, symbolic and imaginary; what it produces is a

material environment, a visual culture and a psychic space. Recognition
of this simultaneity of and in representation does not (necessarily) 'take
us away from materialised social realities', not unless we assume that
representational forms (always) transcend or exist autonomously from
what they represent. As John Phillips notes in his study of Singapore in
this volume, 'symbolic stories [of the city] intersect with the built
environment and with planning grids'. These stories are neither
transparent descriptions of nor abstract substitutes for 'Singapore';
indeed, as Phillips convincingly argues, 'no "text" from Singapore
represents its urban space, for urban space itself is Singapore's chief mode
of representation ... the distinction between material and text is not
pertinent'. To be sure, this sufficiency of Singapore's self-metaphorisation
is not a 'truth' of all cities, rather it is the historical condition of a city
which 'has no history outside or beyond urbanism'. However, Phillips'
reading of the symptomatic spatiality of Singapore is an exemplary interpretation of the simultaneous workings of material, visual and psychic
productions of urban space.

Phillips' essay is also suggestive of the ways in which efforts to 'read'
or 'see' the city function as quests for legibility which will explain much
more than is apparently represented by 'the city'. On the one hand, we
recognise that questions of legibility have long stimulated efforts to 'plan'
or 'map' the city; to render it legible has also meant to make it coherent
and knowable, integral and governable. But we are also conscious that
efforts to read or see the city can produce metaphorical procedures which
all too easily idealise their object and function as quests for revelatory
meaning. Donald Preziosi suggests that,

> what urban studies is clearly after, by and large, is what does not
> (quite) 'meet the eye'; what escapes (almost) the immediate perception
> (or memory) of cities and their parts: what, behind the glittered
> quiddity of the city, can be constru(ct)ed as its (hi)story. The city's
> truth: always to be found (sought) in some *place* – at the city's heart,
> on its margins, in close sweaty rooms up against some freeway, in
> somebody's board room ...[12]

What Preziosi addresses here is our fascination with the ways in which
cities '[touch] upon certain indispensable constructions of our modernity'
and our postmodernity. This search for the city's truth is a central fantasy
of much modern and postmodern urban aesthetics and theorising. With
the modernists it is apparent in the universalising perspectives on the
city 'as a state of mind' in urban sociology, art and literature and in the
heroism of vision of architects and planners.[13] For the postmodernists,
the perceptual distance necessary for such perspectives has collapsed; as
space becomes the 'cultural dominant' of postmodernity there is an
intensified experience of signification which leaves the human subject

disoriented in hyperspace.[14] And yet, the postmodernists cannot resist searches for the truth of the city and the sweep of metaphor they entail: Soja famously finds that 'It All Comes Together in Los Angeles', the paradigmatic site of the global present and template of future urban relations.[15]

Against such sweeping treatments of the city as a metaphor for the condition of society as a whole, we want to present analyses of urban spaces and places which are more particular and partial in scope. At the same time, we do not want to erase the city from analysis for it clearly persists (whatever the bleak diagnosis of planners, or the lofty dismissals of theorists) as an imaginary totality which compellingly symbolises generalised desires and anxieties – often, those configured around the meanings of nationhood, citizenship, urbanity and justice. We also recognise that the desire for legibility is a powerful animus in representations of urban space. Al Deakin, in this volume, shows that the Victorian need to 'domesticate' the city by knowing it whole is interrogated by Charles Dickens' representation of the disabled body as site of 'fear and loathing' in public space. Liam Kennedy also identifies this animus in his analysis of cinematic treatments of postmodern urbanism, where he finds that efforts to synthesise the meanings of Los Angeles in selected films produce images of a 'paranoid spatiality', especially around questions of race and gender. These analyses remind us that urban space and subjectivity are intricately related and that we can analyse the formations of conscious and unconscious responses to urban scenes in literary and visual representations. As psychic space the city resonates with not only conscious but also unconscious impulses; it is often figured as 'uncanny', a space of displacement and dislocation in which repressed material erupts in paranoid or obsessional form. Literary and visual representations of urbanism map the fears and fantasies of urban living, within which – through practices of reading and seeing – we all dwell.

Questions of subjectivity and urban space are also commonly evoked by the notion of place. Places are imbued with affective connotations, charged with emotional and mythical meanings; the localised stories, images and memories associated with place provide meaningful cultural and historical bearings for urban individuals and communities. Some theorists argue that place is being erased by the spatial experiences of late capitalism – the simulacral, the hyperreal, the depthless – and by the global 'flows' of information and images.[16] However, the idea of place should not be hastily theorised away, for it reminds us that space is not only metaphoric but also metonymic in its productions. Places are sites of spatial contiguity, of interdependence and entailment, which take on contours of identity and location through representation. They can, as Peter Brooker argues here, 'provide sites of momentary, memorable definition in lives of heterogeneous flux'. Even as place provides a point of settlement and definition, though, its contours remain contested and porous, and so affective responses to place often make it the locus of struggles over 'representational rights'. Stephen Shapiro refers to such strategies here in his examination of protests surrounding Tompkins Square Park in Manhattan as the focus of local, national and global relations. In our direct attention to place as well as space we want to consider how representations of urban coexistence respond to the lived intersections of urban social relations.

Through the provisional legibility provided by representation the making of urban space becomes available for analysis. In this volume, the study of literary and visual practices in the construction of narratives and images illuminates the processes of this 'making'. Our analyses of narratives and images do not seek to 'prove' theory, rather to supplement it (and, at times, test it) by providing analytical foci presaged by the cultural work of representation. The essays collectively map ways in which study of urban space has become an area of confluence in literary, visual and cultural studies and provide useful trajectories for further critical inquiry. The scope of thematic concerns and arguments is broad but by no means exhausts the relevant lines of critical engagement with representations of urban space. Throughout, questions of space and representation act as key organising concepts around which the essay chapters are structured: space and vision; spaces of difference; and (post)national spaces.

Space and Vision

Urbanism privileges, even as it distorts, vision and the visual. The twentieth century has witnessed a proliferation of new visual technologies, forms and texts that have affected the ways in which the urban landscape is represented and inhabited. Visual representation may be said to bring the city into focus: it frames recognition of urban forms (architectural syntax, street signage); it offers legibility through the reproduction of what is seen (in maps, plans, guides and images); it unites aesthetic and spatial apprehension of the urban scene (levels, planes, perspectives); it mediates scopophilic and voyeuristic desires (to look, to be seen); it technologises the act of seeing (the fusion of the eye and the camera lens). The new forms of visual representation and apprehension have been credited with accentuating the growing abstractions of space in this century and inaugurating the 'society of the spectacle' in urban form. The design and building of the cityscapes of New York and Chicago at the turn of the century, for example, encoded new visual understandings of urban space as spectacle – the expanding production of monumental buildings visualised progress itself and popularised the visual delights of the panorama. Attention to the visual components of urbanism is essential to an understanding of how cities frame and are framed by representation.

It would be possible to write a history of space by tracing the history of different forms and modes of visual representation. This might show us, for example, how the rationality and formal logic of one-point perspectivism gives way to the immediacy and dialectical logic of photographic seeing, and further show us how these different models of vision have worked to structure the position of the viewing subject in relation to social reality. However, such histories of vision can be reductive, ignoring or downplaying what Anthony Vidler calls 'the problem of "carry over"' which emerges due to the survival of what may seem to be historically outmoded optical 'models of spatial structure' (a point taken up by Douglas Tallack's essay in this volume).[17] Moreover, visual experience is not reducible to a formal typology of 'ways of seeing'. There are multiple modes of vision, what Martin Jay calls 'scopic regimes', active at any point in history, and so 'the scopic regime of modernity may best be understood as a contested terrain, rather than as a harmoniously integrated complex of visual theories and practices'.[18] The concept of 'scopic regimes' also summons up questions of power and ideology, reminding us that the operations of the eye are not only biological and formal, but also cultural and psychological. If attentive to the 'condition of visibility' in representations of urban space, we can analyse ways in which space and vision modify each other in producing partial perceptions of urban life.[19] Vision may be ubiquitous but its workings are not all transparent.

This broadened consciousness of the condition of visibility is a concern of many essays in this volume, not just those in the first section. The relationship between power and vision is a recurrent issue, as it functions in the intersubjectivity of looking relations, the sexualising and racialising of vision, the sighting of the body as spectacle, the production of surveillance and the authorisation of images (see the essays by Balshaw, Kennedy and Brooker). The essays in this section examine selective representations concerned centrally with issues of vision and visualisation and consider how space is not simply an issue but also a practice in visual arts and culture. Painters and photographers reconstruct and redefine space in their creative activities, illuminating its constructedness as a component of vision and visibility, while filmmakers have long recognised the plasticity of space – cinema is commonly cited as 'the modernist art of space par excellence.'[20] Painting, photography, cinema and television all disseminate certain techniques of visualising and seeing the city, imaging it in both familiar and unfamiliar forms (mapping transitions in physical and mental space, locating and dislocating the viewing subject's relation to the city as a space of representation). Moreover, critical analysis of these mediums has stressed the spatial relations of vision in the practice and positionality of spectatorship (the very concept of the spectator has come to be understood as a particularly 'modern' urban figure, engaged in a commodified and aestheticised relation to the city, wherein the act of looking is also an act of consumption).[21]

Douglas Tallack's essay engages with current critical theorising on representations of space to question the theoretical suspicion and diminution of 'stubbornly optimistic attempts to represent urban space and achieve a point of view'. In particular, he seeks to question the binarisms of 'mapping' and 'representing' as these have been configured in some discourses of visual theory. He pursues this questioning through analysis of the work of the Ashcan School of American painters whose speciality was the painting of New York city locales in the early twentieth century. While acknowledging the role of traditional perspectivalism and other conventions of representational art, Tallack notes an urge to abstraction in the painting. The result is 'a tension between the dominant representationalism and an incipient modernism', deriving not from an internal transformation of painting itself but from an attempt to 'know' the new spatio-temporal dimensions of the city (both within and beyond the frame of the local scene represented). The most telling indication of this tension is the effort to construct a point of view in the painting which will relate place and space to both centripetal and centrifugal forces shaping the emergent infrastructure of the city. What is being painted is 'a need to know more than could actually be seen', an indeterminate 'space of appearance'. While the point of view sought cannot literally be realised, Tallack argues that the Ashcan painters produce a suggestive anamorphism of barely visible infrastructures of the developing urban economy.

Richard Ings, like Tallack, is interested in the imbrication of space and vision, the coming together of sites of the urban and sights of the city, and the struggle for legibility this can entail. His essay examines how Harlem has functioned as a place of self-definition for black inhabitants and a space of representation for both white and black photographers. More particularly, he analyses the work of the black photographer Roy DeCarava as it appears in *The Sweet Flypaper of Life* (1955), a photo-text that is 'sequenced and stitched together' by the fictional text of Langston Hughes. The book is both a 'snapshot of black life' in a particular time and place, 'a kind of family album' structured around the family of an elderly black woman, and an imaginative reterritorialisation of black culture in urban space. Identifying an 'inner/outer pulse in the narrative' which foregrounds links between the private and public spaces of Harlem, Ings examines how the images draw our attention to the relationship between subjectivity and urban topography, the body and built space, depicting ways in which black people transform an 'unsympathetic urban architecture' (cramped rooms, stoops) into communal and civic spaces.

While Hughes seems seamlessly to suture photographs and narrative Ings detects a discordance between image and text, most notable in Hughes' insistent annotation of ideologemes of 'family' and 'community' to images which are ambiguous in their significations of urban social relations. The disjunction between text and image is itself instructive Ings finds, as it highlights both the interdependence and asymmetry of textuality and visuality in representations of urban space. It implies not just the resistance of the image to narrativisation but its dialectical relationship to the subject photographed – the relationship between viewer and subject, past and present. In Ings' words, 'however compromised the space depicted by the camera, it is also *lived* space'.

Ings and Tallack examine the relationship between the abstractions of the image and the everyday urban life it represents. In doing so they value the possibilities of dialectical insight. For Tallack, this inheres in the anamorphic qualities of the painterly image, the (symptomatic) coordination of a moment of infrastructural change in the city. For Ings, it is the glimpses of 'a community struggling to be seen', not fully indentured to the world of appearances; a world rendered visible not so much in the image of the photograph as in 'the act of photography: the shutter rapidly opening and closing'. Knowledge is not simply secured by vision in their texts, but there are points and moments of apprehension and comprehension in the visualisations of urban space. Such possibilities of critical insight are much diminished in the visual worlds and practices examined in Pascal Pinck's essay on television news and the new technology of the skycam. Drawing on the theories of Paul Virilio and others, Pinck presents a rich discussion of the distinctive temporal and spatial features of television which make it an instantaneous 'interface' with and 'part of the organisation of the city'. Television's intense coincidence with spaces of everyday life instantiates new spatial relations between the private and the public, the visible and the invisible and the familiar and the unfamiliar. The 'flow' of the television image lends an illusory, compensatory continuity to spatial relations, with the image working as a kind of 'revolving window, providing access to disparate, dislocated worlds'. Pinck provides a striking case study for these concerns with the example of the TV skycam; helicopter-based cameras that are increasingly used in local television news broadcasts in the United States. While noting historical origins and precedents of the skycam, Pinck argues that the 'postmodern sprawl of Los Angeles' is 'ideal territory for the airborne lens', bringing a new legibility to a city that is 'opaque from ground level'. The skycam, invisibly tied to the local news broadcast, reinaugurates the modern desire for legibility; it makes the city both knowable and governable through its panoramic surveillance and its 'line-of-sight' access to both private and public spaces. It literally invades the space of appearances, both symbol and tool of 'television's visual and technological dominance'.

Televisual space may or may not be the visual space of our urban futures, but it is an increasingly powerful mode of representation of the urban present. Tallack wryly states 'there is no one place from which to view modernity' and notes that the efforts of one painter to project such a place posits a point of view that is simply not available in physical terms: 'It would have been somewhere in mid-air with no place ... from which this sight could be seen in this way.' Pinck offers an implicit response with his argument that there are multiple spaces from which to see postmodernity, afforded by the skycam technology, 'the optical source is itself visibly mobile as the camera's point of view is cut loose from earthly tethers'. It is this untethered point of view which promises to reenchant our connections to the city (and our belief in the 'urban-real') – notably to the city as a dysfunctional space of natural disasters, crime scenes and traffic congestion – as we survey the erotics of the naked city bared to the insistent, intrusive airborne gaze and are disconnected from the lived space of our urban environments. The consequences of the growing dominance of the televisual city have barely begun to be charted – at the very least it offers a thoroughgoing challenge to our capacities for dialectical understanding of urban space through representation.

Spaces of Difference

Sharon Zukin has observed: 'The ambiguity of urban forms is a source of the city's tension as well as of a struggle for interpretation.'[22] In other words, questions of (il)legibility and (in)visibility are implicated in representation as struggles for power and identity. This is perhaps most obviously marked in the categories of spatial duality – of inside and and outside, of self and other – which often work to naturalise the symbolic order of the city, reproducing social divisons and power relations. The operations of power are everywhere evident in space, for space is hierarchical – zoned, segregated, gated – and encodes both freedoms and restrictions – of mobility, of access, of vision – in the city. Cities exhibit distinctive geographies of social differences and power relations, where space functions as a modality through which urban identities are formed. Major changes in urban forms are experienced differentially and sociospatial restructurings of race, ethnicity, class, gender and sexual identities are key features of modern and postmodern urbanism. Essays in this second section are concerned with productions of difference in urban space and the correspondences between individuals and communities and their urban habitats.

As a space of difference the city is not simply a crucible of ethno-racial relations (the 'melting pot') or a multicultural smorgasbord (the 'urban mosaic'), but a site of intersubjective and collective encounters through which the formation of identity is spatialised. The association of the city with difference and diversity has, of course, a long lineage and has a famous classical articulation in Aristotle's view that: 'A city is composed of different men; similar people cannot bring a city into existence.'[23] This classical conception of the city as a space of difference has resonance in the twentieth century (Western) idealisations of urbanity as the very essence of city life. Urbanity, as represented in the work of urban sociologists and intellectuals across the century, valorises the multifarious forms of social interaction and interdependence in the city – the erotic and aesthetic variety of street life, the close encounters with strangers, the freedoms of access and movement in public spaces – positing these as the necessary conditions of democratic citizenship.[24] Today, this pluralistic view of urban life still has its adherents but is now broadly questioned as the close proximity of strangers in the city refuses to cohere into a civic unity and public space becomes increasingly privatised, commodified and militarised. There is a perceptible crisis of urbanity in Western urbanism (examined as an issue of cinematic representation by Kennedy in this volume) which reflects both the inadequacies of its conventional formulations and its failure to map ideologically the difference of urban social relations.[25]

It is widely argued that the predominant structure of feeling in urban social encounter today is fear and the response is to reduce contact, as Richard Sennett observes when he remarks 'we now measure urban spaces in terms of how easy it is to drive through them, to get out of them'.[26] Perhaps, but there remains the question of who 'we' are in relation to the space of fear. Confrontation with difference in urban space is a positional and relational matter – demarcating the self and the other, the citizen and the stranger – and in some part dependent upon the mental productions and cultural representations of stereotyping. Race can play a significant role here for, as Michael Keith and Malcolm Cross observe, '[it] is a privileged metaphor through which the confused text of the city is rendered comprehensible'.[27] Narrative pathologisations of urban poverty, for example, frequently appear as racialised 'tales of the lower depths', inviting a voyeuristic, even imperialistic, relationship between the implied reader or viewer and the alien urban world depicted. Although these are important considerations we must also question the idea that fear and dissassociation are the dominant modes of urban experience. Even as urbanity falters as a discourse the urges to form urban communities, group identifications and place associations clearly persist and are examined here in the essays by Balshaw and Brooker which, in different ways, seek to delineate the power of imagined communities in narrative and visual representation.

Al Deakin, in his analysis of selected novels by Charles Dickens, argues that nineteenth-century discourses on the city reveal a pervasive impulse to 'provide a controlling language through which the city can be read' as an interrelated fabric of social 'connectedness'. Noting that Dickens absorbed this impulse, Deakin shows that the author was 'equally captivated by the subversive nature of that which defies transparent decoding' in the city and which disrupts the need for urban legibility. This interplay of control and disruption is evident in Dickens' representations of the physically disabled body in the city, particularly as he constructs around it different forms of narrative and signification. On the one hand, he positions it as a product of nature and thus a reassuring signifier of the charity towards 'others' that sustained the Victorian 'fantasy of the city as home'. On the other hand, he positions it as a product of a malleable urban environment and thus an insecure 'riot of signifiers' which exacerbates Victorian horror of the body. Noting that urban space and representation combine both to create and to confound the normalisation of the body, Deakin concludes by commenting upon 'the potential which urban space has both to enable and disable' (echoing Lefebvre's contention that the human body has a corporeal power to *produce* space).[28]

Maria Balshaw is also interested in representations of the body, more specifically in the ways in which it is sexualised and racialised in fields of urban vision. Her essay examines meanings of urbanity in representations of 1920s Harlem through a comparative analysis of Isaac Julien's film *Looking for Langston* and Toni Morrison's novel *Jazz*. Noting the limited attention paid to the notion of urbanity in studies of the Harlem Renaissance Balshaw argues that it should be understood as 'a key shaping element in the development of a racialised aesthetic commensurate to the experience of African American life in Harlem'. Crucial to this aesthetic is the apprehension of Harlem as a visual culture in which both cultural intimacy and spectacle are heightened through the compaction and interaction of strangers in an emergent race capital. Balshaw shows how an 'obsessive visuality' characterises the representation of black urban identity and community in the texts under analysis. *Looking for Langston* uses avant-garde aesthetics to foreground the act of looking as it mediates relations between racial and homosexual registers of identity. In *Jazz* the deceptions of visual perception underlie the ambiguous, modernist treatment of the motifs of death and desire which circle the principal characters. In both texts, Balshaw shows, there is a productive tension between the pleasures of being urbane and the communal imperatives of urbanity. In her critical commentary on the texts' different treatments of this tension she records the relevance of these representations to late twentieth-century debates on the politics of black identity and urban space.

Balshaw's focus on the imaginary community of gay Harlem finds echoes in Peter Brooker's analysis of the work of Paul Auster and Wayne Wang as represented in the films *Smoke* and *Blue in the Face*. Brooker positions his film analysis within a broad and provocative discussion of theories of postmodern urbanism. In doing so he questions what he sees as the 'binarism and simplified historical sense' of certain sectors of postmodern theorising, noting the contradictions and abstractions in notions of 'the city as a space of multiplicity' and the relativisms of a new 'politics of difference'. Brooker begins to sketch an alternative analytic model by carefully exploring the possibilities of enunciating 'the different in the same', the moment of identity and identification in urban coexistence which is inherent in but effectively camouflaged by the routines of everyday life. As Brooker advances his theorising through analysis of the films he considers how they visualise and narrativise intricate relations between identity, place and community as these are localised in a Brooklyn neighbourhood. Of particular significance, he argues, is 'the role of storytelling in establishing a dialogic exchange at the centre of this neighbourhood', most effectively enacted in the bonding of two male characters at the end of *Smoke* as one 'gifts' the other a story. Brooker is well aware that celebration of this moment as suggestive of community relations may seem to sponsor a naive utopianism, but he shows that it is further dialogised as its epiphanic qualities are qualified by tensions and uncertainties of difference elsewhere in the films. The films, he suggests, show that the neighbourhood, as a place of coexistence in the city, demands an ongoing negotiation of relationships between the different and the same, between the self and the other and between settlement and flux.

The qualified utopianism Brooker projects is well measured to the par-ticularities of the films he analyses and the neighbourhood spaces of Brooklyn they represent. Moving to more mainstream cinema, and from Brooklyn to the streets and vistas of Los Angeles, we find in Liam Kennedy's analysis a very different registering of the production of space in which place and community are barely apparent as either physical entities or imaginary environments. The spatial lietmotif of the films he examines is dislocation, reflecting the response of Hollywood cinema to a distinctive social unease about the conditions and effects of contemporary urbanism. More particularly, he argues that selected films allegorise the discourses of urban decline already widespread in American culture and (re)produce a paranoid urban imaginary. Noting that film treatments of contemporary Los Angeles frequently activate this paranoia, Kennedy comments on how the films' projections of urban fears tend to constellate around issues of ethno-racial difference in urban space and foreground the insecurities of white males. Even as he pursues this analysis, though, he also (echoing the arguments of Pascal Pinck) questions the capacity of cinema to cathect viewer and image in repre-sentations of this urban paranoia, suggesting that it is the medium of video (potently demonstrated by the camcordering of Rodney King's beating by Los Angeles police in 1991) which more directly links the optics of postmodernism and the urban scene of paranoid spatiality.

(Post) National Spaces

In many countries the city (often, *a* city) represents the symbolic order of national identity. More and more, we are told that such symbolic orders are being profoundly fissured by socio-economic transformations that connect local cultures to the global system. 'Globalisation' has become a catch-all term for diverse restructurings characterised by the acceleration of global flows of people, capital and information. Some critics have argued that due to these flows 'the importance of place has diminished', but we prefer to argue that the meanings of places are changing and that this process needs to be brought under an analysis that respects the intricately connected transformations in both local cultures and global systems.[29] Attention to this intricacy is evident in Frederick Buell's commentary on the (post) national transformations of the local and the global,

> the movement from a period of globally disseminated nationalism, which reinforced the construction of national identities as objects of faith and focuses for social organisation, to a period of globalism, in which the stereotypical national culture has become increasingly strained, fractured and demystified, and more complex and heterogeneous forms of local culture have been developed to negotiate the larger system.[30]

The essays in this third section consider diverse features of globalisation as they emerge in particular urban locales and representations, and rearticulate meanings of national identity. Globalisation is a potent metaphor which promises to explain much about processes of transnational economic and cultural change, but which can mean very little if not connected to local occasions – these essays examine some of the places where and some of the ways in which it hits the ground in representation.

The cities under analysis here – Paris, New York, Birmingham and Singapore – have all been described as 'global cities', physically extended metropoles which have become (or, in Birmingham's case, strive to become) central 'nodes' in global networks. They all evidence rapid shifts in spatial scales as new relations between cores and peripheries emerge due to global and local dialectics of decentralisation and recentralisation. (They also evidence new temporal scales – of work, for instance, in both formal and informal economies.) As well as the urbanism of 'renewal' and 'regeneration' they also figure in their environments and representational forms the urbanism of 'decline' and 'neglect'. Often, these urbanisms interact, as is the case in many Western cities where new spatial opportunities for some (gentrification) are connected to the restrictions of space for others (homelessness).

Global cities alert us not only to the emergence of 'new ethnicities', but also 'new tribalisms' in urban spaces where the tensions of movement and settlement result in battles over identity. These tensions can be discerned in representations of the cities studied here, all of which are suggestively (post) national, in many ways defined by 'late imperialism' (or the legacies of earlier imperialisms) and the diasporic connections of their inhabitants. What Homi Bhabha terms 'the disjunctive, liminal space of national society' is not necessarily an urban space, but it is widely lived and perceived as such.[31]

The material and imaginary borders of the city/nation are less permeable than the metaphor of 'flows' suggests, nor should global(ising) cities be too hurriedly celebrated as spaces of 'hybrid' and 'syncretic' identity formation. Not surprisingly, the new concentrations of difference and power in global cities have led to fresh efforts to 'read' the city as both a national and an international space. Even as it becomes more difficult to describe a national experience in urban terms or evoke a shared historical consciousness of the city, narratives, myths and images are daily produced to do exactly this. It is notable that many cities seek to produce a 'city image' with which to advertise in the new global networks (of finance, or tourism); a process which has led to an intensification of aesthetic concerns in reshaping and representing urban forms. This is, as Sharon Zukin points out, 'a common cultural strategy that imposes a new way of seeing landscape: internationalising it, abstracting a legible image from the service economy, connecting it to consumption rather than production'.[32] There are also common cultural strategies for narrativising the global city: in this volume Gargi Bhattacharyya examines new myths of Birmingham generated by those with an eye on global markets. Of course, such strategies reproduce stark contradictions; often, city marketing of 'cosmopolitanism' and 'diversity' barely conceals anxieties about the dissolution of national culture. As well as these official strategies of representation there are myriad vernacular representations of the global city, some resonating with the hegemonic city image, some questioning it. There is a growing body of urban writing and imagery being produced by artists, authors and filmmakers who seek to voice the concerns of migrant communities that have strong local *and* global consciousness of their identities – such work is redefining ideas of territory, place, community and culture in new urban cores.

Myrto Konstantarakos finds an intriguing example of transnational codings of representation in the form of the *film de banlieue*. The films critically banded together by this title, 'film of the suburbs', are strikingly influenced in narrative form, stylised action and setting, and in many other generic ways by the American 'hood' films depicting African American ghetto spaces. However, Konstantarakos argues that despite the undeniable formal similarities, the *film de banlieue* is very much localised by its representations of ethno-racial relations and the built space of the city. The films imaginatively condense relations of urban difference and power, which have a broad cultural resonance in contemporary France. Konstantarakos provides a detailed account of how the *banlieue* were constructed in urban social planning, became key sites of discourse in local and national politics, and took on a symbolic focus as an image of societal problems (fusing 'youth, immigration and violence') in media coverage. Although processes of globalisation, such as the migration of decolonised people to French urban centres, do underlie some of the tensions and symbolisations Konstantarakos describes, she also questions the discourse of decentralisation attending such processes to argue that a recentralisation of difference and power is apparent in the 'opposition between Paris and the periphery'. In the films under analysis she finds this recentralisation referred to by the recurrent narrative devices and images signifying the entrapment and immobility of the peripheralised protagonists.

In her influential analysis of the global city Saskia Sassen proposes 'we can think of cities as a new frontier ... charged with the possibility of fundamental transformation in the West'. The global city, she further argues, is the 'premier arena' for battles over rights, independence and identity.[33] The urban frontier metaphor is a tired one but is being theoretically and politically retooled by Sassen and others analysing the distinctive interplay of global and local forces, especially as this is performed in New York City. Stephen Shapiro joins these forms of analysis with a historicising perspective that debates on globalisation often sideline. His title – '"Whose Fucking Park? Our Fucking Park!": Bohemian Brumaires (Paris 1848/East Village 1988), Gentrification, and the Representation of Aids' – suggests the constellation of his concerns, and his plotting between different periods, locales and imaginaries of urban conflict produces a stimulating examination of the meanings of gentrification. His analysis leaps off from an eyewitness account of the spectacle of protests surrounding Tompkins Square Park in Lower East Side Manhattan in the late 1980s – seen by many as an important test case of the politically charged relationships between rent speculation, gentrification and homelessness. For Shapiro, these protests over and in public space function as representational practices manifesting conflicting attitudes, values and priorities. From the immediacy of the moment he analytically backs up to consider how such sites of collision in urban space link global and local symbolic economies. Mediating these economies, he argues, are other crucial representations of power – the state, the city and the body – the relations of which are violently composed by (in Shapiro's Marxist phrasing) 'a historical cycle of primitive accumulation'. The workings of this cycle are evident, he argues, in the historically distant but symbolically related processes of gentrification and bohemianisation in mid nineteenth-century Paris and late twentieth-century New York. They are also evident in representations of these processes – by Puccini's *La Boheme* in the first instance, and by literary and visual representations of gay identity and of Aids in the second. Shapiro shows us that issues of gentrification are complexly played out in the interface of the local/global frontier.

Gargi Bhattacharyya, too, is interested in the relationship between local and global symbolic economies, specifically as these are present in the city of Birmingham. Bhattacharyya somewhat ironically titles her essay 'Metropolis of the Midlands' and the irony resides in her knowledge that 'Birmingham is a city with an inferiority complex'. A common butt of British humour regarding ugly industrial urbanism, it neither fits the tourism stereotypes of 'English' pastoral nor successfully attaches itself to the new regionalism in Britain which brands certain cities as new centres of style and glamour – Birmingham has 'remained an empty in-between place in the national imagination'. But Bhattacharyya detects change, notably in the ways in which a 'new myth' of the city is being formed to market it as a metropolis, at once a national centre and a nodal point of the new globalism. To effect such a transformation, she notes, 'Birmingham must learn to acknowledge both its global population and its complex diasporic connections to economic structures'. Bhattacharyya does not ignore some of the paradoxes involved in this transformation, for Birmingham is a city with a history of strained class and ethno-racial relations. However, she considers more positively the shifts in the city's own 'anti-urban' biases now to present 'workers and foreigners ... as the best products of city space'. While she exhibits some scepticism about the PR exercises surrounding this new mythologisation of the city she lends it qualified support in recognition that it presages a new urban imaginary in which labour, ethnicity and race are revalorised for the urban future.

In her commentary on Birmingham as a city that wants to be a metropolis Bhattacharyya argues that the city 'has to initiate a whole new way of thinking about what is central about urban centres'. This reconceptualisation of the centrality of the centre is demanded of many cities due to the local effects of globalisation. Singapore, in John Phillips' essay, provides a fascinating example for this city is its own state, the space of the city filling the space of the country; Singapore as 'the capital is what it is the capital of'. (Although only implicit in Phillips' analysis, Singapore functions as a salient reminder that the global city theorists, like those who posit postmodernism as a 'cultural dominant', tend to privilege a Western locus and logos – geographically and intellectually *centring* postmodern globalism.)[34] While Singapore is an important site within the systems that organise the global distribution of communication networks and financial circuits, it is also a product of its own 'incessant reorganisation of space'. While a global sign of phenomenal urban development and economic growth, the space of Singapore is conditioned and constrained by the barely visible signs of its historical origins. Phillips refuses to 'read' Singapore as, simply, a postcolonial space. Instead, he coins a new term – 'the empirial' – with which to express the socio-economic management of the tensions between forms of free-market capitalism and rigid state administration in the city. This balancing of tensions is inscribed in the urban fabric of the city and in the modes of speech of its inhabitants, but is peculiarly resistant to conventional forms of textual representation. Challenging any search for the 'essence' of the city, Phillips proposes that Singapore's urban space, always under development, *is* its most characteristic mode of representation.

Phillips' richly textured response to the experience of space in Singapore brings us once again to issues of (il)legibility and reminds us that all representations of cities are partial and provisional – short-sighted, interested, parts (impossibly) standing in for wholes. We are also reminded that the production of urban space generates urgent questions about power, difference and identity that cannot be contained by representations of 'the city'.

Notes

1   David Harvey, *Justice, Nature, and the Geography of Difference* (Oxford: Blackwell, 1996) p. 47. We note Harvey is not sanguine about this process, warning against excesses of abstraction and idealism in contemporary theorising on space and place (p. 46). Others, among many, who have commented upon and/or displayed the cross-fertilisation of disciplines around cultural geography, include: Sharon Zukin, *Landscapes of Power: From Detroit to Disney World* (Berkeley: University of California Press, 1991); Derek Gregory, Ron Martin and Graham Smith (eds), *Human Geography: Society, Space, and Social Science* (Basingstoke: Macmillan, 1994); Doreen Massey, *Space, Place, and Gender* (Cambridge: Polity Press, 1994); David Sibley, *Geographies of Exclusion: Society and Difference in the West* (London: Routledge, 1995); Patricia Yaeger (ed.), *The Geography of Identity* (Ann Arbor: University of Michigan Press, 1996); Linda McDowell (ed.), *Undoing Place? A Geographical Reader* (London: Arnold, 1998).

2   Michel Foucault, *Power/Knowledge: Selected Interviews and Other Writings, 1972–1977*, ed. and trans. Colin Gordon (New York: Pantheon, 1980) p. 70.

3   Henri Lefebvre, *The Production of Space*, trans. Donald Nicholson-Smith (Oxford: Blackwell, 1991).

4   Edward Soja, *Postmodern Geographies: The Reassertion of Space in Critical Social Theory* (London: Verso, 1989) p. 6.

5   Lefebvre, *The Production of Space*, pp. 141–7. We should note that Lefebvre's objections to 'the readable and the visible' in interpretations of space are particularly focused by his aversion to semiology, the procedures of which, he argues, never '[get] beyond mere description of space' (p. 162).

6   Soja, *Postmodern Geographies*, p. 125.

7   Ibid.

8   Lefebvre, *The Production of Space*, p. 144.

9   Rob Shields, 'A Guide to urban representation and what to do about it: alternative traditions of urban theory' in Anthony D. King (ed.), *Re-Presenting the City: Ethnicity, Capital and Culture in the Twenty First Century Metropolis* (Basingstoke: Macmillan, 1996) p. 235.

10   For a related argument, on 'the pairing of transparency and obscurity' in the workings of power, see James Donald, 'The city, the cinema: modern spaces' in Chris Jencks (ed.), *Visual Culture* (London: Routledge, 1995) p. 83.

11   William Sharpe and Leonard Wallock, 'From "great town" to "nonplace urban realm": reading the modern city' in Sharpe and Wallock (eds), *Visions of the Modern City: Essays in History, Art, and Literature* (Baltimore: Johns Hopkins University Press, 1987) p. 17. Sharpe and Wallock contend: 'One of the most useful ways of studying the city envisions the urban landscape as a form analagous to that of a literary composition' (p. 16). It is very much this form of analogy Lefebvre objects to in his critique of interpretive 'reading'.

12   Donald Preziosi, 'Oublier La Cittá', *Strategies: A Journal of Theory, Culture and Politics* 3 (1990) p. 260.

13   For a classic sociological perspective, see Robert E. Park, Ernest W. Burgess, and R. D. McKenzie, 'The city' in Park *et al.*, *The City* (Chicago: University of Chicago Press, 1967) pp. 1–46. William Sharpe and Leonard Wallock define and perpetuate this universalism in their view that 'the idea of the modern city is often difficult to separate from ... the idea of modernism in general' ('From "great town" to "nonplace urban realm"', pp. 4–5).

14   Fredric Jameson defines postmodernism as the 'cultural dominant' of late capitalism. Fredric Jameson, *Postmodernism or the Cultural Logic of Late Capitalism* (London: Verso, 1991).

15   Soja, *Postmodern Geographies*, pp. 190–221.

16   See, for example, Manuel Castells, *The Informational City: Information Technology, Economic Restructuring, and the Urban-Regional Process* (Oxford: Blackwell, 1989), and Nan Ellin, *Postmodern Urbanism* (Oxford: Blackwell, 1996).

17   Anthony Vidler, 'Bodies in space/subjects in the city: psychopathologies of modern urbanism', *Differences: A Journal of Feminist Cultural Studies* 5:3 (1993) p. 32.

18   Martin Jay, 'The scopic regimes of modernity' in Hal Foster (ed.), *Vision and Visuality* (Seattle: Bay Press, 1988) pp. 3–28.

19   Rob Shields comments: 'Both the visibility and the visuality of the city are always incomplete ciphers or parts of the tactile movement of urban life ... The "condition of visibility", the logical and connotative system in which representations are formed, is so powerful as to effectively *create* the things that are the subjects of representation' (Shields, 'A guide to urban representation and what to do about it', p. 235).

20   Anthony Vidler, 'The explosion of space: architecture and the filmic imaginary', *Assemblage* 21 (1993) p. 46.

21   See, for example, Anne Friedberg, *Window Shopping: Cinema and the Postmodern* (Berkeley: University of California Press, 1993), and Lauren Rabinovitz, *For the Love of Pleasure: Women, Movies, and Culture in Turn-of-the-Century Chicago* (New Brunswick: Rutgers University Press, 1998).

22   Sharon Zukin, 'Space and symbols in an age of decline' in King (ed.), *Re-Presenting the City*, p. 43.

23   Quoted in Richard Sennett, *Flesh and Stone* (London: Faber and Faber, 1994) p. 13.

24   See, for example, Jane Jacobs, *The Death and Life of Great American Cities* (New York: Random House, 1961); William Whyte, *The Social Life of Small Urban Spaces* (Washington D.C.: Conservative Foundation, 1980); Richard Sennett, *The Uses of Disorder: Personal Identity and City Life* (Harmondsworth: Penguin, 1971) and *Flesh and Stone*.

25   For an incisive analysis of postmodern revalorisation of urbanity, see Kevin Robins, 'Prisoners of the city: whatever could a postmodern city be?' in Erica Carter, James Donald and Judith Squires (eds), *Space and Place: Theories of Identity and Location* (London: Lawrence and Wishart, 1994) pp. 303–30.

26   Sennett, *Flesh and Stone*, pp. 17–18.

27 Michael Keith and Malcolm Cross, 'Racism and the postmodern city' in Keith and Cross (eds), *Racism, the City and the State* (London: Routledge, 1993) p. 9.

28 Lefebvre, *The Production of Space*, pp. 194–207.

29 Ellin, *Postmodern Urbanism*, p. 1.

30 Frederick Buell, *National Culture and the New Global System* (Baltimore: Johns Hopkins University Press, 1994) p. 144.

31 Homi Bhabha, 'Dissemination: time, narrative, the margins of the modern nation' in Bhabha (ed.), *Nation and Narration* (London: Routledge, 1990) p. 312.

32 Zukin, 'Space and symbols in an age of decline', p. 45.

33 Saskia Sassen, 'Analytical borderlands: race, gender and representation in the new city' in King (ed.), *Re-Presenting the City*, p. 197.

34 See Buell, *National Culture and the New Global System*, p. 172.

Space and Vision

2

Douglas Tallack, University of Nottingham

City Sights: Mapping and Representing New York City

In *Downcast Eyes* (1993) and in debate with other theorists, Martin Jay has been examining and questioning what he calls 'the denigration of vision' in contemporary theory.[1] In reaction against the privilege traditionally accorded sight over other senses (whether in romantic or realist aesthetics), French or French-influenced theory has identified vision and a prevailing ocularcentrism as the site of power relations rather than Enlightenment knowledge. Michel Foucault has been particularly influential here and the well-documented onset of a surveillance-, panoptic-society has given credence to critical hegemonic explanations.[2] In *Techniques of the Observer* (1992), Jonathan Crary has succeeded in adapting Foucauldian thinking to visual culture and theory, while Christine Hollevoet and her coorganisers of the important exhibition, *The Power of the City/The City of Power* (1992) bring together a critique of visual representationalism and urban space in terms of an opposition between a postmodern mapping impulse and 'the scopic pulsion in traditional pictorial representations of cities'.[3] It would be difficult not to be instructed by these and other critical insights into the visual representation of urban space. Nevertheless, in spite of the current authority of a visual hermeneutics of suspicion, it would be a mistake to dismiss as naive or traditional stubbornly optimistic attempts to represent urban space and achieve a point of view. The opposition between mapping and representing, action and vision, might not be quite so sustainable: mapping, after all, has both a street-level and a bird's-eye dimension to it, while representing is an action which cannot but have a degree of conceptuality involved in it. Consequently, this essay will reconsider a group of urban realists, the so-called Ashcan School of American painters, who were, of course, not at all preoccupied with overcoming hegemonic theories of vision but had the more forbidding task of trying to paint late nineteenth- and early twentieth-century New York, an urban environment which threatened defeat for individuals and groups who could not get some epistemological grasp upon it.

Between 1900 and the Armory Show of 1913 – which heralded the arrival of European modernism in the art of the United States – the painting of city sights was the speciality of the Ashcan School.[4] These artists now appear quite traditional in terms of form and style. John Sloan, George Bellows, George Luks, Everett Shinn and other members of the Ashcan group – in their day sometimes known as 'New Realists' – can also be regarded as traditional in their commitment to painting people and communities rather than the abstract cities which characterize the work of John Marin, Max Weber, Joseph Stella and the other early American modernists who were inspired by the Armory Show.

John Sloan's *Sixth Avenue and Thirtieth Street* (1908) is a fairly typical example of Ashcan painting to the extent that it depicts people in the setting of city streets and does not display any obvious self-conscious-ness about representing three-dimensional space on a two-dimensional canvas. A secure viewing position is fairly easy to identify because the painting is not merely organised around traditional one-point perspective but, in painting the receding tracks of the elevated railroad, the cornice-line and the curb of the street, Sloan – in effect – paints in the converging compositional lines which give the painting depth. Consequently, even though the curb disappears behind some figures we remain confident that it invisibly continues towards the point around which the painting coheres. *Sixth Avenue and Thirtieth Street* is, then, a window upon an urban scene which we cannot, of course, now visit in its precise spatial moment but which is recognisable through the conventions of repre-sentational art. This is precisely the kind of art which Jonathan Crary so successfully goes after in *Techniques of the Observer* when he traces a cor-respondence between one-point, Cartesian perspective, the 'technical' paradigm inaugurated by the camera obscura, and the acceptance as reality of this 'optically constructed space'. Crary's demonstration of the constructed or motivated character of this 'ground of vision' is just one aspect of a thoroughgoing scepticism levelled at (in Jay's words) 'the ubiquity of vision as the master sense of the modern era'.[5] Yet, having acknowledged all this, by concentrating upon just a few examples, the Ashcan artists can be shown not simply to be more complicated than their compliance with traditional and straightforward perspectivalism might suggest, but also to have engaged with the kinds of theoretical issues to do with representation and urban space which recent theory – building upon and also modifying the insights of modernism – has foregrounded; though, it might be added, with a decided preference for explaining what cannot possibly be achieved rather than for limited but tangible achievements.

Art history is both helpful and unhelpful in understanding the period in which the Ashcan artists painted New York. It is helpful because it allows us to identify a development: from (apparently straightforward) representationalism to modernism; from the window-perspective representationalism in George Bellows' 1911 painting, *New York*, to the horizontal-abstract phase of representation, or perhaps it should be mapping, exemplified by Piet Mondrian's *New York City 1* of 1941–42. In this kind of explanation Mondrian's late grid paintings are the culmination of a development which increasingly left the realism of Bellows and others behind and issues into an opposition between mapping/action and totalising representational vision which postmodern theory has seized upon. (This perhaps surprising alliance between standard art historical accounts and the refinement of theoretical denigrations of vision is worth noting.)

However, art history is less helpful when making the claim that the key factor behind these changes in representation was not an internal transformation within the discipline of painting (whose ramifications have, by a roundabout route, been felt in contemporary visual theory) but, rather, the attempt, and even the need, to know and understand a modern city, with its new spatio-temporal dimensions. In the field of visual culture knowledge depends, to some extent at least, upon achieving *a point of view*, but getting a clear sight of what was happening in New York was often physically impossible, given the pace and sheer crowded quality of city life at the turn of the century. And, as a spatial form, painting – more obviously than the then new visual form of the movies – labours under the particular difficulty of representing relations between part and whole or particular and general. In Ashcan art, which, one might say, was determinedly short-sighted, the problem posed itself as a relationship between local scene and wider city. How – to put it one way – could painters committed to representing the detail of particular urban spaces also achieve something of an overview: in Michel de Certeau's more recent formulation the view from the top of the World Trade Center (which we might project back into the early twentieth century as the view from the top of the Flatiron or the Woolworth buildings constructed in 1902 and 1913, respectively) and the view from the streets.[6] Or – to put it another way – how could painters represent but also map, be of the streets and yet not be limited to a street-level viewpoint? Beliefs and knowledge, then, were caught up in the effort to know New York City.

Bellows' *New York* (see Figure 2.1 overleaf) reveals New York's fascination with itself and the new kind of urban life which was emerging as a consequence of demographic movements, consolidation after 1898 of the five boroughs into one city, and a transportation revolution which linked those boroughs and altered inhabitants' conceptions of time and space, conceptions which were also being changed by the new perspectives offered by the emerging skyscraper city. *New York* was begun shortly after Bellows had an exhibition of twenty-four paintings of the city at the Madison Gallery and it seems to be an attempt at an overview.

Figure 2.1 George Bellows, *New York*, 1911 (National Gallery of Art, Washington).

As a comprehensive statement of how the Ashcan School artists saw New York in possibly its most dramatic modernising era, Bellows' painting can scarcely be bettered. The foreground is jammed with people, rushing to work and to shop, and at work directing the traffic, driving the horsedrawn carts and clearing snow. In the middle ground (around the ellipse of Union Square) the horse-drawn traffic competes with motorised trolley buses, while the open, public space of Union Square competes with the encroaching skyscrapers which form the backdrop and reduce the sky to an irregular patch at the far end of Broadway.

However, *New York* also conveys some of the formal complexities of the busy but seemingly traditional art of the Ashcan painters. There is a struggle between the almost crude representationalism of the painting and elements, at least, of abstraction in the blocks of tall buildings; themselves 'gridded' by uniform bands of windows and electric signs that cross the piers of the buildings but also climb up them. The flatness of the buildings at least challenges one-point perspective to reassert itself and the illusion of depth which it presents in the converging lines of Broadway. We can perhaps treat the receding streets as a visual equivalent to the depth narratives favoured by Georg Lukács over the flat description of modernist literature.[7] But in Bellows there is a tension between the dominant representationalism and an incipient modernism. The apparent directness of an Ashcan School view of an all-too-real world is further mediated by an intrusive glazed painterly surface, drawing one in to the surface, rather than into the scene depicted.

Bellows' *New York* also poses the theoretical question of how the particular and the general, the part and the whole, could be comprehended and represented. Bellows and his contemporaries faced this question at a time when the speed of life was particularly marked and when, in their professional activities as painters and – in some cases – newspaper reporters, they would probably have encountered competition from film crews at the most well-known city sites. Accordingly, this question had a spatial and temporal dimension: local and city-wide space had to be represented, as did the moment of street life as part of the totality of historical change, the challenge which Lukács maintains only narrative realism can meet. Bellows' desire to live up to his all-encompassing title, while maintaining the close-up view so characteristic of these urban realists, led him to amalgamate elements of Union Square and tall buildings located both to the south and north. Marianne Doezema has pointed out that the green and yellow Broadway trolleys, the red cars of Third Avenue and the Sixth Avenue elevated railway have been re-routed by Bellows.[8] These familiar signs of New York life come together in *New York*; that is, in the space of the painting rather than in the space of the city. Bellows' effort to create a typical New York street scene might be said to have produced an excess of signification commensurate with the meaning of 'New York' (then and since), but beyond what any one city site could generate.[9]

A current and often justifiable suspicion of *visual* representation, allied to a pervasive postmodern scepticism of totalities, could easily prompt a criticism of Bellows' attempt to impose a masterful modern, even potentially modernist, gaze (given the hints of abstraction). As Christel Hollevoet and Karen Jones put it, 'mimetic descriptions of the cityscape ... imply a mastering gaze'.[10] But, in the context of the period, the attempt can also be interpreted more sympathetically. The lack of literality (this is a space which, in its combination of particulars, did not exist when Bellows painted *New York*) suggests that George Bellows is painting a need to know more than could actually be seen. And his inclusiveness suggests that he is also painting a requirement for a public, though admittedly not a civic, space; a space, that is, where some commonality was possible for groups who otherwise might have remained ghettoised.

Although Bellows' *New York* – if only because of its title – has a certain typicality about it, a more characteristic Ashcan painting is of a local scene, with a local title. George Luks' *Hester Street* (1905) provoked two different interpretations in two fairly recent major exhibitions of turn-of-the-century American art. In *American Impressionism and Realism: The*

Painting of Modern Life, 1885–1915, curated by Barbara Weinberg, Doreen Bolger and David Park Curry, *Hester Street* is instanced as a painting in which a hitherto European figure of modernity makes a significant American appearance. In this reading, the key to the painting is the man in the white fedora, standing slightly to one side of the activity of this Lower East Side market scene. He is an American embodiment of the *flâneur* of modern life, and, in the curators' words, is 'the artist's surrogate, observing the exotic culture without immersing himself in it'.[11] But the curators of *Metropolitan Lives* disagree, arguing that the significance of Luks' painting lies in its unresolved contrasts. A youngish woman in a blue blouse and hat with trimmings who is bargaining over a rooster with a shopkeeper seems to be of a different generation or at least outlook from a woman with a shawl who heads towards a group of traditionally clothed men. These men are contrasted with the man in the fedora, perhaps – in the words of the organisers of this exhibition – a 'former resident ... who has taken on modern American ways'.[12]

This disagreement – is the man a 'former [but now assimilated] resident' or a *flâneur?* – is relevant to the questions of urban knowledge and urban points of view posed by this essay. The *flâneur* as he (and it usually is a he), descends to us from Baudelaire, Henry James and Walter Benjamin, knows the city through desultory wandering, and a trajectory which catches the transitoriness and ephemerality of the modern city. And when *flânerie* got updated by Dadaists in the early 1920s, the same lack of intentionality was evident in their plans to visit pointless, boring places.[13] By their very detachment from the usual social referents, these modernists and proto-postmodernists sought to know the city. However, when put together – as in the exhibition, *Metropolitan Lives* – the representational works of the Ashcan School indicate that these painters were different, primarily because they got around the city precisely through not being detached. As former reporters, they were caught up in the routines of the city: newspapers arriving in the early morning; getting to/from work during the rush hour; purposeful shopping; and work. The man in the fedora might indeed have 'taken on modern American ways', but to the extent that he could be interpreted as very involved in the scene: involved as a wheeler-dealer, someone with a detached eye for an economic opportunity in a traditional scene undergoing transformation. The ephemerality which Baudelaire made central to his definition of the modern arises not from the cross-cutting, random route taken by the *flâneur,* but by economic motivation. Arguably, it is Georg Simmel's figure of 'the stranger' who manages to combine the sense of involvement and detachment which Luks has captured. As the following observations confirm, Simmel also seizes upon economic motivation as the key to the stranger:

The stranger ... is an element of the group itself ...

Throughout the history of economics the stranger everywhere appears as the trader, or the trader as stranger ...

... Trade can always absorb more people than primary production; it is, therefore, the sphere indicated for the stranger, who intrudes as a supernumary, so to speak, into a group whose economic positions are actually occupied ...

... Objectivity is by no means non-participation ... but a positive and specific kind of participation.[14]

Simmel helps us to appreciate that Luks is not a local-colour painter. The people depicted in *Hester Street* have come together for identifiable reasons and the painter has followed them to this site to catch the historical resonances of the local scene. But for the same reasons, Luks and the other Ashcan artists should not be associated too firmly with (American) Impressionism, in spite of some similarities of style. *Hester Street* is not a momentary impression, caught by a painter on the move through the city.

Initially, John Sloan's *Six O'Clock, Winter* of 1912 seems to be the kind of scene which a *flâneur*'s interest in movement and spectacle might isolate for detached consumption. Yet Sloan's depiction of a commuter train and rush-hour crowds milling around makes no sense without the larger, implied, picture of the transportation revolution, consequent upon the consolidation of the five boroughs into New York City in 1898. As Oscar Handlin notes in 'The modern city as a field of historical study', a classic essay on the modernising of traditional patterns of life:

The altered situation of the city called also for a new conception of time ... The arrival of all those integers who worked together, from whatever part of the city they inhabited, had to be coordinated to the moment. There was no natural span for such labor; arbitrary beginnings and ends had to be set, made uniform and adhered to.[15]

Another of Sloan's urban scenes, his *Three A.M.* of 1909, gives us a further reason for quibbling with the now-standard definition of modernity as the knowledge of ephemerality and with the association of modernity with such transitory figures as the *flâneur* or the prostitute (or other vaguely related figures). Although prostitution was the lot for some urban women, this does not mean that we have to follow Baudelaire, the Surrealists and, later, the Situationists and define prostitutes as the epitome of the transitoriness of modern life. Baudelaire's critique of bourgeois respectability can slip too easily into a romanticising of the transitory figures of modern urban life. The two women in *Three A.M.* – a painting rejected by the National Academy of Design – are having a cup of tea and one is frying some meat on a large hob. It is a kitchen scene and although they seem to be relaxing after some kind of work they are not wholly defined by their implied work because the details of daily life anchor them to what sustains most people: family, companionship, home and ordinary routines conducted in identifiable spaces.

This is not, of course, a denial of the insights of Baudelaire, Benjamin and others who have so acutely understood aspects of modernity. But it is to say that in the Ashcan School's paintings of modern life there are more signs of relations and an infrastructure – and of the knowledge which this brings – than is sometimes thought to be the case. Modernity was a contradictory phenomenon, containing both traditional and contemporary elements that are not obviously in a teleological relationship.

As already acknowledged, art history can be helpful in seeing what is going on in some of these paintings. Early American modernism was about to overtake Ashcan realism as the preeminent painting of modern life and, in common with European modernism can be discussed in terms of a lack of literality or – similarly – as a need to know more than could actually be seen. Rosalind Krauss has written about the 'invisibility' of modernism, and – in this connection – about anamorphism.[16] Anamorphism is probably best exemplified by Cubism, in which the modernist proposal that what is not 'normally' visible can only be made so through non-representational techniques is advanced through paintings which include a number of different and literally invisible sides of an object or scene all at once. Yet there are glimpses of an alternative and – if it does not sound too paradoxical – more material, notion of invisibility at work in the traditionally painted works of the Ashcan artists: that of the invisible but historically changing infrastructure which gives meaning to an apparently discrete surface scene of local colour. As a further example, it is worth considering not an individual painting – in which can be discerned both a representing and a mapping impulse at work, a local and an infrastructural point of view – but a series of four paintings by George Bellows of the building of Pennsylvania Station.

Bellows was just one of a number of artists who not only saw series or sequences of paintings as a way to map spatial and temporal relations, but was also drawn to buildings under construction because these are places explicitly undergoing change. When time and space intersect the sites/sights change. Bellows must also have felt that the building of Pennsylvania Station offered the opportunity to represent both historical process and causes and have realised that construction changed the conditions of visuality: what could be seen and from what point of view. The vast geographical and technological scale of the Pennsylvania excavation (construction began in 1904 and took six years) was, then, a scene, an event, a process and a space that was once a place, had been turned into a space – as in the first of the series, *Pennsylvania Station*

Excavation of 1907 – and was becoming a different place, as in what is probably the third of the series, also entitled *Pennsylvania Excavation*, begun in 1907 and completed in 1909, and depicting a great building looking down on the building site. This place, then, had become different in itself (the vast hole in the ground is partly filled by a building) but was also in a different relationship with the city. The building of Pennsylvania Station brought people right into the city from the west, rather than depositing them at the New Jersey waterfront. As part of the integrated mass-transit system following consolidation of the boroughs, the new station centralised the area, competing for centrality with Grand Central Station. The meaning of space itself changed, posing questions of how the new station related to the existing grid and how it changed it as it became a new gateway to the city (in the sense that an airport is a curious gateway to a contemporary city). One could say that Bellows uses a local, particular site as a frame with which to try to comprehend the general and rapidly changing picture. Insofar as this paradoxical claim has validity, then Bellows' excavation series is another way of painting New York from that which he later tried in his 1911 painting, *New York.*

An excavation site is the beginning of a 'space of appearance' (to borrow Hannah Arendt's intriguing phrase) and the building of Pennsylvania Station is an especially interesting example.[17] The more official record of photographs of the excavation for the station and of the completed concourse, together with the maps of Manhattan which superimpose the railroad and subway lines on to the street grid, convey a logical process of construction and usage.[18] But, as is apparent in *Excavation at Night* (1908), the second in the series, Bellows offers an infrastructural vision of confused exchange between labour and product, and between the landscape before excavation began and what might emerge from the smoke and infernal machinery.

In an effort to understand what is going on, Bellows tries out a number of points of view in the series and, as the invaluable research of Marianne Doezema has shown, the first of the series, *Pennsylvania Excavation*, is painted from Ninth Avenue looking towards the skyscrapers of New York's commercial district.[19] The grid is less apparent than in some of the photographs of the site taken from a higher angle, but the trestle carrying Eighth Avenue traffic is just about visible, confirming the persistence of the grid in the midst of change; while the tall buildings are incorporated in the background to suggest the integration of transportation and commerce. Bellows uses the indeterminate subject matter of the painting to bring together a vertical/window perspective and at least the sense of an overview, conveyed by depicting the spatial coordinates of the grid.

Amidst the material changes, Bellows looks for places and ways in which people can appear in public and at least partially sustain the belief that this is a human narrative. Where the panoramic views of the Impressionists (American as well as European) assimilate people into the landscape – they are smudges and dashes of paint – Ashcan artists often opted for anecdotes: incidents with implied narratives which have a less than obvious or an ambiguous relationship to the larger process and picture. Sloan and Luks seem at times to make anecdote central to their paintings, whereas in his Pennsylvania Station series Bellows uses anecdote more traditionally to situate figures in a cityscape and to explore oppositions (centre/periphery, foreground/background, where the background is often more significant). Thus, in *Pennsylvania Excavation* (1907) there are two figures in the right foreground who function rather as the hunters, explorers and Indians who appear in the foreground of mid-nineteenth-century Hudson River paintings and suggest a not always convincing relationship between historical movement and human agents. Sometimes, the anecdotes in Bellows have a confirmatory, progressive role: that is to say, they endorse the development of the site by harmonising workers and work. And sometimes, as in *Excavation at Night*, painted a year later, different relationships are set up. The figures around the fire evoke labour disputes and even preindustrial rituals.

Blue Morning (1909) (see Figure 2.2) is a very striking painting. An art-historical type of explanation might easily take off from the title and link *Blue Morning* with tonalism and Impressionism, thereby suggesting a largely positive, even triumphal meaning for what is thought to be the final painting in the excavation series. The painting can be situated differently, though (in an effort to identify a more complicated process of knowing and viewing), by noting the conjunction of three elements: the elevated railroad, labour and the building. By 1909 the El, which had opened its first line in 1871 – and it was the Ninth Avenue El depicted by Bellows as a partial 'frame' in *Blue Morning* – was successful but noisy and eventually lost out to both the commuter railroad, which ran into Pennsylvania Station, and the subway, which had opened in 1904. This kind of competitive scene would be common in the more explicitly modernist painting which took over after the Armory Show. In John Marin's painting, *Lower Manhattan (Composing Derived from the Top of Woolworth)* of 1922, for example, it would seem that with so much happening around him the artist has had to find ways in which to paint such very real abstractions as force, energy and power.[20]

In *Blue Morning*, the use of the El and the curious perspective adopted accentuates the distance between labour and its eventual, soaring product – the grand station building. There is even a suggestion in *Blue Morning* of a rural fence, with someone taking it easy perched on it. Fredric Jameson, writing on Max Weber, employs the term 'vanishing mediator' to describe a practice or an object which functions to ease the transition to modernity, and that might be going on here with the fence, the smoke and the colours.[21] The third element in *Blue Morning* is the building. Pennsylvania Station was a McKim, Mead and White building and

Figure 2.2 George Bellows, *Blue Morning*, 1909 (National Gallery of Art, Washington).

therefore part of an alternative, monumental, anti-modernist, civic definition of the city which competed with the dominant commercial definition. Yet the Beaux-Arts building is partially framed by the Ninth Avenue El. Compositionally, the El emphasises the surface plane, much as in the more common use of a window frame, itself the most common representationalist version of the aesthetic grid.[22] In twentieth-century art the grid (as in Mondrian) broke free of its subordinate role as a template, parallel to the picture plane. As it happens, in Bellows' case it is less necessary to argue for representational versions of the modernist grid because he was fascinated by new geometrical investigations and planned many of his paintings accordingly.[23] However, it is the toing and froing between formal and historical/geographical commentary which best brings out the importance of Bellows' work, so it is important to recall that the El is also part of the surface grid-plan of New York City. As such, its appearance in *Blue Morning* qualifies it as a centrifugal grid, disappearing off Bellows' canvas as the Ninth Avenue El did. Rosalind Krauss offers this helpful definition of the centrifugal grid in Mondrian's work:

By virtue of the grid, the given work of art is presented as a mere fragment, a tiny piece arbitrarily cropped from an infinitely larger fabric. Thus the grid operates from the work of art outward, compelling our acknowledgement of a world beyond the frame.[24]

A brief comparison with Everett Shinn's *Cross Streets of New York* (1899) confirms that Bellows' contemporaries grappled with much the same problem. Shinn's is a street-level scene of individual struggles to keep carts moving in the rutted, snow-covered street and a meeting – it looks like a confrontation – between a man and a woman. But *Cross Streets of New York* was initially an illustration for an article in *Scribners* of the same title and Shinn planned a picture album to be called *New York by Night*, suggesting that he, like Bellows in *New York* and in his Pennsylvania excavation series, was seeking to know New York by combining a broader interest in mapping the city and exploring its spatial relations with a focus on specific scenes.[25] Moreover, the title of Shinn's painting gestures towards the particular way of linking space and time which the New York grid affords; that is to say, that New York's cross streets are a historical cross-section, while the avenues are journeys through time: accelerated journeys once the elevated railroad – depicted crossing this crosstown street in Shinn's work – had been built.

In returning to Bellows' achievement in *Blue Morning*, it is possible to argue that he shifts back and forth between the different dimensions of the grid in order to represent the complexity of New York's infrastructure in and around Pennsylvania Station or – in painterly terms – the complexity of spatial planes. The painting's conventions shift, too, between those of a vertical representation and a horizontal map, between the illusion of three-dimensional space and the reality of two-dimensional space on the canvas. To adapt a deconstructive insight, representationalism would seem always to contain its other – abstraction and the impulse to see all at once – just as an abstract work cannot but provoke the effort to interpret through apparently outmoded representational criteria.

Yet it is the integration of a historical and material perspective into the formalist and theoretical task of composition he faced in painting *Blue Morning* and the three excavation works that preceded it which defines Bellows' achievement most clearly. The different levels and the intersections of horizontality and verticality were changing daily during excavation and construction and Bellows' series of paintings and the individual works in the series constitute a wonderful visual representation of Raymond Williams' dominant, emergent and residual aspects of change.[26] But visually representing space in this manner is very difficult: difficult on the canvas because of the shifting between representing and mapping impulses and their associated conventions; and difficult in the decision when and where to paint because the city was changing so rapidly, and, with each change, it became arguably more difficult to encompass the city, see its point and view it. According to Doezema, the point of view from which *Blue Morning* was painted was apparently impossible to achieve. It would have been somewhere in mid-air with no place, not even a ledge, from which this sight could be seen in this way.[27] Yet it is precisely by contriving a fictional point of view that Bellows seems to have seen in the conjunction of the building, the labourers and the El, and in the representational and abstract aspects of the grid a way of painting what could not be seen. Put rather too straightforwardly and theoretically – certainly in comparison with Bellows' efforts – there is no one place from which to see modernity. This recognition is at the heart of an important strand of both modernism and contemporary theory, but George Bellows, in common with other seemingly traditional Ashcan painters, contrives to get his feet on the ground from which to try.

Notes

1   Martin Jay, *Downcast Eyes: The Denigration of Vision in Twentieth-Century French Thought* (Berkeley: University of California Press, 1993), passim. See also Martin Jay, 'The scopic regimes of modernity' in Hal Foster (ed.), *Vision and Visuality* (Seattle: Bay Press, 1988) pp. 3–27.

2   Michel Foucault, *Discipline and Punish: The Birth of the Prison*, trans. Alan Sheridan (Harmondsworth: Penguin, 1991) pp. 195–228.

3   Christine Hollevoet, Karen Jones and Timothy Nye, *The Power of the City/The City of Power* (New York: Whitney Museum of American Art, 1992) p. 30. See also Jonathan Crary, *Techniques of the Observer* (Cambridge, Mass.: MIT Press, 1992).

4   In addition to Figures 2.1 and 2.2, see, for reproductions, Elizabeth Milroy, *Painters of a New Century: The Eight and American Art* (Milwaukee: Milwaukee Art Museum, 1991), Bennard B. Perlman, *Painters of the Ashcan School: The Immortal Eight* (New York: Dover, 1988), Barbara Weinberg, Doreen Bolger and David Park Curry, *American Impressionism and Realism: The Painting of Modern Life, 1885–1915* (New York: The Metropolitan Museum of Art, 1994), and Rebecca Zurier, Robert W. Snyder and Virginia M. Mecklenburg, *Metropolitan Lives: The Ashcan Artists and their New York* (Washington D.C.: National Museum of American Art, 1995).

5   Crary, *Techniques of the Observer*, pp. 126 and 136; Jay, 'The scopic regimes of modernity', p. 3.

6   Michel de Certeau, *The Practice of Everyday Life*, trans. Steven Rendall (Berkeley: University of Los Angeles Press, 1984) pp. 91–110.

7   Georg Lukács, *Writer and Critic and Other Essays* (London: Merlin Press, 1978) pp. 110–48.

8   Marianne Doezema, ' The real New York' in Michael Quick *et al.*, *The Paintings of George Bellows* (Fort Worth: The Amon Carter Museum; Los Angeles: The Los Angeles County Museum of Art; New York: Harry N. Abrams, 1992) pp. 111–14. See, also, Zurier *et al.*, *Metropolitan Lives*, p. 85.

9   See Douglas Tallack, 'New York, New York', *Renaissance and Modern Studies* 40 (1997) pp. 26–46.

10   Hollevoet *et al.*, *The Power of the City*, p. 7.

11   Weinberg *et al.*, *American Impressionism and Realism*, p. 192.

12   Zurier *et al.*, *Metropolitan Lives*, p. 26.

13   Hollevoet *et al.*, *The Power of the City*, pp. 25–55.

14   Georg Simmel, *The Sociology of Georg Simmel*, trans. and ed. Kurt Wolff (New York: The Free Press, 1950) pp. 402, 403 and 404.

15   Oscar Handlin, 'The modern city as a field of historical study' in Alexander B. Callow, Jr (ed.), *American Urban History: An Interpretive Reader with Commentaries*, 2nd edn (New York: Oxford University Press, 1973) p. 25.

16   Rosalind Krauss, 'The im/pulse to see' in Foster, *Vision and Visuality*, pp. 83–4.

17   Hannah Arendt, *The Human Condition* (Chicago: University of Chicago Press,1958) p. 199.

18   See Marianne Doezema, *George Bellows and Urban America* (New Haven: Yale University Press, 1992) pp. 19–55 and Zurier *et al.*, *Metropolitan Lives*, pp. 30–4.

19   Doezema, *George Bellows and Urban America*, p. 26.

20   See Douglas Tallack, *Twentieth-Century America: The Intellectual and Cultural Context* (London: Longman, 1991) pp. 83–90.

21   Fredric Jameson, 'The vanishing mediator; or, Max Weber as storyteller' in his *The Ideologies of Theory: Essays 1971–1986. Volume 2: The Syntax of History* (Minneapolis: University of Minnesota Press, 1988) pp. 3–34.

22   See Rosalind Krauss, *The Originality of the Avant-Garde and Other Modernist Myths* (Cambridge, Mass.: MIT Press, 1986) pp. 16–18.

23   Michael Quick, 'Technique and theory: the evolution of George Bellows's painting style' in Quick *et al.*, *The Paintings of George Bellows*, pp. 9–95.

24   Krauss, *The Originality of the Avant-Garde and Other Modernist Myths*, p. 18.

25   See Zurier *et al.*, *Metropolitan Lives*, p. 71.

26   Raymond Williams, *Marxism and Literature* (Oxford: Oxford University Press, 1977) pp. 121–7.

27   Doezema, *George Bellows and Urban America*, p. 53.

3

Richard Ings, University of Nottingham

A Tale of Two Cities: Urban Text and Image in *The Sweet Flypaper of Life*

A sibyl, questioned about Marozia's fate, said: 'I see two cities: one of the rat, one of the swallow.'[1]

According to the interpretation of this oracular pronouncement, Marozia is about to be transformed. Today, its people run like rats through its passages, fighting for leftovers to survive on, but a bright new century is about to begin, where they will 'fly like swallows in the summer sky'. At the height of this new era, the narrator returns to find that the promised change does not seem to have occurred, 'there are people who believe they are flying, but it is already an achievement if they can get off the ground flapping their batlike overcoats'. Yet something unusual *is* happening, 'when you least expect it, you see a crack open and a different city appear'. These sudden irruptions in the city walls vanish just as swiftly but leave the viewer with an image of a city 'transfigured ... crystalline, transparent as a dragonfly'.

Like many of Italo Calvino's other fables in *Invisible Cities*, this tale of Marozia can, I believe, provide us with a useful metaphorical starting point for exploring aspects of space, of architecture and of urban life in the city. In Marozia, we may find a trope for the mixture of hope and despair that afflicts city dwellers, or for the promise that the city offers to rural immigrants against the bleak reality of the conditions they must live in. In literally breaking open the surface of the city to reveal a transfigured space, however, the story offers other possibilities: that solid appearances can be deceptive and that, with the right combination of words, actions or gestures, they can be pierced. This intrusion literally changes what we see – or forces us to look at what we might otherwise miss. What

Calvino describes here may be analogous to the act of photography: the shutter rapidly opening and closing, like the crack in the city walls.

Photographic Territory

By intention or accident, photographers take pictures of particular places, districts, buildings, urban situations and so forth as if to establish the city in their own image(s). If these photographs are assembled, the spaces of the city are incorporated into something closer to a fictional narrative than an objective record. For example, Berenice Abbott and Weegee may have occupied the same geographical location at roughly the same historical moment but they tell very different tales of Manhattan in *Changing New York* and *Naked City*.[2]

The Sweet Flypaper of Life, published in 1955, is actually intended to be read as a story of the city, with 140 photographs by Roy DeCarava selected, sequenced and stitched together with a continuous written text over a hundred pages by Langston Hughes, the storyteller *par excellence* of Harlem.[3] Between its first image, of Ronnie Belle, born in the city, and its last, of Sister Mary Bradley, born in South Carolina, *The Sweet Flypaper of Life* attempts to offer a snapshot of black life, as if the recent Supreme Court decision to outlaw school segregation had opened a kind of shutter and it was now time to let some light in on how far black people had come and how far they had to go. The book was a great success, going swiftly into a second edition and winning two awards.

The urban world that Langston Hughes presents yokes Roy DeCarava's photographs to a fictional narrative, adapting a tradition set up by the illustrated magazines (like *Life*) with their photo-stories and the Farm Security and Works Progress Administration projects, out of which a number of photo-texts emerged.[4] Hughes' book was the first fictional photo-text and the first major photographic publication to examine black life from the inside. In locating its images and words in the black community, this book participates, intentionally or not, in a contest over territory, geographic and photographic.

From the early decades of the twentieth century, New York has been the site of fierce territorial competition, most significantly between black migrants and white residents fighting block by block for ownership of the city's space. In the 1930 census, the city plan shows that Harlem had turned black (each block inked in, as it were), and that the utopian thinking behind the Jeffersonian grid had faltered. The grid had not become the site of interchangeability – that is, equality – but of a contest where defeat meant division, containment and ultimately incarceration. Ironically, however, the so-called 'ghetto' that emerged from this trapped location also allowed a space for self-definition against a hostile white world.

Harlem Renaissance writers and black leaders celebrated Harlem as a 'race capital'. For James Weldon Johnson in 1925, Harlem is 'not merely a Negro colony or community, it is a city within a city, the greatest Negro city in the world. It is not a slum or a fringe, it is located in the heart of Manhattan and occupies one of the most beautiful and healthful sections of the city.'[5] While it might be argued that Harlem's relative prosperity, compared with the sections from which the Southern and West Indian blacks had emigrated, blinded observers like Johnson to the fact that it remained a place dangerously set apart within white territory, his sense of pride in a *Negro city* has lingered on as (at the least) a corrective to those who would write Harlem off as a 'dark ghetto'. So, for example, Albert Murray, at another moment of black pride in the late 1960s, chides critics like Kenneth Clark who 'almost always proceed in terms of the liabilities of Harlem', 'documenting the pathological'.[6] On the contrary, Murray flatly asserts, the 'term ghetto does not apply to Harlem' (p. 74).

It is interesting to note that Murray's vigorous restatement of James Weldon Johnson's positive vision of Harlem was written to accompany a 'group of fine photographs' (by Fred McDarrah). Inveighing against 'mass media images' that derive from 'psychopolitical gossip about Negro self-hatred' (p. 76), Murray closes his article with the recommendation that 'those who would help Harlem achieve its aspirations ... approach the people of Harlem with the attitude that good photographers seem to take when they aim their cameras at the streets and the buildings' (p. 77). Murray's exhortation suggests that it is through representations of space or place – 'streets and buildings' – that friends of Harlem can defend and promote their community. It also begs an important question in assigning this task to 'good' photographers. These seem to be photographers who can, through their literal (photographic) and metaphorical point of view, offer an alternative to the negative image served up by the mass media and the doomsayers. They can see (and help us to see) the city of the swallows behind or beyond the rat city with its 'ceilings of stone' that is the favoured image of Harlem in the mainstream media.[7]

This battle over representation has been fought for decades. At one level, it is a simple matter of claiming territory. Although black photographer James Latimer Allen was hailed as a leading interpreter of black life by Alain Locke, Harlem Renaissance spokesman and editor of *The New Negro*, it was (and is) the white writer and photographer Carl van Vechten whose work illustrates most histories and accounts of the Harlem Renaissance.[8] While black studio photographers Marvin and Morgan Smith and James VanDerZee regularly documented the life of the Harlem streets through and beyond the interwar years, it was Aaron Siskind and other white members of the PhotoLeague who produced the 'Harlem Document' that provided the illustrated magazines with images of Harlem.[9]

At a deeper level, it is a matter of interpretation. From Jacob Riis' *How the Other Half Lives* to Weegee's *Naked City*, white photographers had come to black neighbourhoods to take and publish pictures exposing the poor social conditions in which blacks had to live, while black photographers actually living there found few outlets for their images of the city, images that did not set out to expose the negative but to record the positive.[10] Morgan Smith, for example, turned down a commission to photograph Harlem gangs; looking back, he commented: 'My brother and I were striving all the time to present the community in a good light.'[11] The people in the images taken by the Smiths, VanDerZee and others were 'the people the papers don't write about or photograph', identified by Weegee in captioning his own picture of an Easter Sunday church crowd.[12] In this context, *The Sweet Flypaper of Life* appears to be the first major publication that puts the black photographer in control of the representation of Harlem.[13]

A Photographic Narrative

The Sweet Flypaper of Life is set in Harlem but takes as its subject broader issues and concerns about black urban life in general. Although there are references to the particular cultural heritage of Harlem, including portraits of anonymous arts workers and jazz players, the book does not set out to memorialise or celebrate the obvious landmarks, such as the Apollo Theatre or the Hotel Theresa, as a guidebook would. Rather, it takes the streets and interiors of Harlem as the *locus classicus* of black city existence and, directed by the written text, sets out to record and celebrate the everyday life and common heritage of urbanised African Americans. As such, it tends not to focus on specific events and there are no 'newsworthy' images, such as those taken by Weegee in *Naked City*, for example, depicting a Harlem riot. Instead, using the still images as a kind of storyboard or filmstrip, Langston Hughes creates a flow of life – a flypaper to which he sticks his observations.

Hughes structures the book around and through the family of 'Sister Mary Bradley' and its relationship to black history and to contemporary sociocultural trends. From Roy DeCarava's large collection of photographs taken in and around Harlem over the previous five years, Hughes selects a range of images to portray both the members of this fictional family and the wider black community.[14] Significantly, he 'bookends' the narrative with two single images; it opens with a close-up of 'Ronnie Belle', one of Sister Mary's younger grandsons, and ends with a portrait of Sister Mary herself, in her Sunday best – the first and only glimpse we are offered of the narrator through whom Hughes addresses us. What we get in the intervening pages is a kind of family album, which Sister Mary talks us through, perhaps reminding us that the photograph, whether framed on the wall or put in an album, has had a particularly important significance in African American lives.[15] The link between the grandson and the grandmother, however, points to a wider historical frame.

Sister Mary is triggered into telling this narrative by the recent landmark decision of *Brown vs. The Board of Education*, outlawing segregation in schools, which persuades her not to sign for St Peter's telegram calling her to heaven but 'to stay here and see what this integration the Supreme Court has done decreed is going to be like' (p. 2). Born herself, it would appear, in the closing decade or so of the previous century, Sister Mary bridges the history of black struggle for civil rights from the low point of Jim Crowism to this hopeful moment of 1954. Her concern for Ronnie Belle and indeed her whole narrative, which is more a reflective essay on the current issues affecting black people than a conventionally plotted story, seem to stem from a prophetic sense that African Americans are standing on the brink of great change. The narrative can be separated into ten sections or sequences that alternate between Sister Mary's pithy comments on various members of her family and the broader observations and opinions on black urban life that they inspire. The photographs serve to illustrate this inner/outer pulse in the narrative, with most of the family pictures taken inside apartments and those relating to the wider community taken outside, on the streets. This division between interior and exterior space enables Hughes to explore, through Sister Mary's plain speech, a whole range of issues to do with identity, physical and social mobility, and the exercise of power.

The narrative flows, then, back and forth from the personal to the social. Sister Mary's loving puzzlement about her grandson Rodney in the first section (pp. 7–13) leads out into broader commentary on 'young folks in Harlem', the generation gap and the impact of a new consumer society, epitomised by the Cadillac (pp. 14–19). We are next introduced to Mae, who plans to buy a car, and her husband, 'my most up-and-coming grandchild' and a marked contrast to Rodney (pp. 20–1). This produces a longer sequence (pp. 22–34) where Sister Mary muses on the hard struggle for respectability and responsibility and on the temptations of rebellion and fecklessness. We meet members of her family who are doing their best to get on (pp. 35–8), including a daughter who has successfully survived a divorce. 'I got some fine people in my family,' Sister Mary says, 'just like we got some fine people in our race'. This launches another general sequence (pp. 39–40), this time illustrating some of the trades and professions followed by black people in Harlem. Rodney's trade, on the other hand, seems to be his ability to 'say things that makes everybody set up and take notice'.

In one of the longer sequences (up to p. 61), we are introduced first to elderly neighbours, who, childless and houseproud, are compared unfavourably with her daughter Melinda's family who are 'all tangled up in life – which ain't always so sanitary as we might like it to be'. We are taken into the home of Melinda and Jerry and their five children, and see them interacting with each other and with friends who come round for a party in their kitchen. We leave them as Melinda waits for Jerry to come home, ready to 'populate the colored race again'.

As if to illustrate the 'colored race' in all its variety, the next sequence (pp. 62–84) exits into the streets, via the window where people sit and watch the world go by. The following spreads are about life on the streets – people meeting and greeting, celebrating, working, parading, picketing, holding political meetings. This sequence ends as it begins, with a figure silhouetted in a window. We thus return to family concerns, with Rodney and Sister Mary herself in focus. Here, the affinity between the two that has been hinted at is made plain in the grandmother's clear identification with her errant grandchild, who is more 'like a son'. She believes that he would 'do better to marry Mazie ... who don't give a parlor damn about paying Con Edison' and who 'works just hard enough to get along' than the more conventional Ada – a 'decent girl' but not as 'beat up by life' as Mazie and Sister Mary herself have been. As she contemplates the possibility of a new relationship herself, with the widowed janitor, the redoubtable matriarch admits: 'I done got my feet caught in the sweet flypaper of life – and I'll be dogged if I want to get loose.'

Photographic Space

The Sweet Flypaper of Life is a text that annotates and interprets the way in which African Americans live in an almost filmic manner, as Hughes seems to produce a seamless narrative out of a flow of images that he has selected and sequenced to match the flow of Sister Mary's words. However, the fact that we know the photographs were taken, not to his commission but to satisfy the photographer's own agenda, set several years earlier, should remind us of the separate range of meanings that the images may have, once removed from the captioning effect of Hughes' text. It should also alert us to instances where word and image can undermine as well as reinforce each other. Finally, it should indicate that Hughes' written text is partly driven by the images, at least as much as the images are made to serve his text.

Taking up this last point, it does appear that Hughes' portrait of black urban life, by having to refer (directly or indirectly) to the photographs on the page, is thus dependent on and shaped by physical space. This space is both the three-dimensional space depicted (for example, an apartment interior or a street scene) and the two-dimensional space that is filled with the printed image. (There is, of course, a more literal way in which the space occupied by the photographs shapes and dominates the text on the page, breaking up its sentences and reducing utterances to brief captions.) Whether we analyse the written or the photographic text, the same spatial categories emerge: the space of the home, the space of the street, underground space. The treatment of these three types of space by writer and photographer will reveal ways in which the text as a whole ascribes meaning to urban experience, specifically the ways in which African Americans at this precise historical moment define themselves, practise everyday life and resist the conformity and corporatism of white culture.

The Space of the Home
The longest 'family' sequence in *The Sweet Flypaper of Life*, running for nine spreads (pp. 44–61) is set almost exclusively in a single interior, the kitchen in the apartment where Melinda, Jerry and their five children live. Thirty photographs are employed, of which over a half are candid close-ups of family members, singly or in pairs or groups. Although these images contain little if any surrounding domestic detail, the lighting and the pose – usually an embrace of some kind: child with adult, husband with wife – confirm they are of scenes in the family home. The camera pulls back in the other images to reveal family and friends interacting in the limited space of the kitchen. As well as expressions of familial love, this sequence contains a range of social incidents: friends and family singing and even dancing in the kitchen, children tussling, Melinda sewing or reading the paper, the family sitting down to eat, a daughter having her hair braided, the washing up being done. These informal and intimate images of a somewhat chaotic but loving family space support Sister Mary's preference for being 'tangled up in life' and they contrast with the two earlier images of Sister Jenkins and her husband. These elderly neighbours have no children and are able, as the photographs show, to keep a neat and tidy apartment, with antimacassars on the chairs, embroidered tablecloth, and an ordered kitchen area.

The party held in the kitchen for friends recalls the old tradition of 'rent parties', which began as a way of supplementing meagre incomes among city tenants, but more significantly demonstrates the way in which the space of the home is transformed into a place not only of communal display and entertainment, but of cultural continuity as well. Two women are pictured singing and Sister Mary confesses that, still awake in the early hours along with the youngest members of the family, she can be persuaded into singing the blues. This takes her back to her youth and 'Melinda's daddy' back in South Carolina, and forges a link between the past and present generations. The kitchen becomes a theatre for black memory and art, where the performers and the audience are members of the same ongoing community. Nevertheless, while the text emphasises the closeness of family and community ties, the photographs depict a space that is 'close' in the sense of confined, a space barely adequate to contain the lives that are celebrated. The frame is crowded with figures, dancing right up against the fridge, squeezed behind small tables, almost forced into intimacy.

The Space of the Street

> Every so often, every so once in a while, somedays a women gets a chance to set in her window for a minute and look out: New York is not like back down South with not much happening outside. In Harlem something is happening all the time, people are going every which-a-way ... (pp. 62–3)

The two images that this text accompanies are, first, the silhouette of a seated woman looking out of a window and, second, a view of a sidewalk presumably taken from such a window, where half a dozen figures walk up and down. The window presents the spectacle of the streets from the safe space of the home. After a long excursion into the outside world, that has encompassed hints of poverty and manifestations of political unrest, the sequence closes with another figure – a young boy – in a window, seen from the street: 'Yes, you can sit in your window anywhere in Harlem and see plenty' (p. 84). The boy is reading, just as we are reading this text, discovering the variety of life in Harlem.

The street is what distinguishes the city from the rural birthplace of the South. Things here are happening, people are going places or just hanging out. There is a sense of liberation and of anonymity, all of which feeds into the notion of the city as a place of opportunity. However, just as the fictional city of New York turns against the luckless family in Paul Dunbar's turn-of-the-century novel, *The Sport of the Gods*, or betrays Solomon Gillis in Rudolph Fisher's 'The city of refuge', the streets of Harlem present as much a threat as an opportunity to its children.[16] Before we see any street scenes at all, Sister Mary captions a close-up of Rodney with the cry: 'That Rodney! The street's done got Rodney!' (p. 10). This metaphor runs through the written text and expresses Sister Mary's fear of influences other than the family. Even as she celebrates the richness of urban life and its spectacle, she worries over the risk and temptation it represents: 'What do you reckon's out there in them streets for that boy?'(p. 85).

On the one hand, the street is a site of conspicuous consumption; the first photographs of the street are used to demonstrate that they are 'just full of cars' (p. 19) and the car is the ultimate consumer item of the period, a potent symbol of having made it. Rodney's drinking companion Joe 'ties a rope of dreams with Cadillac headlights, and bebop horns and girls saying, "Gimmie a ride"' around his neck (p. 12). Chickasaw, Rodney's polar opposite, and his partner may be considering actually buying a car, but for Rodney, as for many other black Americans, it remains a seductive and paralysing dream. On the other hand, the street is a site of transgression. Although the nature of lawlessness shown and written about here is mild enough, there are clear references to the growth of a street-based culture that replaces the bonds of family with those of peer-group gangs. Rodney, the black sheep of the family, was 'always the first to turn on the hydrant in the street in the summer' and 'always the one who got caught'. The photograph here shows children running around under the hydrant showers in semi-clad abandon, while the following spread of candid portraits purport to be some of the boys involved, with a group of girls egging them on, until 'the cops come – and they have to grab their clothes quick' (p. 23–6 *passim*).

Again, a comparison is drawn between Rodney and Chickasaw, this time emphasised by Hughes' deliberate pairing of two images: the hydrant scene and an elevated view, looking down on a single, elegant figure walking along an expanse of a well-paved avenue. This figure is identified in Hughes' text with Chick's girlfriend: 'Well, where she lives they got an elevator. Pretty streets, clean, it's on the hill' (p. 22). The hill is presumably Sugar Hill and home to the black bourgeoisie. The contrast between the two streets could not be more pointed, one calm and exclusive, elevated literally and in socio-economic terms, and the other very much at 'street-level' and, judging from the jets of spray, explosive. There is only one 'hill', but many streets like this one.

However, Hughes' annotation of the photographs of streets, car lots and urban wasteland in *The Sweet Flypaper of Life* is, by and large, determinedly optimistic. One of the most striking examples of this is his 'caption' to what has become one of DeCarava's most celebrated images (p. 69). A young woman in a glamorous full-length white gown is standing on the sidewalk beside what appears to be an abandoned lot. She is in a trapezium of sunlight surrounded by the shadow of apartment buildings. In the foreground, rubbish has been swept up into a pile in gutter; behind and to the other side of the figure is rough grass and rubble. The woman is standing left of centre; to the right is a dark wall on which a billboard has been pasted, advertising Chevrolet cars with a picture of a family saloon and the slogan 'Style Star of an All-Star Line'.

If examined out of this particular context, DeCarava's photograph seems to belong to a particular kind of documentary image developed during the 1930s and 1940s by members of the Farm Security and Works Progress Administration photographic projects. The deliberate choice to include the car advertisement in a picture that already contains a stark, black and white contrast between an ugly environment and a beautiful and enigmatic lone figure suggests that an ironic social comment is being made. It may be an image about aspiration – it is actually entitled 'Graduation' by the photographer – but it may also be making a subtler point about how the odds are stacked against the aspirant. The poster offers an alternative image – the white middle class in their family car – and recalls a similar contrast in Margaret Bourke-White's 1937 photograph, 'At the Time of the Louisville Flood', where a line of African Americans, queuing up for relief, files past a giant billboard that depicts a happy white family in their car and the slogan 'World's Highest Standard of Living – There's no way like the American Way'.[17] This complex image by Roy DeCarava is, however, reduced in the written text to a fond comment from Sister Mary: 'But it's nice to see young folks all dressed up going somewhere – maybe to a party.' For the next image, showing a shabbily dressed man looking into the closed doorway of a shuttered brownstone, Hughes writes, 'But it's sad if you ain't invited' (p. 70). Whether intentionally or not, Hughes thus undercuts the optimistic note struck against the previous image. The 'party' now seems to stand for the idea of success, even for the American dream – from which some Americans are excluded.

As if disturbed by this brief moment of gloom, Sister Mary goes on to comment over the next two spreads about the challenge of the physical environment of the city for a people raised in the rural South:

> It's too bad there's no front porches in Harlem: Almost nothing except stoops to set on ... or steps ... or doorways to lean in: And in the summertime, maybe a vacant lot: But almost everywhere where there's something to set on or lean on, somebody is setting or leaning. In what few parks there is, some just set on a park bench ... and hold their hands. (pp. 70–4)

In this brief passage, commenting on half a dozen images, Sister Mary both mourns the loss of a communal life based around the front porch and celebrates the way in which black people adapt to and even reshape an unsympathetic urban architecture, turning it into public space. This is the exterior equivalent to their transformation of the cramped apartment into a distinctively African American environment. One of the images thus captioned is of a man on a stoop with his young child. The way he sits may be read as a pose of resistance, the feet planted on the ground, claiming the territory.[18]

The way that African Americans occupy the street as a site of power is depicted in a series of photographs of political action (pp. 79–83): a picket line and street-corner meetings, with crowds of attentive listeners and a portrait of an impassioned orator, arm raised against the night sky. Sister Mary's explanation of the causes behind the demonstrations, that they are about 'Buy black' and 'Africa for the Africans' campaigns, shows how the community is concerned with both domestic and international issues affecting black people. An earlier shot of a parade, echoing James VanDerZee's earlier images of Garveyite Black Cross nurses, reminds us of the significant place that parading has for urban African

Americans, drawn from West Indian traditions of carnival and Marcus Garvey's love of pageant. Cut off from much of the political process, they have developed a long tradition of disciplined street marching, from such celebratory incursions of white territory as the 1919 parade of returning veterans of the 369th Regiment, photographed by VanDerZee and others, through the civil rights marches of the 1960s to the Million Man March in 1995.[19]

The street is a place of display. The famous stroll along Seventh Avenue is recorded and celebrated in a range of stories about the Harlem Renaissance period and has been photographed, though not here by DeCarava, whose images are of more casual walking and loitering. Sister Mary, however, refers to the desire of Harlemites to dress well and put on a show, even when ground down by drudgery and work. Accompanying a picture of a woman resting with her bag at the top of the steps from the subway, the text tells us that sometimes 'a woman goes to work all dressed up carrying her work clothes in a bundle' (p. 33). Sister Mary herself tries to change before coming home, so that 'my grandchildren would see me looking fresh' (p. 34). The subway and its steps here act as a concrete metaphor for the struggle to maintain dignity and a sense of self-worth. Above a picture of a woman descending the steps, glimpsed through the metal bars, Hughes writes: 'And I done climbed up and down a million subway steps: I done rid a million subway cars, and went back and forth to work a million days for that Rodney ...'(p. 31).

The street is a place of work. In a generic echo of the Edwardian street types photographed by Alice Austen in New York or of more recent images of street trades taken by Aaron Siskind in the 1940s for the Harlem Document,[20] DeCarava's photographs used here include informal portraits of a construction worker, a coalman and an iceman, as well as indoor shots of a jazz musician, an actor, an artist, a subway builder and a sign painter. By selecting these images, Hughes hopes to celebrate the diversity and economic health of black life in the city, suggesting in the process that to survive there, you need a defined role, as a worker. Equally, the written text and the selection of images argue that a family role is also vital to survival in a bleak urban environment.

Two sets of images are paired up by Hughes to demonstrate the way the street is less hospitable than the family. In one pair, a sad boy leaning against a lamppost is associated in the text with Rodney's child (born out of wedlock and neglected by his father) and this image (printed in full and in detail, isolating him further) is placed opposite one of another child whispering in a father's ear in an intimate close-up (pp. 28–9). The next page juxtaposes another lonely boy glumly sat in a patch of wasteland ('some children, maybe they don't have nobody') with a son of the same age, tended to by his mother (p. 30). Without a job and without a role in the family, either as a son or a father, you become a Rodney and must find your space underground.

Underground Space

Rodney's failure to fit in with the conventional aspirations of the dominant culture is given a spatial metaphor that assigns him to a literal and metaphorical underground existence. Rodney is never seen outside but in gloomy bars and dark interiors and, at points in the text when Sister Mary is most critical, in the basement drinking with his men friends. As observed earlier, Rodney is compared unfavourably with Chickasaw, who is 'as different from Rodney as day from night' – a telling distinction, associating Chick with whiteness and Rodney with blackness. Unlike Rodney, who 'says daylight hurts his eyes', Chick takes the bus rather than the subway and heads off to work downtown, that is, in the white section of Manhattan. According to Sister Mary, Chick 'could dress himself when he was three years old', gets up early, works hard, has a girlfriend 'on the hill', and is growing up 'all reet, all right'. In these habits and in his evident belief in integration, Chick is a man in the Booker T. Washington mode. Rodney, on the other hand, does not work and 'Never will be integrated with neither white nor colored, nor work, just won't' (pp. 20–3 *passim*).

Rodney's refusal to work or to conform is illustrated by two images of his drinking and rapping sessions down in the basement and in his general lack of movement – or mobility, 'he never moves fast – not even to reach out his hand for a dollar – except when he's dancing' (p. 11). The places he dances and hangs out with a string of different girlfriends are bars and places with jukeboxes. No windows are visible in the photographs used to illustrate this behaviour, and precious little light. The eateries, clubs and dives described in a range of twentieth-century African American literature are often reached by stairs leading underground, from James Weldon Johnson's protagonist (in *The Autobiography of an Ex-Colored Man*) finding the only restaurant in town that will serve 'colored people' below stairs to Solomon Gillis' descent into the club where he is arrested.[21] When Sister Mary exclaims metaphorically that 'The street's done got Rodney!', she goes on to identify a precise place where he may be reached, 'do you reckon my prayers will reach down in all them king-kong basements, and sing with the jukeboxes, and walk in the midnight streets with that Rodney?' (p. 11). The streets at midnight are effectively underground too, hidden from daylight.

At several points in the narrative, Sister Mary comments on Rodney's lack of mobility, upward or actual. There is, however, one exceptional circumstance: 'he only moves fast when he's dancing', being 'crazy about music'. This was, of course, a period when young people had first emerged with a distinctive youth culture, exemplified in this text by jukeboxes, 'cool' jazz and cars. A range of attitudes and poses had also developed, linked to the rebellious writings of the Beat literary movement, itself partly shaped by the new forms of improvisational jazz and a 'black' hipster sensibility. 'When there's music playing', says Sister Mary, adopting the current lingo, 'girls have to just keep looking to see where's he at. *Where's he at? Where's he at?*' (p. 11).

The answer to this existential question is that Rodney is, in effect, in a space of his own creation, shaped not only in his dancing but by his other main activity, talk: 'They say in the neighborhood sometimes Rodney can say things that makes everybody set up and take notice ...' (p. 41). This comment captions an image of four men in serious discussion down in what appears to be a basement, and it follows the series of work portraits of 'some fine people in our race', noted earlier. Rodney's occupation has no immediate, tangible product; his voice starts underground and circulates mysteriously but powerfully around the neighbourhood. It is, in other words, a prophetic voice, like that of Ralph Ellison's *Invisible Man*, telling his story 'on the lower frequencies'.[22]

Photographic Ambiguity

Throughout the text, Hughes struggles to tame the numerous potential readings of DeCarava's photographs and to produce the most optimistic meaning from images that sometimes resist or even contradict the words he puts in Sister Mary's mouth. He has a clear ideological agenda in structuring the text around the twin worlds of the family and the wider community it shapes. Through Sister Mary, Hughes talks into existence a coherent, loving framework where even the most non-conformist member of the group is cherished and absorbed, like a prodigal son. Where this scheme breaks down, however, is in its uncertain and ambiguous attitude towards aspiration and assimilation, on the one hand, and towards unconventionality and refusal on the other. This has its spatial equivalent in the fluctuating interpretation of the street, as both threat and opportunity. Although the space of the home is privileged in the written text, Sister Mary's partial identification with the wilder lifestyle of her grandson Rodney qualifies her disapproval of the underground existence he leads – as if the basements and jazz clubs he frequents recall for her the glamorous days of the Harlem Renaissance.

Another ambiguity lies in the potential conflict or disparity between the written and the visual text, where some images could as easily invite comments on dilapidation and poverty as Hughes' encomiums on black life. This goes to the heart of the challenge facing photographers of Harlem and black sections in other cities. Deborah Willis-Braithwaite has, for example, compared James VanDerZee's photographs of Harlem with those of Aaron Siskind, contrasting the former's sympathy and celebration of his own community with the latter's outsider status and stance.[23] She argues that the difference in their origins and attitudes can be clearly discerned in their photographs. This returns us to 'the attitude that good photographers seem to take', according to Albert Murray, distinguishing those who represent Harlem as a community rather than as a ghetto. A. D. Coleman, a white critic and the first to publish an article on Roy DeCarava in 1970, was also one of the first to argue that outsiders could (or should) not 'go cold into an unfamiliar community' because they would 'come out with images [without] any relationship to truth worth speaking of'.[24]

This argument is supported by current thinking on the intrusiveness of conventional social documentary: somehow the subject of the photograph needs not to be 'subjected' but to have some say in their representation. Stuart Hall, writing about the 'reformist look', argues that its subjects are made 'almost the passive objects of forces that they could not control or actively oppose'.[25] In a detailed critique of John Launois' photograph of an African American family in a decaying tenement room, Paul A. Rogers is concerned by 'the way this static image of dystopia ... signifies "blackness" as an irreducible condition upon whose body poverty is mapped, organized, and finally, firmly ... situated as natural'.[26]

Nevertheless, the essential ambiguity of the photograph or, to put it another way, its dependence on a context (which might be a caption) can problematise this view of documentary photography. Among the images not used by Hughes in *The Sweet Flypaper of Life* is one that has become one of DeCarava's most famous photographs. Called simply 'Hallway', it was taken in 1953 and is formally very simple.[27] It depicts a very narrow dark hallway, dimly lit by bare bulbs. It is, for most viewers, an oppressive and claustrophobic image, with the walls pressing in and the eye drawn along a severe perspective into vaporous darkness. Yet, discussing this photograph recently, DeCarava himself has claimed it as in some ways a comforting image, for the hallway evokes his childhood: 'It just brought back all those things that I had experienced as a child in those hallways. It was frightening ... And it was depressing. And yet here I am an adult ... looking at the same hallway and finding it beautiful.'[28] This double reading may be equally extended to the pictures that Hughes did choose to use. However confined and however compromised the space depicted by the camera, it is also *lived* space: home, in other words.

Removed from Hughes' text and exhibited as art objects, DeCarava's photographs are open to wide interpretation and appropriation but, in *The Sweet Flypaper of Life*, Hughes sees through them to a city of potential. In the spaces that conventional documentary photography has stereotyped as the ghetto, he finds a community struggling to be seen.

Was the oracle mistaken? Not necessarily. I interpret it in this way: Marozia consists of two cities, the rat's and the swallow's; both change with time, but their relationship does not change; the second is about to free itself from the first.[29]

Notes

1   Italo Calvino, *Invisible Cities* (London: Picador, 1979): the following quotations are from 'Hidden cities 3' pp. 119–120.

2   Berenice Abbott (text by Elizabeth McCausland), *Changing New York* (New York: E. P. Dutton, 1939); Weegee, *Naked City* (New York: Da Capo Press, 1985; facsimile of 1945 edition [New York: Essential Books]).

3   Roy DeCarava and Langston Hughes, *The Sweet Flypaper of Life* (New York: Hill and Wang, 1967, c.1955). All further references to this text will be incorporated in the essay.

4   A year after the launch of *Life* magazine, its founder Henry Luce wrote: 'The essay is no longer a vital means of communication. But what is vital is *the photographic essay*' (quoted in Marianne Fulton, *Eyes of Time: Photojournalism in America* (New York: New York Graphic Society, Little, Brown and Company, 1988) p. 136). While illustrated magazines like *Life*, *Look* and *Fortune* published the photographs of the Farm Security Administration and other documentary photographers in the 1930s and 40s, book publishers also brought out a number of books combining text with photographs. Notable examples include James Agee and Walker Evans, *Let Us Now Praise Famous Men*; Erskine Caldwell and Margaret Bourke-White, *You Have Seen Their Faces*; Archibald Macleish, *Land of the Free*; Arthur F. Raper, *Tenants of the Almighty*; and Richard Wright and Edwin Rosskam, *Twelve Million Black Voices*.

5   James Weldon Johnson, 'Harlem: the culture capital' in Alain Locke (ed.), *The New Negro* (New York: Atheneum, 1968 [1925], rep. 1975) p. 301.

6   Albert Murray, *The Omni-Americans: Black Experience and American Culture* (New York: Vintage Books, 1983 [1975]) p. 71. All further references will be incorporated in the text. One target of Murray's criticism is Kenneth Clark, *Dark Ghetto: Dilemmas of Social Power* (London: Victor Gollancz, 1965).

7   Not just in the mainstream media; similar tropes are also used by such writers as Ralph Ellison. In 'Harlem is nowhere', he writes that African Americans migrating North 'made some fatal error of judgment and fell into a great chasm of mazelike passages that promise ever to lead to the mountain but ever end against a wall'. See Ralph Ellison, *The Collected Essays of Ralph Ellison* (New York: The Modern Library, Random House, 1995) p. 323.

8   Alain Locke called Allen 'by far the most outstanding and promising young Negro in this modern field of growing importance – art photography'. See Deborah Willis-Thomas, *Black Photographers, 1840–1940: An Illustrated Bio-Bibliography* (New York: Garland Publishing, 1985) p. 17.

9   Aaron Siskind, *Harlem: Photographs 1932–1940* (Manchester: Cornerhouse Publications in association with the National Museum of American Art, 1991 [1981]). 'The Harlem Document' was never published separately, but images by Siskind and other members of the PhotoLeague were exhibited and published in such magazines as *Fortune*.

10   Jacob Riis, *How the Other Half Lives* (New York: Dover Publications, 1971 [1901]).

11   Morgan and Marvin Smith, *Harlem* (Lexington: The University Press of Kentucky, 1998) pp. 8–9.

12   Weegee, *Naked City*, p. 198.

13   In fact, this might have been the second such publication had a proposed collaboration between Ralph Ellison and African American photographer Gordon Parks come to fruition in the late 1940s. Such combinations of photographs and text were very popular at this time, and could be seen in the most popular photographic exhibition (and book) of the period, *The Family of Man*, curated by Edward Steichen at the Museum of Modern Art in New York in 1955, the same year that *The Sweet Flypaper of Life* was published.

14   After studying painting and drawing at the George Washington Carver Art School in 1944–45, Roy DeCarava (b. 1919) concentrated first on printmaking before turning to photography in 1948. In 1952, DeCarava secured a Fellowship from the Guggenheim Foundation which allowed him a year 'to photograph Harlem through the Negro people'. However, as he recounted to A. D. Coleman fifteen years after the publication of *The Sweet Flypaper of Life*: 'Nobody wanted the pictures, so I took them to Langston.' See A. D. Coleman, 'Roy DeCarava: "thru black eyes"' in his *Light Readings: A Photography Critic's Writings 1968–1978* (New York: Oxford University Press, 1979) p. 25. There is a lengthier account of this collaboration in Arnold Rampersad, *The Life of Langston Hughes*, Vol. 2 (New York: Oxford University Press, 1988) pp. 242–9 *passim*.

15   Describing 'black image production' in the South, bell hooks writes: 'Significantly, displaying those images in everyday life was as central as making them. The walls and walls of images in southern black homes were sites of resistance. They constituted private, black-owned and-operated, gallery space.' See bell hooks, 'In our glory: photography and black life' in Deborah Willis, *Picturing Us: African American Identity in Photography* (New York: The New Press, 1994) p. 47.

16   Paul Dunbar, *The Sport of the Gods* (Miami: Mnemosyne Publishing, 1969; rep. of 1902 edition [New York: Dodd, Mead & Co.]); Rudolph Fisher, 'The city of refuge' in Locke, *The New Negro*, pp. 57–74.

17   This photograph may be found in Sean Callahan, *Margaret Bourke White: Photographer* (London: Pavilion Books, 1998) p. 94. (The caption given here is 'Breadline during the Louisville flood, Kentucky, 1937'.)

18   In an essay on DeCarava, Peter Galassi notes with reference to this and similar images: 'we are sometimes able to read the expression of the face, but the psychology of these pictures is expressed as much through the posture of the body.' See Peter Galassi, *Roy DeCarava: A Retrospective* (New York: Museum of Modern Art, 1996) p. 18.

19   Examples of VanDerZee's street scenes can be found in Deborah Willis-Braithwaite and Rodger C. Birt, *James VanDerZee: Photographer* (New York: Harry N. Abrams/National Portrait Gallery, 1993).

20   Alice Austen was active in street photography from the mid-1880s onwards. Her portfolio, *Street Types*, was deposited at the Library of Congress in Washington.

21   James Weldon Johnson, *The Autobiography of an Ex-Colored Man* (New York: Penguin Books, 1990 [1912]) pp. 40–1.

22   Ralph Ellison, *Invisible Man* (Harmondsworth: Penguin, 1952) p. 469.

23   See Willis-Braithwaite and Birt, *James VanDerZee*, pp. 20–5.

24   A. D. Coleman, 'Fundi: the nuances of the moment' in *Light Readings*, p. 63.

25   Stuart Hall, 'Reconstruction work', *Ten-8* 16 (1984) p. 7.

26   Paul A. Rogers, 'Hardcore Poverty' in Willis, *Picturing Us*, p. 161.

27   This image may be found in Galassi, *Roy DeCarava*, p. 105.

28   Galassi, *Roy DeCarava*, p. 28.

29   Calvino, *Invisible Cities*, p. 120.

4

Pascal Pinck

From the Sofa to the Crime Scene: Skycam, Local News and the Televisual City

Don DeLillo writes in *White Noise*: 'For most people there are only two places in the world. Where they live and their TV set.'[1] Though flip, the point rings true: our experience of TV land and our experience of lived space each apply to disparate worlds, both familiar yet strangely unrelated. My apartment would look out of place on television; TV actors would look out of place in my apartment. Music videos, cartoons and sitcoms don't seem to take place anywhere at all. Some fear losing touch with the physical world while watching television, even as they secretly wonder what they are missing once the set has been turned off.

There is one notable exception to DeLillo's rule: during the local news, television seems to coincide with where we live. News producers present their product as live, local and up-to-the-minute: part of your world rather than an alternative to it. In America, this emphasis holds true especially in large and medium-sized cities, where multiple affiliates find themselves competing for viewers even as they cover the same events. Will folks stay tuned for stories that affect not their neighbourhood, but their region or their country? Many news directors think not, and believe that more on-scene coverage from more angles at more locations close to home is *the* way to boost ratings.

In this essay, I will explore the visual significance of television news as it relates to our lived experience of urban spaces. Although we may recognise the typical forms of our home metropolis on screen – especially if these forms are visually distinctive as in New York or Seattle – television's architectural cues revise our *idea* of the city: what it looks like, how to live there, and how it may be navigated. Framing, lighting, captioning and graphics provide not a simple representation of urban space, but a hybrid that emerges simultaneously in the picture tube and in the street: a televisual city.

Technology has encouraged this trend, and satellite vans, microwave trucks and better cellular networks have brought the city into sharp televisual focus. One pivotal contributor is the television skycam – helicopter-based cameras that provide live images, day or night, in striking magnification and resolution. Traffic updates, high-speed chases, images of natural disasters stream into living rooms, all seen from a bird's-eye perspective. The images of the TV skycam render the economic, political and aesthetic currents of the televisual city uniquely visible, as demonstrated in North Hollywood, California during the spring of 1997. Cops and heavily armed bank robbers clashed in a western-style shoot-out, airborne reporters provided the commentary, and neighbours watched the spectacle from the comfort of their sofas and reclining armchairs. I will devote a portion of this essay to the skycam phenomenon as a case study.

Life Through the Tube

The relationship between architecture and the moving image is a rich area of academic debate, though film scholars have begun to examine questions of urban space only recently. In his introduction to the anthology *The Cinematic City*, David B. Clarke writes: 'So central is the city to film that, paradoxically, the widespread *implicit* acceptance of its importance has mitigated against an explicit consideration of its actual significance.'[2] While disciplinary politics have certainly contributed to this chasm, we can recognise a kind of common sense that would challenge the connection between film theory and urban studies. After all, the bulk of feature films are shot on sets or in sound stages. Location sequences are rarely what they seem – Newark or Toronto can be easily made to look like Chicago or London. Even the darkness of the theatre seems to separate the exterior landscape from the illusionistic space of the cinematic image. Indeed, one of the great pleasures of movie-going is its promise of access to another world.

In an effort to combat this intuitive resistance, some humanities scholars have sought to frame the emergence of both cinema and the modern city as parallel symptoms of the same historical process. Clarke's summary is succinct:

> The spectacle of the cinema both drew upon and contributed to the increased pace of modern city life, whilst also helping to normalise and cathect the frantic, disadjusted rhythms of the city ... [it] reflected and helped to mould the novel forms of social relations that developed in the crowded and anonymous city streets; and both documented and

helped to transform the social and physical space that the modern city represented.[3]

In other words, critics now see cinema as playing a key role in the transformation of urban fabrics. But if we are to investigate the effect of moving images on the pace and social relations of the modern city, it is necessary to include television's role as well. Despite the formal, optical, perceptual and ideological differences between the two technologies, TV and film both normalise and cathect, reflect and mould, document and transform spectators' experiences of urban space.

For Paul Virilio, video images are the key to a novel way of seeing. The cathode ray tube provides not a representation of the world, nor the manifestation of a concept, but rather a membrane, a doorway, literally a structural element. Television provides an interface, a way of engaging a threatening exterior expanse in a manageable fashion, a logic that makes the outside world familiar and legible to the viewer. Virilio identifies this unique role in explicitly architectural terms:

> TV doesn't function at all as a medium like radio or newspapers, but as an architectonic element: it is a portable window, insofar as it can be shifted. It's part of the organisation of the city, a definitive, final, terminal city.[4]

Like a building, television news sets up spatial hierarchies and arranges encounters. Consider the different ways competing affiliates respond to a natural disaster or crime scene. Camera crews are set up at different locations – some closer, some further away, others on the roof of their trucks – each trying to provide clear, immediate visual access. Indeed, many reporters use spatial tricks outside of breaking news events to keep the picture interesting. Walking into the frame or towards the camera to make a point, or having the camera follow the reporter through a cramped interior, are all ways of subtly altering the viewer's encounter with televisual space.

But Virilio's argument goes well beyond television's methods of spatial manipulation. In *The Lost Dimension* he juxtaposes the formal stability of the TV image with its inherent technological instability. Television's system of instantaneous, electronic transmission, and its ability to switch viewpoints and locations at a moment's notice, call the notion of a continuous urban fabric into question. Especially significant is Virilio's distinction between technologies that transform relations of distance and technologies that transform relations of time:

> For the attentive observer, the slicing of physical space into different geometric dimensions [as with the telescope], and the durable separation of geographic and constructed spaces [as with cinema], is

replaced by the momentary break, due to the imperceptible interruption of different sequences of view-points and the perceptible interruption of broadcasting and reception. The new produced and projected space has less to do with lines, surfaces and volumes than with the minutiae of view-point, the dynamite of tenths-of-seconds.[5]

Television's status as a real-time transmission device, then, collapses the boundaries that separate discrete moments and discrete locations. TV news makes little distinction between the geographies of shooting and the geographies of viewing – a uniquely uncinematic feature. Film footage is shot months or years before it arrives in theatres; backlot sets and multiplex theatres operate as dislocated spaces. But the spatial and temporal territory of TV news is remarkably familiar, literally close to home.

Furthermore, television news allows us to inhabit multiple spaces and watch multiple events at the same time – as is often illustrated during major event coverage. American cable news stations are particularly fond of this convention, and will think nothing of jumping between four or five reporters and main anchor to tackle all facets of a given scandal or disaster. Virilio might say that viewers have given up the representation of space in favour of a thoroughly new spatial experience. This explosive transformation of spatial relations recalls the genesis of the cinematic *flâneur*, but television's viewers are anti-*flâneurs*.[6] Rather than transporting the viewer into faraway lands, arranged for his/her consumption, TV's structural system is based on the inverse, on the inertia of the viewer at home. Myriad non-continuous spaces flash before the eye, yet are unified by the familiarity and solidity of the TV set as a piece of furniture. This domestic privilege, for Virilio, enhances the explosive power of the televisual aperture: 'The television screen is an introverted window, one which no longer opens onto adjoining space but instead faces beyond the perceptible horizon ... The television set posted before the sofa is an object that punctures the walls. [It is] a threshold of transformation.'[7]

Besides Virilio, a number of theorists have recognised television as a site of spatial dynamism. In her now-classic 1983 article, Jane Feuer argues that 'notions of liveness lend a sense of flow which overcomes extreme fragmentation of space'.[8] Like military imaging technologies such as radar and sonar, television was indeed designed to communicate information instantaneously; to provide highly specific sensory information about a current set of conditions; to operate, not as a visual archive, but in real time. Feuer proposed that although production practices have changed dramatically, television's inherent 'liveness' has remained uncontested:

Due to its electronic nature, television is far more capable of affirming its own mode as one of absolute presence ... by postulating an equivalence between time of event, time of television creation and transmission-viewing time, television as an institution identifies all messages emanating from the apparatus as 'live' ... In this way, television as an ideological apparatus positions the spectator into its 'imaginary' of presence and immediacy.[9]

Television's rhetorical and technological biases, in other words, conspire to unify the sum total of televisual output – regardless of channel, genre or production method. I would argue that television's capacity to unify disparate architectural spaces is rooted in the *formal* system of the television image as well. The TV screen presents a surface upon which anything can be projected, in any order, without an inherent need for systematised pacing or continuity.[10] This potential for heterogeneity makes the quick succession of different formal categories of a television newscast possible, i.e. graphics, text, still photos, film clips as well as straight video. Indeed, the control-room staff is faced with the challenge of switching between these many sources in a smooth and visually appealing way, and most directors resort to the use of stylised transition effects. These effects – flashy wipes from one image to another, setting one image into another – are built into almost all professional video switchers and used regularly not just in television news, but in a range of genres that have reason to define themselves as expressly televisual like infomercials or MTV.

Mary Ann Doane has commented on television's temporal heterogeneity, and like Virilio locates the medium's power in its manipulation of time. For Doane, the staccato flow of news items, previews, commercials and trailers dissolves the rigid temporal structure found in the cinema, and demands a new kind of unity. This common denominator can be understood as units of electronic information, packets that transcend their own visuality. Thus, in Doane's reading the spasmodic texture of television news actually severs the link to representational modes of imaging:

Television news is distinguished by the very absence of the rationalised renaissance space we have come to associate with film – a perspectival technique which purports to *represent* the truth of objects in space. Instead, the simultaneous activation of different, incongruous spaces (the studio, graphics, footage from the scene, interviews on monitor) is suggestive of the writing surface and the consequent annihilation of depth. Television does not so much *represent* as it *informs*.[11]

The Skycam

The American style of broadcast news, then, sets up the TV image as a revolving window, providing access to disparate, dislocated worlds. But this window is hard to pin down, it jumps and changes, seemingly with a mind of its own. At times, the frame of the TV set contains a portal that promises adventure and escape, as when newscasters introduce a 'live shot' with the words: 'we take you now to …' At other times, this frame contains a mirror in which we are invited to see ourselves – as when ordinary passers-by are asked to comment on events beyond their control. It is a surface that can accommodate various layers, each of which are lifted to reveal yet another – as when graphics wipe to video, and video wipes to captions superimposed on a head shot. The images of television news generate a kind of manic drafting board, a space that wants to include all things at once.

Although the range of visual material is near infinite, news directors prefer some genres of televisual imagery over others – and, as ratings seem to prove, so do audiences. One of the most popular sources are TV skycams, helicopter-based cameras that cover natural disasters, traffic tie-ups and crimes-in-progress. Though broadcast affiliates around the United States regularly sent airborne camera crews to cover fires and floods in the 1980s, the skycam has been transformed in the last five years from an occasional gimmick to a widespread, commonly understood mode of representation. This phenomenon provides a unique illustration of the forces at work within the televisual city. While the skycam has a rich set of historical precedents as a technology of the airborne gaze, it is specific to television news. Helicopter-based cameras are indeed used in film production, but the live skycam must be understood as a whole system of meanings that includes an airborne anchor/reporter and a specific way of looking at the world. And while its use is limited to urban and suburban regions, the skycam has found popularity across America and increasingly worldwide. Affiliates in certain markets weigh their newscasts more or less heavily towards the skycam – success stories include San Diego, Phoenix, Dallas-Fort Worth and Miami. But the dawn of skycam mania can be traced to Los Angeles and June 1994, when it was introduced into the public consciousness during the nationally televised O. J. Simpson Bronco chase. Less than a month after the event, the *New Leader* commented:

> Movies like *Grand Canyon* and *Boyz N the Hood* have taught us about LAPD helicopters, but not until that Friday did the country, especially the backward East, learn about local TV helicopters. Every newsroom in Los Angeles has one. They were bought to spot traffic jams but soon became handmaidens of 'live action' news … By the accepted precept

that what happens in California will soon happen to the rest of us, News From Above is surely coming to us all.[12]

Though California may have popularised skycam images, the technology that made them possible has its origin elsewhere. The most significant innovation was developed by the Canadian company Wescam Inc., which introduced a gyro-stabilised camera mount in the mid-1980s. Designed to provide a stable image regardless of vibration or tilt angle of the platform, this system was first marketed to law enforcement and military agencies, but quickly caught on in the arena of civilian film and TV production. In 1990, the skycam's inventors won an Academy Award for their technical wizardry.[13] Within four years, every television news operation in Los Angeles had acquired a gyro-stabilised system, produced either by Wescam or by FLIR Systems of Portland, Oregon. Why did a repurposed military technology suddenly appear so desirable to TV executives? The key may be found among the painful lessons learned during the Los Angeles riots: ground-based camera crews were slow and cumbersome at best, easy targets at worst. Just as the LAPD deployed airborne units during tactical alert situations, so news directors needed an arsenal of video weaponry at their disposal. An affiliate helicopter ensures that a reporter will arrive at the scene of a major event at the same time as the police, if not beforehand – and provides a secure platform from which to transmit a live picture. The pilot need not even descend to automatic-weapons range. Wescam boasts that the rock-solid stability of the gyro-stabilised mount allows for magnification up to 220x, enabling 'this system to read a vehicle's license plate from a distance of well over 1000 yards'.[14]

It is no accident that tactical concerns of this kind emerged in the suburban jungle of southern California. Not all cities are equally conducive to airborne operations; urban forms tend to exhibit distinctive visual prejudices. In other words, an urban centre may make itself logical by different means – this is especially true of cities that were built in different eras. The medieval section of the Swiss town of Berne, for instance, would not be suitable for the skycam's gaze. The town's density makes its patterns illegible from above. Interestingly, it is visually unreadable from the inside as well: too many nooks and crannies; all the buildings are just high enough to block one's view, but not tall enough to stand out. Instead, the logic of Berne makes itself known in the act of walking, in circling the town centre on foot. In the case of a modern metropolis like New York, the overhead view provides little insight as well. The streets are too narrow to be read clearly and the density confounds the airborne eye. But unlike the medieval city, New York is highly readable from below, before the viewer takes a single step. The even right angles, strong vertical gestures and repeating parallel lines invoke the logic of linear perspective, giving an instant sense of geographic orientation. Most important, New York's unique articulated shapes of bridges and skyscrapers serve to render the city visually transparent from the inside. As I emerge from the subway, I stop and look upwards; these shapes locate me instantly within the city's boundaries.

The postmodern sprawl of Los Angeles, on the other hand, is an ideal territory for the airborne lens. Southern California is above all else horizontal: urban critics like Edward Soja and Mike Davis emphasise the oppressive sense of boundless space, iterations of little houses into infinity. Like the medieval city, the postmetropolis is visually opaque from ground level, inaccessible to those invading by land or sea. Many tourists express befuddlement at the freeway system that seems to simply connect anonymous suburbs with more of the same.

But this mind-numbing expanse is perfectly logical to the region's millions of residents, who employ a schematic visual system based precisely on an overhead point of view. The grid system of the so-called *Thomas Guides* – book-length street maps that list every last cul-de-sac – locates each neighbourhood within Cartesian coordinates, circumscribed by a web of freeways. The skycam, in turn, makes the neighbourhoods and the freeways visible, attests to their three dimensionality, reminds us that the city which we cannot see is really there. Southern Californian suburbanites have learned to use airborne technology to make their city more accessible; the same technology, we might add, used by the LAPD to keep the inner city under guard. News directors invite alienated suburbanites to own, to construct a personalised sense of civic community.

Here we are at the crux of the visionary territorialism inherent within the framework of aerial imaging. The history of the airborne camera in the twentieth century traces the process of making familiar what is invisible and unknowable – a process that is equally applicable at home or abroad, in wartime and peacetime, with respect to the past and to the future.[15] Frome explains:

> Before its use as a military reconnaissance technique, the aerial view had been available only to the celestial eye of God ... [it] also inverted the subordinate role traditionally imposed in church – the upward gaze toward the dome of heaven. Soaring vicariously above the earth, man could now imagine that he could control all that lay below.[16]

Considering aerial photography's implication in the logics of classification and destruction, it is intriguing that the 1960s and 1970s brought unprecedented success for the airborne image as a source for aesthetic and artistic claims. The rise of commercial air travel in the postwar years is partially to blame: the experience of seeing the earth from above with one's own eyes had become accessible to more and more individuals, certainly to many artists as well. One such artist is the Swiss photographer Georg Gerster, whose books *Grand Design: The Earth as Seen from Above* (1976) and *Below from Above* (1986) address several key aesthetic components of the airborne image. In his introduction to the latter volume, Gerster writes:

> The aerial photographer has an advantage over his earthbound colleagues – the advantage of altitude. Even close to three thousand hours of photo flight in chartered small aircraft fail to diminish my amazement at how dramatically the world changes when seen with the eagle's eyes ... this perspective alone both alienates and concentrates, allowing a visually exciting tight-rope walk between information and abstraction.[17]

Altitude and viewing angle dictate an entirely distinctive visual regime: as details disappear and scale becomes relative, we witness the transformation of a familiar, human-sized and human-centred view into something altogether different. Gerster's images treat parking lots, waste dumps, coral reefs and marshlands equally – a kind of standardised overview. This view invokes a language that denies familiar codes of the representation of real objects, is removed from the passage of time, and is disassociated from any specific context – we might call it the 'aesthetic of above'.

I favour this expression, because the word 'above' points to a key spatial relation for the airborne camera. The photographer is always *above* something, by definition something scenic; privy to a landscape laid out for his/her viewing pleasure. That is, we may add to the previously discussed metaphysical privilege of the celestial eye an equally important aesthetic one. Gaston Bachelard writes: 'From the top of his tower, a philosopher of domination sees the universe in miniature. Everything is small because he is so high. And since he is high, he is great, the height of his station is proof of his own greatness.'[18] We find an eerie preview of this aesthetic of above in the writings of Antoine de Saint-Exupéry. From his seat in a French fighter plane, all objects below remain out of reach, and are yet united by these totalising mechanics of vision. Saint-Exupéry writes:

> All I can see on the vertical is curios from another age, beneath clear, untrembling glass. I lean over crystal frames in a museum; I tower above a great sparkling pane, the great pane of my cockpit. Below are men – protozoa on a microscope slide ... I am an icy scientist, and for me their war is a laboratory experiment.[19]

Saint-Exupéry's characterisation of the artist-scientist, in love with his power and in love with his microbes, provides a key to the skycam's privileged position not just within the genre of TV news, but within American culture as a whole. This technology is successful in its incarnation as aerial image machine, because it promises to fulfil multiple kinds of desire: aesthetic, political and metaphysical. In addition, the skycam retains an unparalleled air of technological and scientific credibility. Liveness and technical sophistication invite a reborn myth of documentary, and lend exactly the kind of authority and truth-value long gone from other media. Marcus Aurelius Root could celebrate photography as the 'Pencil of Nature' in 1864, and Dziga Vertov could hope to capture the essence of the Soviet Union on film in 1924, but in the 1990s, we are only likely to believe what we see on TV.

Thus, though the skycam's gaze is indebted to photography, it must constantly position itself as unphotographic. This is emphasised, in part, through the instability of the skycam image, electronically and kinetically. In television news, action and movement are key, and indeed the scene changes moment by moment, police cars give chase, high drama unfolds on screen. Furthermore, the optical source is itself visibly mobile as the camera's point of view is cut loose from earthly tethers. Virilio claims that we have learned to watch TV by looking through a car windshield; if this is true, then the intuitive familiarity of skycam images will be hard to beat indeed. Furthermore, the skycam does not actualise its freedom to soar quite like the airborne still camera. News producers demand a close-up that the still image never does – in aerial photography, higher is better. Skycams need proximity, not just action, and even with super-zoom technology, lower is always preferable. Thus, the skycam enters into a relationship with the observed in a way the high-flying still camera disavows; here, surveillance technology overpowers its subjects. There can be no stealth skycam, or at least, not yet.

The News in Your Front Yard

We have, then, positioned the skycam along the axes of mobile/static, fast/slow and high/low. In concluding this look at the TV skycam, I would propose a brief consideration of the skycam's role in the playful tension between inside and outside – a tension that appears throughout television news. This bias seems to germinate in the genre's propensity for spatial manipulation, and is especially noticeable if one tries to locate the interior of the news studio within Cartesian coordinates. In a sense, this is impossible: the studio itself is completely interior to television, and purports to be linked to the outside world only through its window-monitors. So where is the space of the skycam image? On the one hand, it depicts events located ostensibly in the real: the outside world. But this outside view is mediated by the airborne anchor/reporter, sitting inside the protected bubble of the helicopter. None the less, the spatial logic of television positions the airborne anchor 'in the field', that is outside the contained sphere of the studio. All of this, of course, seems to be happening inside your television set, which in turn is an object inside your house. But the rhetoric of broadcast reporting demands that TV 'take you there', that is, for your sofa to be whisked outside, into the scene of breaking news.

The constant *potential* for breaking news, the threat that the city might be instantly transformed into a skycam's backdrop, seems to cause Virilio a great deal of uneasiness. His writing is characterised by a feeling of crisis, especially in work from the 1990s like the boldly titled essay 'Speed and information: cyberspace alarm!'[20] Technology threatens to explode and annihilate, to signal the advent of an architectural apocalypse. But I think we can be a bit more precise: television is not really *dismantling* the outside world of the cityscape. Though reporters may manipulate space, and the TV set may warp it, television's status as an architectural medium suggests it has too much in common with urban space to become an electronic Godzilla.

But Virilio is right to call attention to the consequences of television's visual and technological dominance. This elision of electronic and architectural environments erodes a basic function of built spaces: the ability to obscure. He reminds us that, at one point, the same buildings that protected us against inclement weather also protected us from curious glances – now, a tactical mindset demands line-of-sight access to public parks, jail cells and bedrooms.[21] Movies like *Blue Thunder* celebrate the dawn of an era when buildings can no longer protect from curious ears or curious glances. Conspiracy theorists fear surveillance within our 'own four walls', and nostalgically recall the time when privacy was possible. Television, especially local news, has made the city more familiar and the living room less so. Indeed, we need only to turn to a 1993 *Los Angeles Times* article for a dramatic example:

Jose Ornelas was watching television at home Thursday when suddenly the pictures changed from Carol Burnett on a morning talk show to live helicopter shots of police cars in hot pursuit of a hijacked pickup truck. It looked just like another one of those live police chases that Los Angeles TV loves to cover. But then he looked again: a neighbour was on the screen. 'Wait a minute, that's my friend Fish,' Ornelas, 23, shouted at the screen. 'And that's my friend Fish's house. This is happening right outside our house!' Ornelas was among many residents of this Santa Ana neighbourhood who followed the police chase on TV only to find that the drama would roll right up to their doors: 'You're watching TV, and suddenly you fear for your life – you realise he could suddenly run into your house,' [one neighbour] said. Even after the suspect was taken away, Gloria Rodriguez, 48, was still shaking her head and holding one of her four children tightly.

Rodriguez lives on Manitoba Drive, near the end of the cul-de-sac where the chase ended. 'One of my daughters called me from Riverside and told me to watch the TV, and I said, "I've got to go, Crystal, he's in front of my house!"' Kent Chavez, 31, who had watched part of the chase on TV earlier in the morning, left his home in the neighbourhood to pick up a nephew from school. He was almost broadsided by the pickup. 'I couldn't believe it, though. He was just leaning out the window like, "Go ahead, make my day,"' Chavez said about the gunman. 'It was just like on TV. He was real close, too. I thought, damn, he could kill me.' Many residents milled around for much of the day talking about the drama. 'No one minds a good police chase,' said Ralph Rodriguez, 23. 'But this one was too close to home.'[22]

This example represents one instance when television news can be said to have moved firmly out of the TV set and into the real world. Indeed, in looking at the skycam's role in television news, it becomes quite evident that links between televisual spaces and the built environment are ubiquitous. Consider themed shopping districts like Universal Citywalk in Los Angeles or South Street Seaport in New York, where an urban utopia is presented as a packaged consumable – high-profile brand names superimposed on a familiar landscape, safe and sanitary and fun for the whole family. One might also point to the link between cop shows and markers of urban authority like surveillance and security cameras, or televised spectacles of civic order like the New Year's Day Rose Parade in Pasadena, California. It would also be worth pursuing Mary Ann Doane's arguments in 'Information, crisis, catastrophe' in order to investigate the importance of wrenches in the machine – events that disrupt the city's sprawling electronic surface. What is the significance of televisual crisis: terrorism, hazardous material spills, natural disasters?

Though this initial foray into the televisual city is hardly complete, it is clear that television invites us to experience our built environments in an altogether novel way. The spatial dynamics of TV news propose that what we think of as urban real space and what we think of as televisual space are nothing more than two interlocking points of entry into the same domain. That is, we have learned to engage the city and television on a similar set of terms. The explosive transformation is happening not in the realm of buildings, or even in the realm of images, but rather in the realm of individuals' points of view. We feel that there must be a distinction between the city streets and our TV set, but it has become surprisingly difficult to articulate what that distinction might be – urban life and television news feel oddly, disturbingly interchangeable.

This was made particularly clear in early 1997, when skycams and police choppers descended on a sleepy neighbourhood in North Hollywood, California. A group of heavily armed robbers had barricaded themselves inside the Bank of America; a situation that culminated in a shoot-out between cops and robbers, all transmitted live, direct and with phenomenal ratings. But whereas witnesses in the Santa Ana car chase expressed mostly surprise at the unusual parallels between TV and real life, the following *Los Angeles Times* report made clear that in North Hollywood, the intersection of the architectural and the televisual had more disturbing ramifications:

> 'I could hear the shooting at the Bank of America,' said Ken Ogger, who lives three blocks away. He saw and heard the helicopters from the police and television news. He went inside the house and turned on the television. Feeling safe because the bank was three blocks away, 'I thought I would just sit home with the dog and be quiet and watch.' But the police had shot one of the bandits in front of his house. 'I ran into the laundry room and crouched down with my dog,' he said.[23]

Ken Ogger fled the living room, when he heard the choppers over his house, but he could not escape the crime scene. Sometimes, a free trip to TV land can ruin your whole day.

Notes

1   Don DeLillo, *White Noise* (New York: Penguin, 1986) p. 66.
2   David B. Clarke, *The Cinematic City* (London: Routledge, 1997) p. 1.
3   Clarke, *The Cinematic City*, p. 3. See also Leo Charney and Vanessa R. Schwartz (eds), *Cinema and the Invention of Modern Life* (Berkeley: University of California Press, 1995).
4   'The third window: an interview with Paul Virilio', translation of an interview in *Cahiers du Cinema*, April 1981, published in Cynthia Schneider and Brian Wallis (eds), *Global Television* (Cambridge, Mass.: MIT Press, 1988).
5   Paul Virilio, *The Lost Dimension* (New York: Semiotext(e), 1991) p. 76.
6   See Charles Baudelaire, 'The painter of modern life' in *My Heart Laid Bare and Other Prose Writings* (London: Soho Book Company, 1986), quoted in Anne Friedberg, *Window Shopping: Cinema and the Postmodern* (Berkeley: University of California, 1993) p. 29.
7   Virilio, *The Lost Dimension*, pp. 79–80.
8   Jane Feuer, 'The concept of live television: ontology as ideology' in E. Ann Kaplan (ed.), *Regarding Television: Critical Approaches* (Frederick: University Publications of America, 1983) p. 19.
9   Feuer, '*The concept of live television*', p. 14.
10 I don't mean to say that pacing is not an important part of TV news, or that a well-paced show will seem more appealing than a poorly paced one. Rather, my point is that there are few built-in *compositional* restrictions on the types of images that may follow one another – compared especially with cinematic rules.
11 Mary Ann Doane, 'Information, crisis, catastrophe' in Patricia Mellencamp (ed.), *Logics of Television* (Bloomington: Indiana University Press, 1990) p. 225.
12 Reuven Frank, 'An evening of perfect TV', *New Leader*, 4 July 1994, pp. 20–1.
13 For more information on the Wescam system, see Dan Hawaleshka, 'Steady shooter: Canada's Wescam focuses on the Olympics', *Maclean's*, 11 December 1995, p. 38.
14 See the Wescam Inc. website at http://www.wescam.com.

15   For a comprehensive history of aerial perspective, see Margret Dreikausen, *Aerial Perception* (Philadelphia: Art Alliance Press, 1985). For an overview of aerial photo techniques, see Beaumont Newhall, *Airborne Camera* (New York: Hastings House, 1969).

16   Karen Frome, 'A forced perspective: aerial photography and fascist propaganda', *Aperture*, 132 (Summer 1993) p. 77.

17   Georg Gerster, Introduction, *Below from Above* (New York: Abbeville Press, 1986).

18   Gaston Bachelard, *The Poetics of Space* (1958; New York: Orion Press, 1994) p. 173.

19   Antoine de Saint-Exupéry, 'Pilote de Guerre', *Oeuvres* (Paris: Gallimard, 1959) p. 297.

20   Paul Virilio, 'Speed and information: cyberspace alarm!', *Canadian Journal of Political and Social Theory*, 18: 1–3 (1995) pp. 82–9. See also http://www.ctheory.com/a30-cyberspace_alarm.html.

21   See Paul Virilio, *The Vision Machine* (London: British Film Institute, 1994) pp. 59–77.

22   David Maharaj and Jon D. Markman, 'TV drama turns alarmingly real for some viewers', *Los Angeles Times*, 12 March 1993.

23   Bill Boyarsky, 'A violent script that defines our lives', *Los Angeles Times*, 1 March 1997.

Spaces of Difference

5

Al Deakin, University of Westminister

Fear and Sympathy: Charles Dickens and Urban (Dis) Ability

In a recent essay, Steven Connor has observed contradictory energies at work in Charles Dickens' representation of urban space, energies which simultaneously assert and subvert the need for an urban 'legibility'. Dickens, he suggests,

> needed to surrender his writing to the crammed, dissolving energy of the streets, to their characteristically modern scene of traffic and tumult. But he also needed to take possession of those streets pacing them out and imaginatively introjecting them; in abandoning himself to the disorientations of the street, Dickens strives to make them his own.[1]

Elsewhere, Connor has suggested that the coexistence of impulses towards both dissolution and control can be traced in the interplay of metaphor and metonymy in the novels.[2] The representation of urban flux (typified by Dickens' love of sprawling, unwieldy lists) is frequently contained and controlled by an overlying metaphor which provides the paradigm from which a stream of metonymic detail is drawn. There are numerous, obvious examples of this in Dickens: the opening passages of *Bleak House*, for instance, where the chain set off by likening London in November to a period of prehistoric apocalypse finds its limit in the image of a Megalosaurus waddling up Holborn Hill; the metaphor of the city as diseased organism which contains the movement of the streets in certain passages of *Dombey and Son*; the metonymic and metaphoric evocation of the prison in *Great Expectations*. Such examples of the interplay of linguistic poles suggest a desire to define boundaries which render the city coherent, which order its chaos and channel its subversive currents and which make urban space finally knowable.

The need to provide a controlling language through which the city can be read is a typical mid-Victorian impulse. Nineteenth-century social engineers consistently employed mechanical and organic metaphors to assist them in this task and these same totalising concepts find their way into Dickens' fiction. In fact, the paradigm of the urban which we can trace throughout Dickens is partly an articulation of the nineteenth-century 'discovery' of society as an interrelated fabric which throughout his writing career becomes an increasingly ambitious attempt to dramatise the 'connectedness' of everything. Dickens' language, like those of social reformers as diverse as Sir James Kay-Shuttleworth[3], Henry Mayhew[4] and Friedrich Engels,[5] struggles to produce modalities which force the city to cohere and give some sense of a knowable object at work.

The difference between a novelist and those working in non-fictional genres, however, is that the former's prose does not have to show these ideas that much respect. If the desire to render the city legible constantly asserts itself in Dickens, he is equally captivated by the subversive nature of that which defies transparent decoding, by the dark carnival of characters like Fagin and Quilp and the Artful Dodger in the early novels, by the exhilaration of new technologies like the railway later on, and by the overwhelming, polysemic nature of the crowd throughout. These are elements which rupture the signifying structures built to contain them and which demonstrate the provisionality of any fixed reading the text may apparently endorse.

In this essay, I want to explore how these contradictory energies are brought to bear on the representation of the interaction of the body with urban space in Dickens' early fiction and how the result is two very different versions of the relationship between physical ability and disability. The first version is constructed around a binary logic of physical normality/abnormality which naturalises disability as a biological fact whose presence can be located upon an isolated human body – in this case, that of Tiny Tim – and thus cancels all environmental considerations. The second suggests different kinds of physical *ability* being produced and repressed by the shifting environment of the city; it suggests that disability is a condition which is relative to certain social formations as opposed to being a biological given. The two novels which demonstrate this most clearly, and which I shall look at here, are *A Christmas Carol* and *The Old Curiosity Shop*.

Physical Impairment and Disability

A major theoretical influence here are theories developed in the social sciences which have defined disability as a sociocultural construct.[6] In order to emphasise the concept of disability as a *reading* of certain physical states rather than something emanating from 'nature', the following twofold classification has been incorporated into and widely accepted by those working around the subject:

- *Impairment*: lacking part of or all of a limb, or having a defective limb, organism or mechanism of the body
- *Disability*: the disadvantage or restriction of activity caused by a contemporary social organisation which takes no or little account of people who have physical impairments and thus excludes them from the mainstream of social activities.

What this differentiation suggests is that disability is produced by the interaction of the body with the urban environment; that, for instance, it is inaccessible buildings and transportation systems which disable those with mobility problems rather than the difficulty they may have in walking. As such, disability can be understood as produced at the moment in which Western societies reached what Michel Foucault has described as the 'threshold of modernity', the point at which a complex of knowledge and technology grant

> a relative control over life ... Western man was gradually learning what it meant to be a living species in a living world, to have a body, conditions of existence, probabilities of life, an individual and collective welfare, forces that could be modified, and a space in which they could be distributed in an optimal manner. For the first time in history, no doubt, biological existence was reflected in political existence; the fact of living was no longer an inaccessible substrate that only emerged from time to time ... part of it passed into knowledge's field of control and power's sphere of intervention.[7]

Modernity is a condition within which human beings are able to reflect upon and maximise physical ability. This optimisation, however, is always produced through the power/knowledge relationships of specific social formations. Foucault demonstrates that in the West these relationships have developed increasingly refined techniques for the location of physical disorder, or what we might more accurately term physical inefficiencies, which do not effectively respond to the dominant economy of power. As a result, individuals are differentiated from each other and placed in a hierarchy according to a principle of normalisation; the ideal normal body is the one whose capacities can be maximised most effectively within the power relationships of a given society.

While this is clearly a reduction of Foucault's theory of bio-power, it none the less helps us to understand further the concept of disability as a category which is defined as other according to a principle of biological normalisation. Furthermore, it allows us to see representations of the interaction of the body with urban space, in fact to see the very production of urban space itself, as a process which is forced to engage with a normalised biological 'archetype'. One possible result of such an engagement is the othering of disability and, as I hope to demonstrate, it is this which is naturalised in *A Christmas Carol* through the domestication of urban space and the legitimation of a specific version of charity. In *The Old Curiosity Shop*, however, disability is still constructed as something other but, in the hyperbolised and grotesque performance of Quilp, the notion of physical ability/disability as a natural and universal binary is subverted.

A Christmas Carol: Disability, Charity and the Domesticated Urban

'And how did little Tim behave?,' asked Mrs Cratchit when she had rallied Bob on his credulity and Bob had hugged his daughter to his heart's content.

'As good as gold,' said Bob 'and better. Somehow he gets thoughtful sitting by himself so much, and thinks the strangest things you ever heard. He told me, coming home, that he hoped the people saw him in the church, because he was a cripple, and it might be pleasant to them to remember upon Christmas Day, who made lame beggars walk and blind men see.'[8]

Tiny Tim is the most straightforward example in Dickens of the angelic disabled child; the boy who is as 'good as gold' despite his condition, whose 'childish essence was from God' (p. 123), and whose only direct words in *A Christmas Carol* – '"God bless us everyone"' (p. 97) – encapsulate the need for benevolence which the story affirms. Even in the aftermath of his death, as shown to Scrooge by the third spirit, his patience and mildness is evoked by Bob Cratchit as a reason for remaining passively content with small mercies despite the family's ill health and poverty (p. 123), and it is, of course, the need to save Tim which brings about the change in Scrooge's character.

In fact, as the above quote tacitly acknowledges, Tim's only role in the narrative is as a signifier by which other people's charity is measured; he is both a victim of an unhappy social formation and a touchstone for the values which that formation might lack. The ideal Victorian object of charity, he is passive, well behaved and almost completely silent, as well as selflessly aware that he is 'a cripple' whose presence can only ever represent a personal tragedy. As a result, the meaning of physical disability in *A Christmas Carol* is confined to Tim's isolated body: an object which engenders the desire for miracles, for the lame to walk and the blind to see, while simultaneously providing a spectacle in the church which enforces the dividing line between the physically normal and abnormal. In this way, disability is naturalised as an isolated biological fact.

This naturalising of disability upon the body is compounded by the portrayal of the city as a kind of extended domestic space in the text. Urban space as something which simultaneously demands and resists excessive modes of signification is here cancelled in favour of the fantasy of the city as home. Christmas is a time in which all the people of London from 'the Lord mayor, in the stronghold of the mighty Mansion House' to 'the little tailor whom he had fined five shillings on the previous Monday for being drunk and blood-thirsty in the streets' (p. 52) are united in a spirit of goodwill. The crowd, that polysemic mass which threatens and exhilarates elsewhere in Dickens' work, is transformed into hundreds of people 'flocking through the streets in their best clothes and gayest faces' (p. 91), or 'shovelling away on the housetops, jovial and full of glee, calling out to one another from the parapets, and now and then exchanging a facetious snowball – better natured missile far than many a wordy jest – laughing heartily if it went right and not less heartily if it went wrong' (p. 89).

Under the paternal gaze of the Christmas spirits, the public spaces of the city are reshaped in the light of an idealised middle-class domesticity. London is represented primarily as a series of homes; that of the Lord Mayor, the tailor, Scrooge's nephew, Mr Fezziwig, the Cratchits and so on. The family harmony found here extends out into the streets,

> as Scrooge and the spirit went along the streets, the brightness of the roaring fires in kitchens, parlours and all sorts of rooms was wonderful. Here the flickering of the blaze showed preparations for a coy dinner, with hot plates baking through and through before the fire, and deep red curtains ready to be drawn, to shut out cold and darkness. There all the children of the house were running out into the snow to meet their married sisters, brothers, cousins, uncles, aunts, and be the first to greet them. (p. 99)

The city-wide spirit of familial reconciliation which allows both the Lord Mayor and the tailor to synchronise their activities is given its most explicit representation at Mr Fezziwig's party where the signifiers of work are cleared away to create 'as snug, and warm, and dry, and bright a ball-room, as you would desire to see upon a winter's night' (p. 76). Here, everyone from Mrs Fezziwig to 'the housemaid with her cousin, the baker' and 'the boy from over the way, who was suspected of not having enough board from his master' (p. 76) join together in the Christmas party (p. 76). This replication of the domestic at all levels in *A Christmas Carol* makes the city a finally knowable presence, a 'knowledge' which enables Scrooge to forsake his harsh Malthusian view of the world for the paternal role which he should have adopted all along (p. 134). A recognition of the city as home, then, with its wealthy playing the role of caring parents, allows us finally to define urban space as 'good'.

Within this domestic totality, Tiny Tim's disability becomes something that can only ever be cared for by the stronger or more able, a process that naturalises him as ultimately subordinate to other people's benevolence. The extreme passivity of Tim and his family compound this; throughout the text, Tim and the Cratchits exist only to illustrate the absence of a more powerful hand which might alleviate their suffering and reward their performance as model examples of the deserving poor. Tim's survival can only be ensured when Scrooge takes the role of 'a second father' to him (p. 134), a role which ensures Tim's subordinacy since it is Scrooge's either to give or take.

It is here that *A Christmas Carol* resolves certain contradictions in the Victorian view of charity. The Victorian articulation of the discourse of charity was one which was preoccupied with the effects of it upon the recipients: indiscriminate alms giving was seen as something which could simply encourage the lazy and the indolent, which might ruin the poor's own attempts at self-help. Although Dickens was deeply hostile to the Malthusian attack on all forms of poor relief, he periodically raged against those who saw charity as their right and created numerous characters who prove that they are worthy of help through their reluctance to ask for it.[9] As such, the version of charity which emerges from his work is one which falls squarely within the Victorian consensus concerning the policing of charity and which affirms the distinction between the deserving and the undeserving poor. The injustice which is attacked with greatest frequency in Dickens is the failure accurately to identify the deserving poor; the distinction itself is more or less taken as a given.

Gareth Stedman Jones has suggested that this desire to prove the worthiness of the object of charity has its roots in the mutations of traditional modes of perception caused by urbanisation.[10] Drawing on the work of Weber and Mauss, Stedman Jones suggests that urbanisation 'deforms' the meaning of the charitable act so that its purpose and outcome become frustrated. In premodern social formations, he argues, the principal effect of the act of giving was to improve the status of the giver and to endow him with social prestige. This can be unpacked into three structural features that Stedman Jones, after Marcel Mauss, sees as inherent in every act of giving. In the first place, the gift implies a sacrifice, primarily to God, which averts the vengeance of Nemesis upon the rich for enjoying excessive wealth and happiness. Importantly, the receivers are incidental to this process, acting only as passive receptacles for the generosity of the wealthy and significant only because of their need: the focus is entirely upon the giver. Second, the gift operates as a symbol of social superiority, inscribing a power relationship in which the receiver becomes subordinate and a mere client of the giver. In this sense, the gift can be seen as operating as a method of social control, imposing an obligation on the receiver to behave in an acceptable manner, if only through the expression of gratitude and humility. Third, the gift is a one-to-one relationship between two persons, a feature that anchors the first two since it ensures that the power relationship is close and personalised and therefore difficult to abuse, at least from the 'receiving' end.

Stedman Jones suggests that these features were quite compatible in a rural society in which the rich would be more familiar with the poor and were therefore less likely to have to give to strangers. However, the wholly personalised form of the gift is clearly an impossibility in the city of the nineteenth century and as a result its role as a kind of social cement becomes frustrated:

> The gift as a sacrifice no longer implied the gift that would lead the poor in the path of virtue ... The original integrity of the gift relationship had been replaced by a promiscuous compound of indiscriminate alms giving and careless Poor Law relief. In either case, the relationship between persons had disappeared, and with it, the elements of prestige, subordination and obligation.[11]

It is precisely these contradictions which are overcome in the text by forcing the city to adhere to the dimensions of the domestic. With the help of the ghosts, Scrooge is able to see the city as a whole, to 'know' all the potential recipients of his charity within it and as a result, the one-to-one relationship between giver and receiver is miraculously restored. The conclusion of the novel sees the dominance of the giver reconstructed through the paradigm of the domestic, with Scrooge as the idealised father figure. The fantasy of urban legibility which the text produces, then, is one which orders the city according to the power relationships of the middle-class home and which confines disability to the body, constructing it as never anything more than a potential object of charity.

The Old Curiosity Shop: Urban Ability

If the family hearth provides a moral centre of gravity to the London of *A Christmas Carol*, in *The Old Curiosity Shop* the urban cannot be contained by any single signifying structure or paradigm. As a result, there are no straightforward oppositions between the impaired and the able bodied in the text, no easy physical delineations. Rather, it presents us with a variety of types of physical ability, types that are enabled or disabled according to the shifting urban and non-urban environments that they inhabit. There is for instance, the narrator of the opening chapters, whom we know to be lame but who initially inhabits the usually able-bodied position of paternal carer for Nell because of his comparative wealth. There is Nell's increasingly senile father who is safe and able to function within the confines of the curiosity shop but in need of constant help once he has been made homeless. And there is Nell herself, the 'dear, gentle, patient, noble' child, the contrast between whose abilities (her 'strong affection and consciousness of rectitude' enables her to look after her father on the street) and disabilities (her physical frailty means that life on the street increasingly weakens her) fuels the melodrama of the narrative.[12] For all of these characters, physical ability is relative to their position within the urban environment. While they all have impairments (lameness, senility, consumption) it is the interaction of these with urban space and the ideological formations which have produced it and are produced by it which engender varying levels of ability and disability.

This can be explained further if we turn to the character who dominates the text, Daniel Quilp, the dwarf whose body is spectacularly enabled by the city. When Nell and her grandfather embark upon their journey of escape into the countryside, they encounter a group of fairground entertainers, one of whom runs a small freakshow and is described as owning 'a giant' and a lady without arms and legs (p. 204). The financial merits of giants are discussed and it is agreed that they are a bad investment when old since they 'go weak in the legs' and are only useful for looking after dwarfs. While they agree that one of the most lucrative attractions is a man with a wooden leg, they all praise the merits of the dwarfs: '"The older a dwarf is, the better worth he is," returned Mr. Vuffin, "a grey headed dwarf, well wrinkled, is beyond all suspicion"'(p. 83).

In this non-urban environment, dwarfs are 'beyond all suspicion,' contained and controlled as objects of voyeuristic fascination, referred to only through their value as freaks. Quilp, however, the dwarf in the city, is empowered and liberated, uncontained and uncontrolled in an environment which spectacularly and, as it is coded in the novel, horrifically enables his body. Quilp represents one of the strongest challenges in Dickens to the concept of disability as confined to the body; if, in the countryside, he would have been nothing but a subordinate curiosity, in the tangled, chaotic streets of London he is 'a small lord of creation' (p. 124), the city a space which he is able to manipulate with 'uncommon agility' (p. 124). In subverting that which is so meticulously naturalised in *A Christmas Carol* (and less successfully so elsewhere in *The Old Curiosity Shop*), it is almost inevitable that Quilp should be identified as grossly unnatural; he is grotesque not only because his character hints at the deconstruction of the physically normal/abnormal binary, but also because his body monopolises the urban spaces which resist transparent decoding.

While he admits that he is 'not quite small enough to get through keyholes' (p. 124) he is constantly appearing suddenly and out of nowhere; as a sinister and living curiosity to startle Nell and her grandfather in her grandfather's shop, or hiding in his own living room watching his wife and associates mourn for him when she assumes him to be dead, or shocking Richard Swiveller, for whom London has dissolved into an alcoholic mist, by appearing out of it:

> 'Then,' said somebody hard by, 'let me be a father to you.'
> Mr Swiveller swayed himself to and fro to preserve his balance, and, looking into a kind of haze which seemed to surround him, at last perceived two eyes dimly twinkling through the mist, which he observed after a short time were in the neighbourhood of a nose and mouth. Casting his eyes down towards that quarter in which, with reference to a man's face, his legs are usually to be found, he observed that the face had a body attached; and when he looked more intently he was satisfied that the person was Mr Quilp, who indeed had been in his company all the time, but whom he had some vague idea of having left a mile or two behind. (pp. 236–7)

If the presence of the paternal spirits in *A Christmas Carol* allows the text to deliver the city to us as home, Quilp's grotesque urban abilities dissolve all sense of fixed perspective, of the individual and domestic boundaries which are the prerequisites for any such ownership of the urban. He is the 'small lord of creation' because the interaction of his body with the environment seems to invent new dimensions to it, and as such he is the diametrical opposite of the Christmas Spirit or the reformed Scrooge, something which the ironic offer of fatherhood from a city which has become a hazy mist would seem to confirm.

At one level, these are the cliched, 'he's behind you!' tactics of the pantomime and, as Paul Schlicke has demonstrated, *The Old Curiosity Shop* utilises elements of the folk or fairy tale in both its form and content.[13] But Quilp is not simply a more riotous version of Mr Punch or the fairground freaks; he represents the meeting of the traditional pleasures of folk entertainment with a peculiarly modern and urban set of anxieties; articulated through the many comparisons made between Quilp and creatures of myth and folklore – the goblin (p. 81), the salamander (p. 239), the vampire (p. 665) – in the recognition of new kinds of physical ability: abilities which modernity itself makes possible but which frustrate the available metaphors for imagining them. The riot of signifiers which describe the horror of Quilp's body, then, are also an articulation of the potential which urban space has to both enable and disable. Significantly, within this shifting, polysemic environment Quilp is eager to have as much control over the ways in which his body is described as possible. When, hiding in his home, he overhears Mrs Jiniwin describe his nose as 'flat' he cannot help but leap from his hiding place: '"Aquiline!" cried Quilp, thrusting in his head and striking the feature with his fist, "Aquiline, you hag. Do you see it? Do you call this flat? Do you? Eh?"' (p. 460).

Where Tiny Tim in the church surrenders his body to the meanings which others give it, Quilp refuses all such descriptions and violently claims the right to represent himself. This is always encoded as an obscene threat or inhuman act, but the restless polysemy by which it is signified, the exhilaration of the language used, suggest the empowering possibilities which the city makes available to the human body. *The Old Curiosity Shop*, then, while still a text which resolutely 'others' disability through the employment of grotesque and melodramatic codes, is one which accompanies that othering with a recognition of physical ability as taking on different meanings within the context of the urban. In this sense, Quilp's role is the diametrical opposite of that of the spirits in *A Christmas Carol*; if they have the universal perspective aspired to by so many mid-Victorians, the gaze which fixes the city as a knowable, stratified community, Quilp's improvised physical abilities – made available to him by the very formations which disable other 'normal' bodies – frustrate and defy all such attempts at a normalising ominiscience.

Conclusion

If, as Steven Connor has argued, the representation of the city in Dickens is characterised by the contradictory impulses towards ownership and surrender, in relation to physical ability this contradiction produces at least two textual features. The first, which is exemplified by the relationship between Scrooge and Tiny Tim in *A Christmas Carol*, sees the representation of the impaired body falling within the controlling arms of the discourse of charity, a process which constructs disability as the property of charity in that the sympathy of the philanthropist affords a kind of ownership of the object of charity. The second, determined more by the impulse towards surrender or dissolution, sees the diverse physical abilities engendered by the city as things that can become dangerously and intoxicatingly out of control.

Paradoxically, the fear which surrounds such transgressive abilities in *The Old Curiosity Shop* is where urban space's potential to physically *enable*, as well as disable, is signified.

Notes

1   Steven Connor, 'Space, place and the body of riot in Barnaby Rudge' in Steven Connor (ed.), *Charles Dickens* (London: Longman, 1996) pp. 211–29.

2   See Steven Connor, *Charles Dickens* (Oxford: Basil Blackwell, 1985) pp. 54–60.

3   See Frank Mort, *Dangerous Sexualities: Medico-Moral Politics in England Since 1830* (London: Routledge and Kegan Paul, 1987) pp. 19–21.

4   Henry Mayhew, *London Labour and the London Poor* (Harmondsworth: Penguin, 1985).

5   Friedrich Engels, *The Condition of the Working Class in England in 1844* (London: Allen and Unwin, 1892) pp. 45–54.

6   See Michael Oliver, *The Politics of Disablement* (London: Macmillan, 1990) and David Hevey, *The Creatures that Time Forgot* (London: Routledge, 1991).

7   Michel Foucault, *The History of Sexuality Vol. 1* (Harmondsworth: Penguin, 1990) p. 142.

8   Charles Dickens, *The Christmas Books, Vol. 1: A Christmas Carol and The Chimes* (Harmondsworth: Penguin, 1985) p. 94. All further references will be quoted in the text.

9   The most exaggerated example being the character of Betty Higden in *Our Mutual Friend*. See Alexander Welsh's discussion of Betty in his *The City of Dickens* (Oxford: Clarendon Press, 1971).

10 Gareth Stedman Jones, *Outcast London* (Oxford: Clarendon Press, 1971).

11 Ibid., p. 252.

12 Charles Dickens, *The Old Curiosity Shop* (Harmondsworth: Penguin, 1985), p. 654. All further references will be quoted in the text.

13 See Paul Schlicke, *Dickens and Popular Entertainment* (London: Allen and Unwin, 1985) pp. 93–136.

6

Maria Balshaw, University of Birmingham

Elegies to Harlem: *Looking For Langston* and *Jazz*

Nobody says it's pretty here; nobody says it's easy either. What it is is decisive, and if you pay attention to the street plans, all laid out, the City can't hurt you. (Toni Morrison, *Jazz*)

The Harlem presented in this essay is a city of urbanity and urban sophistication, particularly as this defines a race capital in Harlem as the focus of a *modern*, urban mode of existence for African Americans. This raises important questions about the centrality of urban experience in understanding the meanings of race in African American cultural production, and the relationship between African American art and critical conceptions of modernity.[1] Isaac Julien's film *Looking For Langston* (1989) and Toni Morrison's novel *Jazz* (1991), discussed in this chapter, deal in different ways with these issues, particularly through their fascination with urbanity as a key shaping element in the development of a racialised aesthetic commensurate to the experience of African American life in Harlem.[2] This race aesthetic would understand African American subjectivity as mediated by the impact of new forms of spatial organisation that develop in the Northern urban centres and most typically and substantially in Harlem. The typical Harlem subject represented by this aesthetic articulates the dislocated and unsettling aspects of urban life as a characteristically modern, fragmented subjectivity. There is a fascination with the visual impact of Harlem and with the imbrication of race and sexuality in the formation of subjectivity. These issues will be explored as the essay unfolds, for now we must simply note that peculiar and interesting configurations of urban space emerge from Harlem's iconic status as an urbane and cosmopolitan race capital.

Racialised Urbanity

The notion of urbanity as the expression of a peculiarly modern form of urban consciousness – the projection of an urban mode of being and self-awareness of what it means to be a citizen in a rapidly changing urban polis – has been the subject of much critical analysis.[3] The modern origins of this concept can be traced back to the writings of Robert E. Park and his contemporaries (particularly Louis Wirth) and the foundations of the Chicago School of sociology.[4] The meanings of urbanity are manifold, but what emerges most clearly from the writings of Park and his contemporaries is that it refers to the evolution of civic consciousness and responsibility and stresses the importance of the life of the mind, in terms of everyday customs, artistic endeavour, human communication and philosophy, in the construction of what it means to live in the city. It is also crucially dependent on the idea of the coming together of strangers who construct the city through social interaction that is not based on kinship or group membership. In Park's most famous formulation the city is,

> a state of mind, a body of customs and traditions, and of the organized attitudes and sentiments that inhere in these customs and are transmitted with this tradition. The city is not, in other words, merely a physical mechanism and an artificial construction. It is involved in the vital processes of the people who compose it; it is a product of nature, and particularly of human nature.[5]

This notion of the civilised and civilising human organisation of the city is one which has been questioned profoundly in the years since Park wrote, both in terms of the subsequent development of the cities he wrote about and his theoretical conception of them. The concept of urbanity has also accrued rather different meanings as the twentieth century has progressed, coming to stand less for the active striving toward civic responsibility and more for a social and cultural sophistication, a self-consciousness about how to project the manners and mores of urban living: being urbane rather than practising urbanity. It is useful though to remember the connections between urbanity and civic consciousness and being urbane as self-consciousness, because the Parkian stress on the importance of communication and social interaction, with the arts as an integral part of this urban social interchange, does connect importantly to the other sense of urbanity as proficiency in negotiating what becomes known as cultural capital.

Urbanity as a concept is not something that has been held to have much relevance to African American urban experience. The histories of

Harlem, Chicago's Southside or many other racialised urban centres one might name would seem at first glance the antithesis of the experience of urbanity. The optimism of Robert Park's understanding of urban space in 1925 is easily undermined if one considers the lack of progress in economic or political terms that has characterised black urban experience in the decades since the 1920s. Yet, urbanity does have key significance to African American writing, particularly during the 1920s but also beyond this period. The influence of Parkian thinking on the key players in the Harlem Renaissance can be traced in direct terms through figures like Charles S. Johnson, as George Hutchinson and others have shown.[6] It has a broader influence, however, if one sees that the particular mode of 'uplift' or racial improvement that leaders of the New Negro movement like Alain Locke advocated was one which was plainly concerned with the cultivation of urbanity as both civic responsibility *and* as an artistic attitude of mind. In this sense the race aesthetic advocated by New Negro philosophers could be termed racialised urbanity. Furthermore, the stress in Chicago School work on the significance of the coming together of strangers in the public spaces of the modern metropolis gives us a useful context for understanding the fascination with racial spectacle, in the form of cabarets, balls, dances and bars, in the work of many Harlem Renaissance writers.

One would surmise, however, given the economic and political developments in Harlem in the later twentieth century, that this sense of urbanity dissipates, if not disappears. Certainly we are more familiar with the 'ghettocentric' representation of black urban space, where one might argue that the only cultural capital generated is the culture of poverty itself (manifesting itself often through the supposed 'authenticity' of the experience of immiseration).[7] But, the fetishisation of the authenticity of the streets (one could cite Chester Himes, Spike Lee, Walter Mosley, John Singleton as cultural producers whose work cultivates such resonances) does not, in my view, fully explain the still evident fascination with the ghetto capitals of African American life – such as Harlem, or Southside Chicago, or South Central LA. To understand the still forceful pull of these urban locations we need to take seriously the ways in which discourses of race pride, and racial urbanity, persist (albeit in modulated form) from the 1920s to the 1990s, maintaining – in complex ways – a sense of the race capital as a cornerstone for the formation of race pride. To examine how this works it seems useful to examine two late twentieth-century texts, *Looking for Langston* and *Jazz*, which look back with extreme self-consciousness to the legendary days of 1920s Harlem. These texts present a complex meditation on urban space as the means by which they negotiate the multiple demands of racial, sexual, gender and class location.

An Urban Snapshot

Isaac Julien's film recreates a Harlem of the 1920s in order to intervene in 1980s and 1990s debates on identity and the politics of black representation. Julien's film looks for the always unspoken sexuality of perhaps the most powerfully iconic figure of the Harlem Renaissance, Langston Hughes, but what it represents, to quote Toni Morrison, is 'the necessity of historical memory ... and the impossibility of forgetting', which it discovers through a meditation on black-and-white image making.[8] It does this in order to begin tracing a sexual politics of African American identity, and specifically an historical exploration of formations of black gay identity and image making. The film derives its visual style and many of its theoretical cues from avant-garde cinema, but in the spirit of a black urban aesthetic it takes its most potent visual images from the Harlem presented in the city photographs of James VanDerZee – African American photographer *par excellence*. From the scene of a wake which opens the film to the freeze frame of the dancing bohemians which closes it, the film repeatedly recreates 'moving' (in all senses of the word) versions, or critical recreations, of still images by VanDerZee and other avant-garde photographers (notably Robert Mapplethorpe's black nudes, Carl Van Vechten's portraits of Harlem literati, and Georges Platt Lynes' homoerotic photography).

Jazz too derives much of its power from its self-conscious construction of scenes of heightened visual pleasure, from the interior exploration of the unnamed narrator's pleasure in looking, 'worth the trouble if you're like me – curious, inventive and well informed' (p. 137), to descriptions of the intimate point of connection between the body of a woman and the surface of a building: scenes that map out an architecture of desire,

> sitting on a stoop with a cool beer in her hand, dangling her shoe from the toes of her foot, the man, reacting to her posture, to soft skin on stone, the weight of the building stressing the delicate dangling shoe, is captured. And he'd think it was the woman he wanted, and not some combination of curved stone, and a swinging high-heeled shoe moving in and out of sunlight. He would know right away the deception, the trick of shapes and light and movement, but it wouldn't matter at all because the deception was part of it too. (p. 34)

The desires and obsessions which are mapped out in the novel are repeatedly figured through the medium of a photograph, most notably through Violet and Joe's shared haunting by the picture of Dorcas that lives on their mantelpiece, an image which captures and torments the two central protagonists of the novel. This is merely the most obvious of the images which capture the characters whose fates are revealed in Morrison's mournful recreation of Harlem; images which work as a rich memory-text of Harlem's visual culture. Morrison's duplicitous narrator, who leads us and seduces us through the novel, presents a visual panorama around which the ambiguous love story is woven. Morrison has admitted part of the inspiration for the story came from her encounter with the photographs of James VanDerZee, particularly the numerous funeral pictures that are collected in his *Harlem Book of the Dead*.[9] The 'drums' that accompany Morrison's account of the famous July 1917 protest parade (pp. 54–5) and echo through the narrative are also the aural correlative of the many photographs of this parade, which have become one of the paradigmatic Harlem images. The sequences derived from these photographs are used in the novel to organise memory and emotion and develop powerful relationships between characters, their urban environment and their history as African Americans.

Looking For Langston and *Jazz* are curiously bound together in this utilisation of a counter-history of African American photography and in particular they pay homage to the Harlem constructed through the work of VanDerZee. Both texts start with a death and expand outwards from the scene of mourning to recreate the lives of the living and the historical connections between the urban past and the present. This is made most explicitly clear in *Looking For Langston*, where Julien himself is the body in the coffin in the opening scene, but the text also stands as elegy to a Harlem, gay Harlem, that has been lost to history and to the men who made up the gay literati, most notably Bruce Nugent – whose 1926 short story 'Smoke, Lilies and Jade' forms the central memory text in the film – but also James Baldwin, whose words are read out by Toni Morrison during the wake and to whom the film is dedicated. We might also add the names of the gay blues singers whose songs make up the soundtrack to the film and Florence Mills, whose funeral brought Harlem to a halt and whose wake, also photographed by VanDerZee, is connotatively connected to the funeral scenes in both texts.

The obsessive visuality seen in both texts cultivates a mode of urbanity that is the aesthetic – but also the political – keynote of each text. That is, to use a common 1920s trope, they 'pass' between one form of urbanity and another.[10] Embracing the superficial graces of the urban bohemian, and the seductions of the ever-changing, ambiguous city scene, they also use this to carve out space for some *other* histories of urban African American experience. Preferring not to give up the aesthetic celebration of racial space for a rather more material history of African Americans within the city, both texts produce indeterminate – seductive and dangerous – comments on the politics of identity and community for African Americans within urban culture. Both texts derive their urbane-ity through their critical appropriation of visual texts, but also as we shall see through their engagement with concepts and proponents of the avant-garde and by setting themselves in critical relation to contemporary debates about African American identity.[11] They make it very clear that contemporary debates about sexuality, race, gender and urban identity are too the concerns of the 1920s, and in fact it is the historical dialogue between past and present, particularly in *Looking For Langston*, that allows new and productive commentary on these issues. The passing structure of both novel and film presents an oscillation between different modalities of identity at the same time as they perform an act of beautiful historical recreation. This passing structure suggests that this ambivalent visual field is a necessary component of a politicised relativism, a politics of identity and community which pays attention to postmodern notions of performance and fragmentation whilst holding on to a grounded notion of opposition to dominant cultural representations.

Looking At ... or For?

We see this process of passing identification most clearly in one of the film's central scenes that I want to examine in some detail. The opening of the film presents a wake (troping on VanDerZee's funeral pictures) with the body of Isaac Julien in the coffin surrounded by a group of mourners who are dressed as Harlem literati. This ceremony takes place in the upstairs of a nightclub that recreates the Cotton Club as a gay nightspot. The film then moves to a history lesson about Harlem, the Harlem Renaissance and homosexuality, which counterpoints a reading by Stuart Hall with archival footage of 'sissy' artists, and we then return to the Cotton Club, where the major fictional episodes in the film take place. As with so many important moments in the film we start from a still image, of the 'jazzers' in the club, nostalgically evoking a Harlem scene only too familiar in its night-time allure. As we close in on the still and the jazzers start to move, this familiarity is confirmed and critically destabilised as it becomes clear all the dancing couples are same sex. The scene begins, then, by situating itself in relation to – taking its visual language from – a number of clearly recognisable cultural discourses: stereotypes of Jazz Age Harlem, the chiaroscuro light of early black-and-white cinema, avant-garde cinema and photography. On the soundtrack Bessie Smith sings 'Freakish Man,' conjoining the blues as the paradigmatic African American expressive form with the history of homosexuality.

The camera draws in to a close-up of the face of Alex, lit to precisely divide his face along its vertical axis, giving us a perfectly realised image of passing identity – between black and white, gay and straight – and we move from his face through a series of profoundly extended glances to exploration of a triangulated scene of desire. The scene gives us Alex staring at a black man called Beauty and the jealous reaction of the white lover with whom Beauty sits. As Alex and Beauty exchange glances, the white lover bangs his champagne bottle on the table to discipline Beauty and reclaim his erotic attention. The slowness of shot movement and the construction of *mise-en-scène* and lighting mark the film's debt to avant-garde cinema. The film cuts from the shot of Alex's face divided into black and white to Beauty's face framed through an iris shot. This works in a very complex way to reverse the coding of colour (and race) associated with this sort of shot. Common in silent films, this shot is used to particular effect in D. W. Griffith's *Birth of a Nation* (1915), where, as Richard Dyer points out, it works to emphasise the whiteness of the film's heroine, Lillian Gish.[12] Whiteness becomes more-than-white, a cinematic as well as racial ideal which must be defended from the assault of darkness (in *Birth*, the black and mulatto characters who appear as monstrous figures and move in and out of the dark edges of the frame). This shot sets Julien's camerawork in relation to this tradition and works a transformation upon it.

As the iris frames Beauty's face he is lit so as to lighten his skin, making him appear almost white. Yet at the same time the camera dwells sensuously on his lips, an obviously provocative strategy given the stereotypes of thick Negro lips. There is a disjunction between the lightening of the epidermal signifiers of blackness and the hyper-valorisation of other corporeal signifiers of race, which mirrors the doubled discourse of identity that underpins this scene. As a scene of racial recognition the shot flirts with some pernicious stereotypes, but from another perspective this kind of 'look' becomes the inscription of homosexual desire as the camera dwells on Beauty's lips as a site of erotic pleasure. The look is a seduction that draws the viewer into a passing structure which problematises simplistic conceptions of identity. Each interpretation inhabits the other, something that is only emphasised by 'Freakish Man' on the soundtrack, underlining the contention that the construction of race in this scene has also to be read through the construction of homosexual desire.[13] This recoding of racial representa-tion is also extended to the white man in this scene as we see his face lit so as to drain the colour from his face. Traditions of cinematic lighting are revealed in their racial specificity as white skin is quite clearly the marked exception rather than the normative centre of the film. Thus, the dubious racial motives for this man's participation in this scene of desire and his imperious attitude are mirrored by the formal organisation of shot and scene, at the same time as he is allowed to articulate his homosexuality by jealously competing for Beauty's attention.

In a scene a little later this exchange of glances is recapitulated to explore the disjunction between discourses of black pride (in their New Negro and post-sixties black power versions) and those of homosexuality. If the previous scene flirted with a racist homoerotic this scene deals with homophobia within black cultural discourses. Placing the articulation of black pride (a song, 'Beautiful Black Man', by Blackberri) against the visual exchange of looks between Beauty's white lover, Alex, and a third unnamed 'dark' black man, the scene allows the viewer to draw out suggestive analogies. Although the song to the 'beautiful black man' would be appropriate to the articulation of both forms of 'pride' (as it is obviously intended to be) it is also a fact that the rhetoric of black pride – in the 1920s as now – has tended to articulate a positively homophobic stance, as Stuart Hall's early commentary points out: 'Homosexuality was considered an affront to the race so it had to be kept a secret, even if it was a widely shared one.' Once again the scene is characterised by a seductive doubleness which allows a pleasure in looking but suggests at the same time a rather more uncomfortable 'other' scene writ within the desiring exchange. The beloved in this sequence is shown to have the (nascent) ability to refuse the objectifying gaze of the white looker/lover. This suggests that there are in fact two orders of looking being negotiated in the exchange of glances; one consensual and erotic that is valorised in the sequence, and one commodifying and objectifying that is critiqued.

The scene starts with the injunction 'Look at me' on the soundtrack, and as the 'beautiful black man' walks into the club the aggressive gaze of the white man attempts to transfix and shame the black man. Another order of looking is suggested, however, by the sideways looks of the light-skinned Alex at the face of the dark man. The close-ups of his steady gaze work to suggest a meditation on the power of looking as his own face is examined in detail as he looks with desire at another man, and the narcissim of desire is elaborated as the camera acts as a mirror to his own beauty. His 'looks' appear to be supported by the soundtrack that calls for the black man to look up, to return his glance and 'be proud of his race', but his staring is a sexual invitation as well. Julien trades here on the characteristic rhetoric of the New Negro in the service of a politics of sexuality, which inhabits the inside of the racial discourse the soundtrack pronounces. A language of race typically associated with the New Negro movement (and which also finds its way as artefacts into the historical section of *Looking For Langston*) is here doubled to mark sexuality's manifest absence in these originary texts and to suggest the erotic instability of identity within the fantastic and spectacular urban scene that forms the film's visual content.

As the scene develops the look of the white man that attempts to objectify the black man is returned, refused and critiqued. He as observer feels the power of the gaze turned upon him as he becomes the observed, in a contrary movement to the shaming of the black man that is protested in the soundtrack. In an even more pronounced manner than the earlier scene as blackness is lit for maximum sensuous effect whiteness is presented as a deathly pallor, in a witty reversal of the supposed hyper-visibility of blackness. His vampire-like appearance stands as a visual metaphor for the draining and demeaning order of looking associated with him. He is also, we should note, presented as an urban gay stereotype – with kiss curl, cigarette holder and foppish demeanour – and we should view this exaggerated nature of his white gayness as a risky fetishisation in the same vein as the focus on Beauty's Negroid lips in the earlier scene. While it makes possible the doubled racial and sexual vocabulary we see at play in this scene, it also moves deliberately close to stereotypes of gayness, pointing again to the powerful organising energies of social stereotyping. The exchange of sexually charged looks between Alex and the other black man becomes the means by which certain kinds of voyeurism and racial and sexual objectification are critically explored. It is the means by which we experience the pleasures of voyeurism (having our critical cake and eating it) as a passing both/and formulation.

The film is also, as critics have noted, peopled largely by light-skinned black men, something which Julien claims is dictated by the social and cultural conditions of the 1920s, but can also be seen as provocatively linked to the construction of the Cotton Club as gay space in the film.[14] One might argue that the film shows black men passing as white in order to identify as homosexual or at least that related category, the bohemian. The film flirts with this suggestion, ultimately to undermine it, as a critical commentary on the seductions of avant-gardism and to point up the whiteness of stereotypes of bohemianism and modernism that the film takes on. At the same time it emphasises the ambiguous address of the film because the seductive valorisation of avant-gardist style is part of the film's homoerotic challenge to certain tendencies within black cultural discourses. My emphasis here is on the contradictory doubleness of looking and identity which is at the heart of Julien's stylised recreation of Harlem, a doubleness which stresses the interconnected histories of racial and sexual identity as a shared feature of the 1920s and the 1980s, something underlined by the textual embedding of Nugent's 'Smoke, Lilies and Jade' (as one of the very few 'out' Harlem Renaissance texts) as the central erotic fantasy in the film. The film looks back to Harlem, not as utopian urban space but rather for the usefully 'messy ambivalence' (to use Kobena Mercer's phrase) around issues of race and sexual identity that can be articulated through exploration of this iconic African American place.[15] Inside the urbane a more politicised concept of urbanity resides, and the subject of the film is the pleasurable oscillation between the two.

Bitch or Dumpling Girl?

To turn now to Toni Morrison's *Jazz*, a text equally reliant on still photography for inspiration and aesthetic power, one finds that the field of vision proves to be equally deceptive. As with *Looking For Langston* the text opens with a funeral, which is disrupted by Violet's attempts to slash the face of the 'bitch or dumpling girl' (p. 106) Dorcas who has been murdered (in loving destructiveness) by Violet's husband, Joe Trace. This scene, which makes reference again to the funereal tradition of VanDerZee's photography, sets the novel on a course of mourning, but also searching, for the something lost that could explain the drive to murder, passion and desire. While this something lost is not ever straight-forwardly recovered for the characters in the text, it is made clear that the project of understanding is bound up with the slippery truth(s) attributed to the visual and to urban space. Thence, we come to know Violet and Joe and their violent history through their contradictory obsessions with a photograph of the dead girl, Dorcas. Photography, the visual pleasure of architecture and urban space and exploration of the deceptions of visual perception through the figure of the curious and voyeuristic narrator, form the dynamic of the text's relationship to modernism and postmod-ernism, and to its historical subject, Harlem and the Harlem Renaissance; it also marks the limits of its project (at least in relation to *Looking For Langston*). In addition, it goes some way to explain the peculiar absence in the novel of actual Harlem places, jazz joints, famous buildings, events or people.[16] Instead what we have is a love story, and a deliberately abstract aesthetic appreciation of urban space and its parameters.

The love-triangle plot of the novel is recounted on the first page by the narrator, and her gossipy voice tells us the story of the whole book, betraying the ending and her own incapacity as narrator at the beginning of the tale. The text then elaborates the story of Joe, Violet and Dorcas as a narrative of Harlem and desire and identity, weaving this story as a dynamic interrogation of the power and ambiguity of the image. As Joe and Violet tiptoe out in the dark to stare at the photograph of Dorcas on their mantelpiece which Violet has taken from Dorcas's Aunt Alice Manfred, the picture which torments their sleepless nights appears to shift under their respective gazes. For Joe, 'it is the absence of accusation that wakes him from his sleep hungry for her company ... Her face is calm, generous and sweet' (p. 12). But for Violet the face is very different; powerful in a way which suggests the ability to reverse the relationship between subject and object so that the photograph may possess the perceiver with a kind a kind of visual haunting:

> The girl's face looks greedy, haughty and very lazy. The cream-at-the-top-of-the-milkpail face of someone who will never work for anything

... An inward face – whatever it sees is its own self. You are there, it says, because I am looking at you. (p. 12)

This photograph of Dorcas becomes, through a process of introjection, the outward trace of a horribly intimate history of love and loss for Violet. The woman who stole her husband becomes the daughter whom Violet (and Joe) lost (through abortion or miscarriage, the issue is deliberately confused) in their everyday dash to become 'City People'. After the fact the photograph comes to stand for the traumatic loss of a history which never happened.[17]

The scheming bitch ... Or mama's dumpling girl? Was she the woman who took the man, or the daughter who fled the womb? Washed away on a tide of soap, salt and castor oil ... Or was it the city that produced a crooked kind of mourning for a rival young enough to be a daughter? (p. 109)

Violet's identification with and against the image of Dorcas as both daughter and rival (with its deliberately provocative psychoanalytic resonances) is another example of a passing structure, and it is no accident that this at first appears to be a story of a dark woman's fury at a rival light enough to pass. In the end though Morrison takes the tragic elements of the classic passing narrative to present a story of country folk passing as urbanites, and it is the deceptions and seductions of the city, not the temptation to pass as white within it, which are presented as the greatest threat to a racial authenticity that Morrison (unlike, I think, Isaac Julien) wishes to defend against the depredations of a delightful, beautiful, but ultimately predatory urban modernity.[18]

How soon country people forget. When they fall in love with the city it is forever and it is like forever ... There in the city they are not so much new as themselves: their stronger riskier selves ... what they start to love is the way a person is in the city ... Little of that makes for love but it does pump desire. (pp. 33–4)

The reader's deceitful guide to the seductions of the city is Morrison's consummately brilliant narrator, and it is her modernist city passion I want to concentrate on for a moment. The pain and confusion and extreme ambiguity of desire associated with Violet and Joe Trace are held against the insistent, confident, all seeing, *nosy* voice of the narrator who sings a modernist paean of praise to the city, and to her own all-encompassing interpretative passion. This voice, the lyrical centre of the novel, develops a powerful seductive effect on the reader to compare with the risky gorgeousness of the chiaroscuro history presented in *Looking For Langston*:

I'm crazy about this city ... A city like this makes me dream tall and feel in on things. Hep. It's the bright steel rocking above the shade below that does it. When I look over strips of green grass lining the river, at church steeples and into the cream-and-copper halls of apartment buildings, I'm strong. Alone, yes, but top-notch and indestructible – like the City in 1926 when all the wars are over and there never will be another one. The people down there in the shadow are happy about that. At last, at last, everything's ahead. The smart ones say so and the people listening to them and reading them agree: Here comes the new. (p. 7)

This exultant voice steals centre stage in the novel and carries a force which is stirring and hypnotic but is also the novel's most problematic feature. The sheer urban savvy of the narratorial voice attempts to close down the interpretative indecision that is earlier associated with Violet's relationship to her own past (as Violet, or Violent). In her desire to capture the city's essence and sing its praises the narrator falls into a celebratory modernism which is very close to Ann Douglas' 'terrible honesty': the characteristic white modernist attitude in the 1920s.[19] The city in this rendition is characterised by its lack of ambiguity: 'What it is is decisive' (p. 7), and although it is the fate of the narrator to realise that she has fallen in love with the city and missed the action within it entirely, the crystalline brilliance of this writing is not so easily undermined.

As the novel moves toward its end (which is also its beginning, in that it is the section which Morrison wrote first) the knowing narrator of the glittering city becomes increasingly disillusioned with her own inter-pretative powers, particularly when it comes to ascribing meaning to the novel's miscegenation story and its white/black hero Golden Gray: 'What was I thinking of? How could I have imagined him so poorly? Not noticed the hurt that was not linked to the colour of his skin, or the blood that beat beneath it' (p. 160). In fact, as Peter Brooker points out, Morrison suggests a whole other interpretative angle on racial conjoining with her symbolically named passing character.[20] But in describing a genealogy of black/white relations the narrator becomes confused, frustrated with her own desire to see things as categorically black and white; while the story of Wild, Joe Trace's mother (who, it seems likely, is also Beloved, pregnant with Paul D's child) and her connection to Golden Gray, the (black) white child who owned True Belle's heart and possessed the mind of her grand-daughter Violet, goes beyond these opposed polarities tracing a complex pattern of desire and loathing that the narrator simply cannot get to grips with: 'I have been careless and stupid and it infuriates me to discover (again) how unreliable I am' (p. 160). It is also clear that the history hunted down by Joe Trace and Violet is part of a longer, more complex history (of African Americans and their experience of modernity) which *Jazz* takes on as a sequel to *Beloved*

(1987) and of which *Paradise* (1997) is the third section. The city becomes both the site of the destruction of the rememory that haunts Sethe in *Beloved*, and also its apotheosis through the haunting of Wild/Beloved's son Joe Trace by his mother's reincarnation, the bitch/dumpling girl Dorcas: a woman young enough to be his daughter. The convoluted chronology of all this suggests the extreme unreliability of testimony and memory in the novel, perhaps the only way to recover a traumatic history in its pain and poignant energy. But at the same time this unreliability is repeatedly forsaken in the luxuriant pleasures of city sights, which are not simply Joe and Violet's experience but also that of the narrator who gives us their experience. It is this that provides the key to the novel's oddly elegiac tone, and is, whether Morrison intends it or not, the key feature of the novel's aesthetic ambitions.

The narrator is not so much unreliable as belatedly coming up against the deceptiveness of the visual field that she so confidently declares she can read in the early sections of the novel – 'sth, I know that woman' (p. 3). She is forced to admit that interpretation is a matter of positionality and power: 'It was loving the City that distracted me and gave me ideas. Made me think I could speak its loud voice and make that sound human. I missed the people altogether' (p. 220). The narratorial conviction of the outcome of the 'scandalizing threesome' (p. 6) on Lenox Avenue – 'that the past is an abused record with no choice but to repeat itself at the crack' (p. 220) – is undermined by the shifting perceptions of the images and encounters that structure this Harlem world. In its repetitions the story of 'who shot whom' (p. 6) turns out very differently, an effect which follows the ambivalent unconcealings of fantasy and desire that one sees in *Looking For Langston*. In the end, however, the novel is rather less challenging than the film in that it remains wedded to a modernist aesthetic whose redemptive focus is ultimately individualist. The pleasure the narrator takes in her own beautiful experiences is mirrored by the pleasure the text takes in its own language: a heady seduction which seems in the end to override the narrator's (or Morrison's) cautionary admonitions about believing the City's (or the text's) hype. The novel ultimately fails to make the transition from the urbane – as the cult of the individual – to the pursuit of urbanity as a communal project.

We see this most clearly in the closing love song of the novel, which follows the narrator's interpretative disclaimers to authority after the story of Violet, Joe and Felice does not repeat that of Joe, Violet and Dorcas but instead finds itself some kind of future (beyond the seductive malevolence of Beloved's spirit) in the confidently striding figure of Felice who claims the city as her own, 'her speed may be slow, but her tempo is next year's news' (p. 222). Finding herself islanded by her smug superiority and entirely superseded by the agency of the characters who peopled her cityrama, the narrator retires from prying and in doing so is intended to teach us a lesson about historical uncertainty and the unpredictability of human desire; a lesson which would set the text on a similar track to *Looking For Langston*. Ultimately though this does not happen, for even as the narrator insists upon her wrong-headedness and the incapacity of her view – 'I missed it altogether' (p. 220) – for this reader at least the intensely subjective, passionate swan song with which she closes the novel makes one feel that the modernist pretensions of the narrator were spot on after all. It is the most stunning piece of prose from an author who specialises in the painfully beautiful, and the experience of reading it recapitulates the modernist city epiphanies of the earlier sections of the novel:

> That I have loved only you, surrendered my whole self reckless to you and nobody else. That I want you to love me back and show it to me. That I love the way you hold me, how close you let me be to you. I like your fingers on and on, lifting, turning. I have watched your face for a long time now, and missed your eyes when you went away from me. Talking to you and hearing you answer – that's the kick ... If I were able I would say it. Say make me, remake me. You are free to do it and I am free to let you because look, look. Look where your hands are now. (p. 229)

Despite the delight I take in reading this passage, if I remove my hands from the book (or somewhere slightly lower given the sensuousness of the passage) I find this closure to the novel difficult. This paragraph traces again the soaring splendour of the 'I'm crazy about this city' sections of the text and tells us that despite the narrator's protests we were right to love it, and more to the point we were right to love the narrator that gave it to us in this fashion. The 'experience' of the novel becomes ultimately the fleshly contract between reader's hands and the pages of the text. Whilst this might be nicely postmodern it is also individualist in a way that rather undermines the tracing of a community's history beyond the 'abused record' of exploitation and exclusion: a community story which bears testament to this and to the singing pleasures of the Harlem experience. In fact, history (in the form of Harlem in its specifics) and community (in the form of Joe, Violet and Felice) disappear into the self-absorbed song of book to reader and back again. Most problematically the woman whose yellow, pock-marked face, *whose photograph*, occasioned all this love and trouble – Dorcas, the true passing heroine of the novel – is decisively removed from the picture, a sleight of hand which is deeply satisfying in its push toward closure but a slight to a murdered girl nevertheless, as well as a typical fate for a passing woman.

On the other hand, the more fluid both/and formulation of *Looking For Langston* leaves us with an evaporated image of community, which is there in raucous celebration but is also, as powerfully, not there as at the end of the film thugs break into a scene which is gone already and was never really there except in its evocation of a community in process.

Eschewing the seductiveness of the stable image, 'look where your hands are now', for the indeterminacy of the (passing) gaze, *Looking For Langston* presents an avant-gardist meditation on identity without falling into modernist solipsism. *Looking For Langston* develops a representation of city life that can embrace the striving toward urbanity as the construction of community in terms both social and political. The thugs breaking in to the suddenly empty nightclub represent, after all, not the postmodern instability of history but its brutal suppression by the forces of the dominant culture. But the aesthetic celebration of community that makes up the filmic text also suggests we will find the practice of urbanity embedded in the striving toward being urbane. In uniting these oft-opposed meanings of the practice of urban life the film returns to Harlem not to rewrite its history but to explore the multivalent symbolism of the race capital.

Notes

1   For contemporary critical accounts which address the cultural significance of the Harlem Renaissance phenomenon and its relationship to debates about modernity and modernism in the US context, see Houston A. Baker, *Modernism and the Harlem Renaissance* (Chicago: University of Chicago Press, 1987); Walter Benn Michaels, *Our America: Nativism, Modernism, and Pluralism* (Durham: Duke University Press, 1995) pp. 85–94; Ann Douglas, *Terrible Honesty: Mongrel Modernism in the 1920s* (London: Picador, 1996) pp. 73–107, 303–45; Paul Gilroy, *The Black Atlantic: Modernity and Double Consciousness* (London, New York: Verso, 1993) pp. 1–40; George Hutchinson, *The Harlem Renaissance in Black and White* (Cambridge, Mass.: Harvard University Press, 1995).

2   Isaac Julien (dir.), *Looking For Langston* (1989). Toni Morrison, *Jazz* (New York: Alfred A. Knopf, 1992). All further references to both texts will be incorporated in the text.

3   See Kevin Robins, 'Prisoners of the city: whatever could a postmodern city be?' in Erica Carter, James Donald and Judith Squires (eds), *Space and Place. Theories of Identity and Location* (London: Lawrence and Wishart, 1994) pp. 303–30; Richard Sennett, *The Uses of Disorder: Personal Identity and City Life* (Harmondsworth: Penguin, 1971); Michael Walzer, 'The pleasures and costs of urbanity' in Phillip Kasinitz (ed.), *Metropolis: Centre and Symbol of Our Times* (London: Macmillan, 1995) pp. 320–30; Iris Marion Young, 'City life and difference' in Kasinitz (ed.), *Metropolis*, pp. 250–70.

4   See Robert E. Park, Ernest W. Burgess, Roderick D. McKenzie, *The City* (1925; rpt. Chicago: University of Chicago Press, 1967); Louis Wirth, 'Urbanism as a way of life' (1938) in *On Cities and Social Life: Selected Papers* (Chicago: University of Chicago Press, 1964) pp. 60–83.

5   Park, 'The city: suggestions for the investigation of human behaviour in the urban environment' in Park *et al.*, *The City*, p. 1.

6   On Park's influence on the Harlem Renaissance see Charles Scruggs, *Sweet Home: Invisible Cities in the Afro-American Novel* (Baltimore: Johns Hopkins University Press, 1993) pp. 50–4.

7   On the construction of 'ghettocentric' style, see Ed Guerrere, *Framing Blackness: The African-American Image in Film* (Philadelphia: Temple University Press, 1993).

8   'Living memory: a meeting with Toni Morrison' in Paul Gilroy, *Small Acts* (London: Serpent's Tail, 1993) pp. 179.

9   James VanDerZee, Camille Billops, and Owen Dodson, *The Harlem Book o,
    Photographs by James VanDerZee* (Dobbs Ferry, NY: Morgan and Morgan, 19,

10 Passing usually refers to the phenomenon of light-skinned African Americans dei.
    their racial heritage and choosing instead to present themselves as white, though
    recent years the term has been used to refer to the movement from one identity
    formation to another (gay passing as straight, or even white passing as black). The so-
    called passing novel was common in the early part of the twentieth century,
    particularly in the 1920s, reflecting cultural anxieties about the instability of racial
    boundaries in the expanding urban centres, and these novels, in the hands of writers
    such as Nella Larsen or Jessie Fauset, became the vehicle for the discussion of the
    sexual, racial and class politics. For further details on passing literatures, see Werner
    Sollors, *Neither Black Nor White Yet Both* (New York: Oxford University Press, 1997).
    For discussion of the contemporary theoretical debates about passing, see Martha J.
    Ginsberg (ed.), *Passing and the Fiction of Identity* (Durham: Duke University Press,
    1996).

11 For an excellent summary of the debates about identity and representation and the
    interesting frequency with which contemporary black cultural theorists have drawn
    on the Harlem Renaissance for inspiration, see Henry Louis Gates Jr, 'Looking for
    modernism' in Manthia Diawara (ed.), *Black American Cinema* (New York: Routledge,
    1993) pp. 200–07.

12 Richard Dyer, 'Into the light: the whiteness of the South in *The Birth of a Nation*' in
    Richard H. King and Helen Taylor (eds), *Dixie Debates: Perspectives on Southern Culture*
    (London: Pluto Press, 1996) pp. 171–5.

13 See Kobena Mercer, 'Reading racial fetishism' in *Welcome to the Jungle* (New York:
    Routledge, 1994) pp. 171–220 for a reading which elaborates theoretically the
    doubled discourse of race and sexuality one sees in Julien's film.

14 See bell hooks, 'States of desire: interview with Isaac Julien' in Isaac Julien and Colin
    MacCabe, *Diary of A Young Soul Rebel* (London: BFI Publishing, 1991) pp. 128–9 for
    Julien's comments on the prevalence of light-skinned bodies in *Looking For Langston*.

15 See Mercer, 'Reading racial fetishism', p. 209.

16 The absence of any actual jazz places is noted in Peter Brooker's perceptive essay on
    Jazz in his *New York Fictions: Modernity, Postmodernism and the New Modern* (London:
    Longman, 1996) p. 200.

17 On the employment of tropes of 'belatedness' in Morrison's work, see Peter Nicholls,
    'The belated postmodern: history, phantoms and Toni Morrison' in Sue Vice (ed.),
    Psychoanalytic Criticism: A Reader (Cambridge: Polity Press, 1995) pp. 50–74.

18 Morrison's attitude to the city is deeply contradictory; see 'City limits, village values:
    concepts of the neighbourhood in black fiction' in Michael C. Jaye and Ann Chalmers
    Watts (eds), *Literature and the Urban Experience* (New Brunswick: Rutgers University
    Press, 1981) pp. 35–44.

19 See Douglas, *Terrible Honesty*, pp. 3–72.

20 Brooker, *New York Fictions*, pp. 207–8.

The Brooklyn Cigar Co. as Dialogic Public Sphere: Community and Postmodernism in Paul Auster and Wayne Wang's *Smoke* and *Blue in the Face*

All postmodern roads lead to Los Angeles. Or so it often seems. For here, as David Lyons reports, is 'the world's first truly postmodern city'.[1] Lyons cites the city's accelerated deindustrialisation, concentration of high-tech occupations, low-paid service and manufacturing jobs, its 'constantly moving, fragmentary urban flow', squalid slums and gentrified neighbourhoods, airports, hotels and shopping malls as paradigmatic of postmodernity.[2] For Edward Soja, one of the city's leading interpreters, LA is 'the world's most symbolic space of urban decentralisation'[3] and this 'symbolic centrelessness', in particular, says Lyons, makes LA 'a metaphor for postmodern consumer culture in general; all is fragmented, heterogeneous, dispersed, plural – and subject to consumer choices'.[4]

Obviously, much critical discussion and cultural expression have gravitated towards and emanated from LA, but surely the general claims here are questionable. Aside from the troubling idea that here is the centre of centrelessness, can any single instance (city, event or text) be thought to express a pure and achieved postmodernism when the descriptions and dimensions of this are so evidently fluid and contentious? Does LA represent the common destination of other contemporary cities, even of other major North American cities? How well does it apply, for example, moving back across the continent and back in time through the layers of modernity, to New York City, founded on the grid system which is such a graphic emplotment of Enlightenment principles?[5] The substantial growth of banking, financial services and other nationally and internationally dominant aspects of the 'producer service sector' in this city, along with the growing influence of the culture industries, dramatically altered employment patterns, ethnic composition and consequent social polarisation make New York a postmodern city in its own right, indeed a 'paradigmatic example'.[6] In one view of this development, Saskia Sassen argues that the advanced economic sectors of global cities such as London, Tokyo and New York share a 'transnational urban space' marked by the concentration of control and management in downtown financial districts, and that this is contrasted in a hierarchy of urban forms with gentrified residential areas, 'old working class districts and immigrant communities', with their own supporting subeconomies and a 'growing mass of poor, displaced people who occupy devastated areas of the city'.[7] Thus, if in one version of postmodernism, 'decentralisation' produces LA as the quintessential postmodern city, another model, concerned to identify the forms and effects of globalisation, sees New York as a leading example. Where, in one account, there is heterogeneous sprawl, there is, in the other, a dual agglomeration of functions and marked social and economic division.

But if globalisation, along with internal social and economic differentiation and inequality, make New York a postmodern city, these trends have arguably only intensified features in an earlier phase of monopoly capitalism, immigration and employment patterns. Rather than the linear development Lyons proposes, therefore, where the 'premodern city, such as Venice' and 'the modern city, such as New York' give way to the postmodernism of LA, we are witness to an uneven development in which New York presents a palimpsest of layered times and economic and cultural forms, the talismanic skyscrapers of its modernist moment rubbing shoulders with the postmodern buildings of a Philip Johnson.[8] A further set of relations comes into view, moreover, if we look beyond Manhattan, which is the object of Sassen's analysis, to consider its relations with the Boroughs, which of course have their own distinctive physical character and social and economic histories. How do the Boroughs relate to the 'centre' of Manhattan, itself so internally differentiated? Are the Bronx and Brooklyn postmodern or modern, or anti-modern or premodern, or some combination of these?

All this suggests that in thinking about the postmodern city, as in thinking about postmodernism at all, we need a flexible analytic model, alert to newness and the traces of the modern in postmodern times as well as to the spatial relations and consciousness associated with postmodernism in the new cultural geography. This is true also of notions of place and community which have proved an important if fraught topic in this field and form the guiding theme in the present discussion. I want to survey some of this commentary below before sketching the development, principally of relations between the self and other, in the work of Paul Auster and the further exploration of this in the two films *Smoke* and *Blue in the Face*, made by Auster and Wayne Wang. I should make it clear at the outset that I do not view these texts as the proof of a given theoretical argument, or as a solution to theoretical or empirical questions, but as an illustration of the need for complexity in thinking about the issues of identity, public space, and the interleaved and uneven relations of the modern with the postmodern in the city. Auster's work and these films are also concerned with narrative or storytelling, and this too, I suggest, is instructive in conceptualising relations of the self and other and thus of forms of dialogic urban social exchange.

Maps and Movement

Iain Chambers writes of how we need maps to get around in the city, but how this modernist device – 'with its implicit dependence upon the survey of a stable terrain, fixed references and measurement' contradicts the 'fluidity of metropolitan life'.[9] 'The fluctuating contexts of languages and desires', he says, 'pierce the logic of cartography and spill over the borders of its tabular, taxonomic, space' (p. 92). Chambers consequently urges us to leave the modernist map behind, to go to encounter the disturbance of the everyday in the gendered and ethnic city, 'the territories of different social groups, shifting centres and peripheries' (p. 93). These 'complexities of fugitive, heterogenous ideas and experience are opposed', he says, to 'linear argument and certainty' and present 'us' in the city or the modern metropolis, especially, with 'a reality that is multiform, heterotopic, diasporic', whether this city is Lagos, London, Beijing or Buenos Aires (p. 93).

Chambers talks of challenging what 'passes for critical "common sense" in this field' (p. 111). However, his vocabulary and libertarian rhetoric place value, indeed 'reality', all on the side of migrancy, borders, drift, mobility and a series of other cognate terms – apertures, intervals, interruptions – in what is only the newer common sense of postmodernist or postmodernised cultural studies. Here, in a world of differences, 'subjects, languages, histories, acts, texts, events' exist, he writes, 'under the sign of "homelessness"' (p. 98). In an unrecognised double contradiction, Chambers treats these perceptions of urban living as a universal experience, most revealingly in an assumed equation in his own prose between the first person singular and plural pronoun, between 'I 'and 'we', and, second, reinforces the binary thinking he would otherwise seek to topple in the denigration, on the bad side of his dividing line, of the ideas of home, community, continuity, or the activity of mapping. These, he argues, posit an impossible authenticity or are conservative and reactionary.[10]

Chambers' writing provides a relatively unqualified example of a common polemic in the field of the new social or cultural geography; one whose deconstructive postmodernism reads all too unfortunately like the romanticised self-projection from the very narrow base of a nomadic and privileged intellectual middle class. An earlier, influential, but also problematic statement on urban identities, emerged from within the feminist engagement with deconstruction and postmodernism. In 'The ideal of community and the politics of difference', Iris Marion Young brings a deconstructive perspective to what she sees as the homogenising notion of 'community'. In privileging the supposed transparency of face-to-face relations, this ideal, she argues, 'devalues and denies difference in the form of temporal and spatial distancing'; excludes where it cannot assimilate; and is politically unrealistic, if not indeed incipiently racist, chauvinistic, or sectarian.[11] Contemporary mass urban societies set strangers in proximity with each other, she argues. A more appropriate ideal will therefore acknowledege that 'city life is the "being-together of strangers"' who cannot hope for an immediate, mutual and reciprocal understanding, and will aim instead – in a key formulation – to achieve an attitude or ethos of 'openness to unassimilated otherness'. This Young defines as the utopian norm of 'the unoppressive city'.[12]

A 'politics of difference' is thus opposed to a universalising and essentialist ideal of social relations. The problem with this argument, however, is that this conservative tendency is imputed to the ideal of community with little evidence or reference to community's variant historical or political forms. A Mormon community is not the same as that established in a rural English village, no more than a Masonic Lodge is the same as a fan club, though these too might constitute communities. Nor within the city is the community of an African-American neigh-bourhood the same as that of an environmentalist lobby, a gun club, a criminal network, or a revolutionary working-class splinter group. Moreover, face-to-face contact in such groups is by no means necessarily privileged above relations with strangers connected at a physical distance; nor is shared subjectivity, which Young attributes to the ideal of community, assumed as a fact or aim. Some groups or communities might be exclusive, closed totalities, but some will be more open; some communities are conservative while some are radically progressive, some will be of long, others of short duration. Obvious though these reservations are, Young's has been an influential argument, directly and indirectly endorsed in recent writings.[13] In similar vein, the editors of *Space and Place. Theories of Identity and Location* introduce the essays in their volume as questioning neo-liberal and essentialist or communitar-ian notions of identity, location and the public sphere. 'The presumed certainties of cultural identity', they write, 'firmly located in particular places which housed cohesive communities of shared tradition and perspective, though never a reality for some, were increasingly disrupted and displaced for all'.[14] The broader assumption supporting this thinking is offered by Sophie Watson and Katherine Gibson in their collection *Postmodern Cities and Spaces*. They conclude:

> In the new conceptualisation of identity politics the old binary oppositions of class and gender and race are disrupted and dispersed, and new formations and alliances come together in different forms to erupt in new places and new forms. Instead of assuming single subject positions it is now commonplace to recognise that people represent several groups at once and occupy multiple subject positions and identities which shift and change all the time.[15]

Indeed, it *is* commonplace to talk this way. But the kind of overstatement in these formulations is again questionable. How and why is it that identity is now disrupted for all, but was in the past ambivalently and unevenly experienced? Isn't the view of past identities as 'single' and new contemporary identities as 'multiple' more of the same old binarism that is said to be superseded? Are the 'people' (a unifying category), referred to as representing different subject positions and identities, to be understood as 'everyone', 'everywhere'? Is this a surreptitious, unacknowledged and inconsistent universalism? And are people's multiple identities, if we concede this much, to be understood as shifting and changing 'all the time'?

Of more positive interest here, perhaps, is the implication in the first statement by Carter *et al.* above, that such 'presumed' identities were themselves narrative or ideological fictions which, it is allowed, 'continue to resonate throughout the imaginations of displaced communities' (p. vii). Unlike Chambers, the editors here see the force of such past fictions of identity and 'aim to show how and why they are so powerful as a prelude to acting on them' (p. xiv). They accordingly seek a newly conceived heterogeneous public sphere 'of contestation between groups of distinct, located identities' (p. xiv); an agenda in which older notions of individual autonomy or cohesive communities are to be 'acted on'; that is to say, critiqued and surpassed. Watson and Gibson talk similarly of a postmodern politics of strategic contestation, which 'allows for optimism and possibility, since it celebrates struggles and new possibilities at many sites – both marginal and mainstream – recognising that victories are only ever partial, temporary and contested ... shifting with the fast-changing circumstances of cities today'.[16]

As I suggested, this discourse is coming to comprise an academic common sense on place and identity, one which accords with the work of Edward W. Soja in cultural geography and seeks a politicised Baudrillardian or Derridian take on postmodernism. In fact, however, as Kevin Robins shows, a range of contrasting but often still 'post' modern alternatives to this idea of place and community has been quite evident in the realm of theory and public discussion. Cultural critics, planners, architects and British royalty have invoked the need for a sense of the local, of tradition and community in terms which have been conservative, even aristocratic in perspective, but also radical and progressive. In the fuller extent of this debate, as Robins shows, Prince Charles' appeal to neo-classical and vernacular styles and its associated idea of an organic community takes its place alongside Mike Rustin's observation, for example, that, 'territorial locations remain nodes of association and continuities, bounding cultures and communities' and Mike Featherstone's view (echoing Chambers above) that postmodernism in the city presents a 'no-place space' of consumer and leisure sites (malls, museums, theme parks, shopping centres and the like) in which urban identities can be eclectically and differentially composed and recomposed.[17]

A further important contribution to this discussion has been made by Doreen Massey who questions the stark contrast of an idealised sense of place and community and postmodern fragmentation and disruption and along with it the assumption that a sense of place or community is necessarily static or reactionary. Communities, Massey argues, are thoroughly mixed in their ethnic composition, political groupings and historical development, as well as in the copresence they exhibit of the global and local. Mobility, ownership and control advantage some and disadvantage others. Formulating 'an adequately progressive sense of place', she argues, means questioning 'the idea that places have single, essential identities', dissociating communities from a fixed place, understanding their internal structures and conflicts and the many linkages connecting local experience and activities with global economic and communication networks and political events.[18] 'In this interpretation', Massey writes, 'what gives a place its specificity is not some long internalised history but the fact that it is constructed out of a particular constellation of social relations, meeting and weaving together at a particular locus ... each "place" can be seen as a particular, unique, point of their intersection'.[19]

There is therefore a conflicted discourse on notions of place and community. I do not think the answer to this is to take sides, so as either exclusively to favour a lexicon of complexity, displacement, dispersal, heterogeneity or contestation, or to defend the fixed stabilities of home, the claims of continuity or linear argument. I am more sympathetic to the first, more usual postmodern discourse, but opposed to its simplifications of the past, and thus of the present and future, and unsympathetic to a dismissal of notions of stability, coherence, tradition or community as if these are always experienced and imagined as fixed and unbroken, and are not – differently conceived – necessary to any contemporary progressive politics. Relevant here is Stuart Hall's argument in the seminal essay 'Minimal selves' that the discourse of difference must come to a temporary stopping place, a point of punctuation in a continuing narrative of identity, when the individual says: 'But just now, this is what I mean; this is who I am' for there to be a necessary consciousness of solidarity.[20]

A second issue, as Robins suggests, is that all of these arguments – from Iain Chambers to Prince Charles – involve attitudes towards modernity. This, as he says, lies at the heart of current debate on the crisis of the city. Invariably, modernity is seen as abstract, impersonal, universalising, as eliding or repressing difference and particularity, and these vices are then seen as invested in homogenising notions of place, community and identity. For all their differences these discourses are therefore commonly 'postmodern' but give to the prefix 'post' the meaning of anti- or non-modern. This demonising of modernity along with the assumption that the 'epoch' of modernity is simply over, leaving no trace or vestige, is, however, of a piece with the binarism and simplified historical sense of these otherwise opposed views. Once more, a way forward lies not in endorsing either position, but in developing a vocabulary adequate to the complex particularities of city life in its uneven transition from the modern to the postmodern which will recognise the imbrication of one set of terms in the other.

A Time for Stories

The films *Smoke* and *Blue in the Face* were respectively written and directed and codirected by Paul Auster and Wayne Wang. Auster is known chiefly for *The New York Trilogy* (1985), whose abstract use of the popular genre form of detective fiction in a sequence of three related self-referential stories about language, writing and identity have established it as an acclaimed postmodern text. These are persistent themes in Auster's writing, refracted through the figures of author, narrator, protagonist as writer, editor, notetaker: each a version of the other, like boxed Russian dolls, and on occasion bearing Auster's name or initials. In Auster's world of chance and contingency, identity is plainly unstable; a casualty of postmodernism, thrown between the limited perimeters of a lonely room and peripatetic quests across city and country to pursue what is lost: friend, father, family and, beneath these of course, the self. Pattern, but not order, is brought to this existence through coincidence, itself an unnerving because unmotivated sign of resemblance or repetition; like twins, or in the most troubling resemblance of all for Auster, the kinship expressing continuity and separation between fathers and sons.

The New York Trilogy had been preceded by *The Invention of Solitude*, a prose work in two parts, 'The Portrait of an Invisible Man', written after the unexpected death of Auster's father, and 'The Book of Memory'. In the second he maintains in a conception of 'myself as everyone' and of the 'multiplicity of the singular', repeated elsewhere, that the truly solitary individual connects through introspection and memory with others.[21] This is less a postmodernist than a modernist conception of the self and the world. Indeed, many of Auster's literary essays, on Mallarme, Hugo Ball, Celan, Kafka and Ungaretti, would confirm his affinity with European modernism, or more accurately, Symbolism, since it is Mallarme's 'ideal book' and Rimbaud's '*j'est un autre*', directly cited by Auster, which give the most obvious expression to this idea of monadic plenitude. This leads him to talk – somewhat perversely, I suggest – of 'The Book of Memory' as a 'collective work', since the intertextuality of voices discovered in looking down to the bottom of the self 'speak through me'.[22]

There is a contrary movement, however, in Auster's work and thinking which releases the self and text into a different kind of non-appropriative relationship with the other.[23] He talks of his early poetry as a 'clenched fist' and of prose as an opening up, 'a letting go', and of letting go further in being a parent, when, as he writes, 'you can find yourself wanting to tell stories'.[24] He tells classic fairy tales, especially the story 'Pinocchio' to his son, and comes to describe himself as a storyteller and realist. Oral tales recommend themselves, he adds, in their anonymity, economy and openendedness.[25] Moreover, a story breaks down walls of solitude because 'it posits the existence of others and allows the listener to come into contact with them'.[26] A further opening of the clenched fist of the all inclusive universalising self occurs, I suggest, in *Smoke* and *Blue in the Face*. These works move Auster beyond a concern with the self and the other who is kin, or twin to, or lies deep within the self into collaborative, improvisatory and creative, communal relationships. The films are both about these themes and a demonstration of them, in their composition and production. I want to consider this second aspect first.

The story on which *Smoke* is based, 'Auggie Wren's Christmas Story', was first published, in an irony Auster clearly appreciates, in *The New York Times*, the paper of record, on Christmas Day 1990. It was read there by Wayne Wang, director of *Dim Sum* and *The Joy Luck Club*, who determined to make it into a film. *Smoke* was completed over the next four years to Auster's rewritten script in an evidently happy collaboration between Californian Chinese American filmmaker and New York Jewish novelist. Wang describes Auster as 'my friend, my brother and my partner' and Auster comments on 'the atmosphere ... of respect and equality' between director, writer and the editor, Maysie Hoy: 'there were no hierarchies', he says, ' no intellectual terrorism'.[27]

The second film grew like a dancing, misshapen footnote from this working ensemble. It was made in six days from left-over time and film stock and Auster became codirector. There was no script: celebrities like Jim Jarmusch, Lou Reed, Madonna, and Rosanne Barr took cameo parts for standard or no fees alongside local people. The crew were joined by Harvey Wang, who shot documentary video footage, incorporated in brief montaged snatches into the film, of Brooklyn streets and citizens. Jewish, Asian and black inhabitants delivered statistics directly to camera at the door of the cigar store on Brooklyn's rivers, its mixed population, even its potholes. The whole film was improvised and only given shape, says Auster, in an 'ongoing triangular conversation' between himself, the photographer and video filmmaker, Wayne Wang, and the editor Christopher Tellefsen (p. 160). All this, says Auster, was 'wonderfully in keeping with the spirit of the project ... strange unpredictable doings set against a backdrop of diversity, tolerance and affection' (p. 200). The film is a comic statement of 'great human warmth' in which, with appropriate contradiction, characters argue, yell and insult each other, are obnoxious, opinionated and angry, and in which 'Nearly every scene ... is about conflict' (p. 161).

Auster says *Blue* has no plot, but it has. Vinnie, the owner of the store, wants to sell the store to replace it with a health food shop. Auggie's defence of the cigar store as a public forum where the old and young come for their papers, their candy, their cough drops and simply to hang out, against the demands of 'dollars and cents', is a story of how the living memory of the Brooklyn neighbourhood can withstand commercial progress, and is also entirely in keeping with the film's aesthetic of spontaneous, collectively inspired amateurism, a blip of dissent and diversity in a homogenising, hugely commercial film industry.[28] Auggie's case is aided, moreover, by the speech of the ghost of the Dodgers baseball star, Jackie Robinson, the first black to play pro-baseball. The best of old Brooklyn, its stand against prejudice and profit speaks in the present, not as nostalgic whimsy but as a living and active influence.

Smoke, to return to this text, has at least two main stories as well as some internal storytelling – about how to weigh smoke and how Mikhail Bakhtin smoked his only copy of a manuscript while in exile. The first main story is about a writer, Paul Benjamin, recovering from the death of his wife and from a writer's block and who needs a Christmas story, and Auggie Wren, who provides him with it. The second story is about a young black boy from the projects, Rashid/Thomas Cole, whose mother is dead, who is estranged from his father, and is on the run from local black hoods after finding some stolen money. He assumes different names and identities in his double flight from his pursuers and his search for his father. His life crosses with Paul Benjamin's and Auggie's and theirs with his. The stolen money circulates between them until it is passed on as a gift. Paul Benjamin and Rashid pose as father and son and (impossibly) as son and father before Rashid confronts, fights with, and is reluctantly accepted into his natural father's present family. They sit at the close of Rashid's story at an awkward picnic lunch with Paul and Auggie as silent guests and in which the only exchange is not words but a cigar. Rashid is also an aspiring artist and he presents his father with a drawing of his garage as a secret gift. Auggie too is an artist, his project a multivolumed series of photographs of the corner opposite his store, shot every day at the same time. Until instructed by Auggie Paul cannot see any difference beneath the apparent sameness of these photographs, but it is there. Auggie is the witness to the community's varied daily life, the chronicler of its routines and vitality whose project gives it definition and life, even in the picture his albums include of Benjamin's dead wife.

Open Endings

There is much to comment on in these films. A major concern, I think, is the role of storytelling in establishing a dialogic exchange at the centre of this neighbourhood, in particular between men. Paul Benjamin requires a Christmas story and Auggie gives him one in a scene occupying the last ten minutes of *Smoke* in which the story he tells – which is no less than Paul Auster's own published story of 'Auggie Wren's Christmas Story' – is intercut with the story on film, in black and white. Auggie chases a black youth who has thieved from his shop and finds his pocket book with photos inside, including one of his grandmother Granny Ethel. When Christmas comes Auggie goes to return the wallet. Granny Ethel lives alone in the projects and is blind. She mistakes Auggie for her grandson and he goes along with this. They eat Christmas dinner and he prepares to leave, but before he goes takes a camera from a pack of stolen cameras in the bathroom. This is the story and the camera is the camera he uses every day. Is it a true story? Does it show Auggie in a good light or as a thief?

The film ends on Auggie and Paul Benjamin's smoke-wreathed smiles, as they share the ambiguity of the story – that's what friends are for they agree, to share your secrets with. Clearly, the scene confirms their friendship, but the filming suggests something more of the terms of this friendship. Early scenes of the film are shot in wide shots and masters, giving way to more close shots and singles as the characters become more involved with each other. During the telling of the story the camera is almost exclusively on Auggie's face and closes in on Auggie's mouth, 'apparently', says Auster, 'as close as it ever will' (p. 13). But then it moves in further in an unexpected intimacy. 'It's as if the camera is bulldozing through a brick wall', says Auster, 'breaking down the last barrier against genuine human intimacy' (p. 13). Thus visual and emotional conventions are broken down in a moment that confirms the bonding between the two men. The mouth speaking and smiling is an erotic opening between them, as language, the body and friendship are shown as intimately connected. The mouth which occupies the screen is also, of course, the mouth of the storyteller, who gifts this story and is also, we might say, the mythologist (echoing still the Greek '*muthologist*') the figure of the historian as storyteller who passes on the tale of the tribe by word of mouth. Anthony Giddens reminds us in *The Transformation of Intimacy* how rarely men form and sustain close friendships. He reports how in a group of 200 American men and women two-thirds of the men could not name a close friend and that those who did named a woman friend. Three-quarters of the women meanwhile could easily name one or more close friends and these were invariably other women.[29] In foregrounding a friendship between two white, heterosexual males, *Smoke* presents a gendered and, we might think, limited perspective on positive relations within the community. Nevertheless, in the developing intimacy, respect and mutual dependence between Auggie and Paul Benjamin – in their dialogic relations in short – the film challenges the stereotype of competitive, uncommunicative, non-caring relations between men. In the context of Auster's own work it moves beyond the concept of the introspective, universalised individual, releasing the male self from the mirroring relation of father and son while suggesting another emotional connection than the fragile triangle of father, mother and child.[30] The scenes between the two men establish a non-sexual but emotionally charged intimacy; a bond of friendship founded on the act of giving, primarily the giving of a story which is a giving of the self: a letting go.

In *Blue*, a communal Brooklyn identity is reaffirmed with the saving of the store. The neighbourhood spontaneously rejoices in the carnivalesque dancing in the streets at the film's close as lovers, friends, strangers, men and women, short and very tall, white, Asian, African American, Hispanic, Puerto Rican are led in the 'Brooklyn shuffle' by the drag dancer, RuPaul. Thus a mixed and montaged narrative mode combines in collaborative creative work to celebrate intimacy between men, neighbourhood values and ethnic diversity. No doubt this sounds nostalgic, conservative and sentimentally utopian all at once, echoing the verdict on the ideal community of Iris Marion Young and others above. The films affirm face-to-face friendship – characteristically privileged, in Young's view, in the conservative ideal of community – and further install the valued neighbourhood space of old Brooklyn in the preservation of the cigar store. I do not wish to defend a conservative idea, nor do I think this is what is entailed. The problem is that the binary model of the old ideal and the new ideal is simply inadequate.

Auster and Wang's films, I suggest, represent the site of an urban community as it is lived, imagined and contested with a greater complexity than Young's model can sustain. The local community is valued, certainly, but shown as mixed and heterogeneous, without a unitary history or identity and as functioning on differentiated and contradictory levels. First, the films alert us to a range of relationships in the community which Young's description fails to consider. For here, non-assimilative relationships embrace face-to-face friendship as well as a 'being with strangers' in a network of near and far connections across time and space where these can and do also change. Second, both films, and *Blue in the Face* in particular, show how the place of the neighbourhood as one important coordinate of cultural identity might 'continue to resonate' as an active and positive force in the very process of rearticulating the networks of social relations in the city.[31]

If this conception of people and place is nostalgic and utopian, then both terms stand in need of some redefinition. Nostalgia, as bell hooks writes, is 'that longing for something to be as once it was, a kind of useless act', and as such is to be distinguished, she says, from 'that remembering that serves to illuminate and transform the present'.[32] This 'politicisation of memory' applies in Auster to the evocation of an earlier Brooklyn, most evidently in the embodied memory of Jackie Robinson, who pleads the case of 'sense' against 'cents' and of a combative, anti-racist culture against commercial gain. The best of the past is thus felt as a living memory and active influence in the present. This is neither wishful thinking nor the pastiched recycling of the postmodern 'nostalgia mode'. Elizabeth Wilson describes in similar terms how this kind of 'retrieval' rather than passive 'remembrance' of the past can prompt an 'active responsibility both for the past and for the future'.[33] As such, this kind of interpretive historical imagining is closely connected with utopian thoughts of a better world. Like nostalgia, utopianism is, of course, commonly associated with escapism; with a distracted, unrealistic gaze towards a perfect future rather than preferred past. Thus, the 'ideal community', says Young, is 'undesirably utopian', 'wildly utopian and undesirable'.[34] Here too, however, the important question concerns the relation of this better world to the perceived imperfections of the present and the possible strategies which would convert one to the other. Thus, although Young rejects the utopianism of the community, she does so in favour of an alternative 'ideal' or ' vision of the good society', achievable, she believes, through a 'politics of difference'.

What kind of utopianism, therefore, do these films present? *Blue in the Face*, said Auster, is a 'hymn to the republic of Brooklyn'.[35] Park Slope, where he has been a resident for fifteen years and where the film is set, he describes as 'one of the most democratic and tolerant places on the planet. Everyone lives there', he says, 'every race and religion and economic class, and everyone pretty much gets along' (p. 14). This is in spite of the 'terrible ... wrenching ... unbearable things' that go on in Brooklyn, not to speak of the 'hellhole' of New York as a whole (pp. 14, 15). In the texts of the films this utopianism is expressed not so much in the characterisation of a whole life or 'vision' of the good society as in valued moments or epiphanies: the scenes, notably, once more, between Auggie and Paul Benjamin and the dancing in the streets which celebrates the victory of saving the store. As Angela Carter once said, the heroic optimism stories produce for us is of a kind that says, 'one day we might be happy, even if it won't last'.[36] The comic community spirit of *Smoke* and *Blue in the Face* is not built to last, but its utopianism is no more naive or unqualified than is its nostalgia. The final scene shows a harmonious multiethnic community congratulating itself on its now reaffirmed identity. However, its positive value does not lie in any suggestion of a permanent victory over the bad times of the present but in the way a small, better moment (involving some 600 people) is embedded in and arises from that world. Like the memory of a better self which returns to shape the present, the joy of this moment triumphs for now in a world of spite, jealousy and dissatisfaction between men and women, and of suspicion between blacks and whites.

This is worth some further comment. Auggie and Paul are evidently the centred figures of the films' jointed narratives. Yet, as I suggested, their respective and shared stories connect them with others, including their past wives and new women partners and non-white characters, especially African Americans. Taken together, these connections contextualise and relativise the stable bond they achieve as friends. Women characters (for example, Ruby and Madonna) enter the community or the store (the waitress, Auggie's woman friend Violet) from a place outside, or they do not enter the physical sphere of this male-centred world at all (Paul's student girlfriend, April), or like Rosanne Barr's character they wish to leave. Women come second to baseball or business, or simply the boys. If things work out, as they do for Rosanne who gets to go with Vinnie to Las Vegas, or for Ruby, the road is rocky; marked by suspicion, insults, deception and stand-up rows. None the less, these relationships have their ambiguities and include moments of assertivenesss and independent action by women and of a non-invasive mutual recognition between women and men. Ruby, for example, is the one storyteller to match Auggie and Paul. Her story that her pregnant daughter, Felicity, is Auggie's child is a ploy – perhaps – to get the money to help Felicity off drugs. Auggie at first rejects this account outright, and is rejected by Felicity, yet he and Ruby arrive finally at a non-manipulative and affectionate understanding. The stolen money which circulates through *Smoke* passes to Auggie and he gives it to her, as freely as he gifts Paul Benjamin a story. With a wink he accepts the fifty-fifty chance that Felicity is his daughter. This scene effectively returns the ambiguity of fiction as lie and truth to Ruby's story, much like his own, and in the same gesture acknowledges her enigma as other to himself.

Relationships between blacks and whites and the question of ethnic identity are similarly shown as complex. Blacks live not in Park Slope but in the adjacent projects in Boerum Hill. The men are unemployed or struggling economically, involved in the informal economy or in theft. Auggie and Paul's stories connect them with black lives through Grandma Ethel (whose grandson Auggie pretends to be) and Rashid /Thomas (who poses with Paul as father and son). *Smoke* tells us how difficult, if not in 'real' terms impossible, these relations are. Thus, Auggie can only pass as Grandma Ethel's grandson because she is blind and Rashid/Thomas simply cannot be Paul's son. Rashid/Thomas' aunt implies that Paul has to be 'some kind of pervert' to have taken an interest in him, and Rashid makes it plain that Paul's taking him in for a few days is not a miracle cure for racial inequality: 'Let's not get too idealistic' they agree (pp. 58, 83). Rashid/Thomas' newfound family, including his father's second wife and child, sit in silence, with Auggie and Paul on the margins: the whole a tableau of compounded personal, familial, gendered and racial uncertainties. The more positive signs of coexistence and fluid identity, therefore – the street celebration and the coming together of white, Puerto Rican and African American males in the store, over sport, but again over song; Auggie's successful relationship with the Spanish American Violet; the video footage of racially mixed shopping areas, the interviews with and statements by Brooklyn citizens of mixed race, all of which occur in the more relaxed *Blue in the Face*, have to be seen in this more fully differentiated context. The utopian moments of joyful union work, that is to say, because they qualify and are in turn qualified by the tension demonstrated elsewhere.

The nostalgia and utopianism of the films are therefore neither sentimental nor weakly idealistic; nor are they 'undesirable' in terms of the ideal of a 'non-oppressive society' or a dialogic relation with 'unas-similated others'. Their moments of self-aware and negotiated coexistence offer less a vision of another, better world than a glimpse of the possible in this imperfect present. The community is defined by both, in an anthology of intersecting and contesting narratives of the good and less good life. Its positive moments of non-intrusive affection, tolerant social interaction and combative reaffirmation draw on the strengths of association with a place, notably the store and its immediate Brooklyn environs. These places, we might say, provide sites of momentary, memorable definition in lives of heterogeneous flux.

Kevin Robins suggests that the experience of combined 'settlement and flux' has comprised the most vital tension of the modern city and that this is now undermined by the new globalising flow of information networks which traverse the borders and boundaries of community, region and nation without impediment.[37] The postmodern city is therefore viewed as a thoroughly permeable space without settlement or stability. This distinction subsumes the series of distinctions informing other contemporary arguments on the city – between community and migrancy, belonging and homelessness, continuity and dispersal, the local and the global, the modern and the postmodern. What, then, does this suggest finally of the representation of the community and city in *Smoke* and *Blue in the Face*, where a tension between settlement and process is retained? Are they, after all, 'modern' or, at least, not yet postmodern? As above, I believe things are more uneven and two-sided than these distinctions suggest. In one respect, this Brooklyn is a technological backwater, entirely bereft of information technologies and media flows, Walkmen, faxes, and e-mails; a place where authors use typewriters rather than word processors and where the only TV is a dud black-and-white set. But it is also the Brooklyn where, as Auster summarises, '"We don't go by numbers"' (p. 161): a Brooklyn of spontaneity and cosmopolitan diversity rather than calculation and sameness; a 'supplement' to the city which counters the mathematical grid and rational categories of the still modernising Manhattan with its own anarchic postmodern and improvised, eccentric mayhem.

The best illustration of this bifurcated allegiance to the modern and postmodern is Auggie's photographic project. The exact timing, dating and apparently totalising ambition of this project, for which Auggie uses a still camera on a tripod rather than the postmodern apparatus of roving video camera, suggest a modernist sensibility keen to order the randomness of the everyday. Here too is the controlling male gaze of modernity's predominantly visual regime. At the same time, however, Auggie's albums of 14 years' photographs, numbering above 'four thousand pictures of the same place' (p. 42) comprise an anonymous, public chronicle rather than an authored artwork. The project proposes no hierarchising evaluations, no telos; there is no centre to its narrative of serial snapshots; its gaze is equalising and democratic rather than predatory or invasive. Also, although the photographs are 'stills', collectively they present movement and change over time in a continuing negotiation between 'settlement and flux', or the impulses of the modern and postmodern. Above all, as Auggie has to point out to Paul Benjamin the photographs require a way of reading: 'You'll never get it if you don't slow down, my friend', he says, '... They're all the same, but each one is different from every other one' (p. 44). As Paul looks more closely and comes upon a photograph of his dead wife, so the photographs become a moving personal as well as public memoir. They record the individual in the collective, the exceptional and contingent in the routine and commonplace, the different in the same. The result is neither modernist nor postmodernist as usually understood, but what we might think of as a deconstructed modern in the postmodern.

Auggie's project, like these films as a whole, tell us that absolute distinctions between the modern and postmodern, the local and global, continuity and contingency are too simple. The known place and community and the strange and distant run but do not merge together. Moments of stability are not necessarily enclosing or oppressive, nor are intense emotions and focused identities sentimental, nostalgic and conservative. It is fitting that Auggie's cultural project in the film represents these complexities since it is my contention that cultural texts have precisely this value in relation to theoretical commentary. They do not supercede or superannuate theory, of course, but remind us of the need for a correspondingly adequate complexity of description and definition. In a sense, the lesson they offer, like Auggie's, is in how to read. To appreciate the different in the same (whether in notions of community, identity, modernity or postmodernity) we need to slow down, putting the 'victories', however fleeting they may be in a postmodern politics, on rewind and on freeze frame, pressing the pause button to introduce an uneven, contradictory counter-time in 'the fast-changing circumstances of cities today'.[38] Current discussion suggests that we need to pay more attention to such moments of provisional stability, to the still photograph and close-up, and thus by analogy to the moment of identity and effective social action as well as to the process which takes this moment with all its constellated meanings speeding by.

Notes

1   David Lyons, *Postmodernity* (Buckingham: Oxford University Press, 1994) p. 59.
2   Ibid., pp. 59–60.
3   Edward W. Soja, 'Heterotopologies: a remembrance of other spaces in the citadel – LA' in Sophie Watson and Katherine Gibson (eds), *Postmodern Cities and Spaces* (Oxford: Blackwell, 1995) p. 23.
4   Lyons, *Postmodernity*, p. 61.
5   See Peter Brooker, *New York Fictions* (London: Longman, 1996) pp. 27–8, 220–1.
6   Anthony, D. King (ed.), *Re-Presenting the City: Ethnicity, Capital and Culture in the Twenty-First Century Metropolis* (Basingstoke: Macmillan 1996) p. vii.
7   Saskia Sassen, 'Rebuilding the global city: economy, ethnicity and space' in King (ed.), *Re-Presenting the City*, pp. 23, 29.
8   Lyons, *Postmodernity*, p. 59.
9   Iain Chambers, *Migrancy, Culture, Identity* (London: Comedia/Routledge, 1993) p. 92. Further page references are given in the text.
10 While he recognises that recent developments can have mixed, contradictory effects beyond simple binaries, Chambers still appeals to a 'we' he assumes is positioned on his side. Thus, he notes how 'deterritorialisation produces both diasporic identities and a new fundamentalism ... how older formations stubbornly, often brutally, re-emerge and impose themselves on *our* differentiated but increasingly connected lives, forcing *us* to acknowledge murderous tendencies that insist on localised ethnicities, virulent nationalisms and religious fundamentalism ...' (p.110); '*our* destiny', he avers, in a similar citation of racism, xenophobia and virulent nationalism, 'is now clearly elsewhere' (my italics). The alternative to this thinking is not simply to take 'the other side', nor to invoke an uncommitted neutrality, but to recognise that 'we' are caught *within* such contradictions.

11   Iris Marion Young, 'The ideal of community and the politics of difference' in Linda J.
      Nicholson (ed.), *Feminism/Postmodernism* (London: Routledge, 1990) pp. 302, 301.
12   Ibid., pp. 318, 301.
13   See, for example, Paul Patton, 'Imaginary cities: images of postmodernity' in Watson
      and Gibson (eds), *Postmodern Cities and Spaces*, pp. 112–21; James Donald, 'This, here,
      now: imagining the modern city' in Sallie Westwood and John Williams (eds),
      Imagining Cities. Scripts, Signs, Memory (London: Routledge, 1997) pp. 181–201.
14   Erica Carter, James Donald and Judith Squires (eds), *Space and Place. Theories of Identity
      and Location* (London: Lawrence and Wishart, 1994) p. vii. Further page references are
      given in the text.
15   Watson and Gibson (eds), *Postmodern Cities and Spaces*, p. 262. Further page references
      are given in the text.
16   Ibid.
17   Cited in Kevin Robins, 'Prisoners of the city. Whatever could a postmodern city be?'
      in Carter *et al.* (eds), *Space and Place*, pp. 310, 311.
18   Doreen Massey, 'A global sense of place' in Ann Gray and Jim McGuigan (eds),
      Studying Culture, 2nd edition (London: Arnold, 1997) pp. 236, 237.
19   Ibid., p. 239.
20   Stuart Hall, 'Minimal selves' in Gray and McGuigan, *Studying Culture*, p. 137.
21   See Paul Auster, *The Invention of Solitude* (London: Faber, 1982) pp. 79, 114, 136,
      139, and for these two quoted statements, 'Interview with Larry McCaffery and Sinda
      Gregory' in Paul Auster, *The Red Notebook* (London: Faber, 1995) pp. 136, 147.
22   Auster, *The Red Notebook*, p. 144.
23   Of interest here are Auster's essay on and interview with Edmond Jabes, *Ground Work.
      Selected Poems and Essays, 1970–1979* (London: Faber, 1990) pp. 183–9, 190–210.
24   Auster, *The Red Notebook*, pp. 130, 132, 134. It might be noted that the figure of the
      storyteller in *The Country of Last Things* supplants the keeper of the city's documentary
      record which goes up in smoke when the library burns.
25   Ibid., pp.140–1, and see p. 153 on Auster's *The Music of Chance* as a fable.
26   Auster, *The Invention of Solitude*, p. 152. Auster's remarks on storytelling recall Walter
      Benjamin's essay, 'The storyteller' in *Illuminations* (London: Fontana,1970). Here
      Benjamin distinguishes between 'the novel', the written product of bourgeois indi-
      vidualism and mechanical production processes, and the older, oral and communal
      form of 'the story'. The latter is marked crucially, in his account, by a dialogic
      exchange between the copresent narrator and listener, between the self and other, and
      by repetition, in which the listener may become in turn the storyteller. Auster's
      distinction between his own poetry and prose writing and his emerging perception of
      the role of story is cast in similar terms.
          In *Psychoanalysis and Storytelling* (Oxford: Blackwell,1994), Peter Brooks suggests
      that we view Benjamin's invocation of 'the sociable situation of storytelling' as a
      strategic protest against the implications of 'solitary consumption' in the age of the
      novel (p. 86). One might argue similarly on behalf of Auster and other contemporary
      writers that to mobilise this 'superannuated' form is a way of contesting a dominant
      cultural narrative from a residual but oppositional position. Thus, the more
      democratic, communal form of storytelling provides the source of a 'counter post-
      modernism' which looks not to the hypermodern, but to an earlier, premodern and
      oral mode. Brooks adds that Benjamin 'proposes ... the notion of narrative as gift: an
      act of generosity' (p. 87). This, also, is very apt in the light of the exhange of story
      and experience between Auggie and Paul Benjamin in *Smoke*.
27   Paul Auster, *Smoke* and *Blue in the Face* (London: Faber and Faber, 1995) pp. viii, 11.
      Further page references are given in the text.
28   '"The whole neighbourhood comes in here", says Auggie, " ... It's a hangout, and it
      helps to keep the neighbourhood together"', ibid., p. 255.

29   Anthony Giddens, *The Transformation of Intimacy. Sexuality, Love and Eroticism in Modern Societies* (Oxford: Polity Press, 1992) p. 126, and see Chapter 10, 'Intimacy as democracy'.

30   For the key instance of relations between man, woman and child see Auster's story, 'The Locked Room' in *The New York Trilogy* (London: Faber and Faber, 1985). The narrator reflects: 'By belonging to Sophie, I began to feel as though I belonged to everyone else as well. My true place in the world, it turned out, was somewhere beyond myself, and if that place was inside me, it was also unlocatable. This was the tiny hole between self and not-self, and for the first time in my life I saw this nowhere as the exact centre of the world' (p. 232).

31   Sharon Zukin reports how identity is negotiated in neighbourhood shopping streets in contrast to commerical downtown areas. 'Despite their problems', she writes, 'these streets produce the quality of life that New Yorkers prize, the public space that makes neighbourhoods liveable, and attaches people to place'. 'Space and symbols in an age of decline' in King (ed.), *Re-Presenting the City*, p. 58.

32   bell hooks, *Yearning, Race, Gender and Cultural Politics* (Boston: South End Press, 1990) p. 147; quoted in Joseph Sciorra 'Return to the future. Puerto Rican vernacular architecture in New York City' in King (ed.), *Re-Presenting the City* in connection with building of *casita* by Puerto Rican inhabitants in New York City. These dwellings are not solely the actual remembered dwellings from the Caribbean, but, Sciorra writes, 'also an ideal and imagined site; memory given form to serve future possibilities' (p. 78).

33   Elizabeth Wilson, 'Looking backward, nostalgia and the city' in Westwood and Williams (eds), *Imagining Cities*, p. 139.

34   Young, 'The ideal of community', pp. 302, 316.

35   Auster, *Smoke*, p. 16. For a more sceptical view see Jan Rosenberg, 'Park Slope: notes on a middle-class "utopia"' in Jim Sleeper (ed.), *In Search of New York* (New Brunswick: Transaction Publishers, 1989) pp. 159–61. Rosenberg reports on the 'community politics' of 'the neighbourhood's concentration of leftists and liberals' and their self-organisation 'against the tide of privatization' and also on how Prospect Park 'serves as more of a barrier than a meeting ground between white upper-middle-class and black and Hispanic Brooklyn'.

36   Angela Carter, *The Virago Book of Fairy Tales* (London: Virago, 1991) p. xviii.

37   Robins, 'Prisoners of the city', see pp. 316–21.

38   Watson and Gibson (eds), *Postmodern Cities and Spaces*, p. 262.

8

Liam Kennedy, University of Birmingham

Paranoid Spatiality: Postmodern Urbanism and American Cinema

The cores of American cities have been radically transformed in the last twenty years, with white flight to the suburbs, decentralisation of economic enterprise, the privatisation of public spaces and the concentration of a new urban underclass changing the spatial, cultural and political form of the city. Many commentators now argue that 'the city' as a synthetic totality has lost coherence and legibility; it has been ruptured as a coherent sign as it has imploded into fragmented spaces and exploded into metastasized, polynucleated urban agglomerations. And yet, the city continues compellingly to define the condition of American society as a whole and is the symbolic locus of ideological debates and moral panics about problems of crime, drugs, homelessness, immigration and demographic change. With its various decentrings and recentrings the city may be said to provide 'a spatial fix' for a generalised crisis of urbanity which encompasses both the material and imaginary restructurings of postmodern urbanism.[1] In the formulation of the classic tradition of American urban studies urbanity is the phenomenon of collectivity which emerges from the close proximity of strangers and face-to-face relations in public space. Today, the discourse of urbanity reflects the inadequacies of this formulation and asks anxious questions: What are cities for? What does civic identity mean? 'Can we all get along?'[2] In this essay I will comment on some general features of this crisis of urbanity and examine how it has been treated as an issue of representation in Hollywood film. Before turning to film, though, I want to comment briefly on some contexts for my study of what I shall refer to and shortly attempt to illustrate as a paranoid urban imaginary in Hollywood film.

Paranoid Spatiality

Almost forty years ago Lewis Mumford, in *The City in History*, commented upon what he perceived as 'the intensified struggle within' urban culture, suggesting that urban life encourages a 'paranoid psychal structure'; the city, he observed, is 'the container of disruptive internal forces, directed towards ceaseless destruction and extermination'.[3] Mumford's vision of the psychodrama of the city, in which chaotic feelings of fear and anxiety signify a collectivised paranoia, has had no clear influence on mainstream urban studies in the United States. However, ideas of urban paranoia have found a fresh resonance in the work of American analysts of postmodern urbanism, most notably in studies of what is often described as the privatisation of public space. Mike Davis provides an influential example in his study *City of Quartz: Excavating the Future of Los Angeles*, published in 1990. Davis analyses the spatial geography of social differences and power relations in the postmodern city. He describes Los Angeles as a 'fortress city' which is 'brutally divided between "fortified cells" of affluent society and "places of terror" where the police battle the criminalised poor'. It is a city of apartheid, he argues, in which 'genuinely democratic space is all but extinct', where social relations are structured around race and class wars, and where 'underlying relations of repression, surveillance and exclusion ... characterize the fragmented, *paranoid spatiality* towards which LA seems to aspire' (emphasis mine). For Davis, the segregation and policing of urban spaces in Los Angeles is plotted in political and urban planning to the benefit of the white middle class to create a spatial grid of exclusions separating this class from the 'Third World service proletariat' and urban poor and homeless.[4]

Davis is only one of many critics in recent years who have drawn attention to the social imperatives which demand increasing control and privatisation of space. The 'fortress' aesthetic he identifies in the planning and building of malls, office towers and private homes in Los Angeles is one that has proved to have broad appeal among middle-class homeowners and professionals in the United States. By now famous examples include the inward-turning shopping mall, the indoor 'atriums' of corporate office buildings, the proliferation of theme parks and 'festival market places', all spaces which are rigorously disciplined through practices of gating, signage and surveillance. It is an aesthetic that denotes an escapist and exclusionary urbanism in which 'form follows fear' as much as it follows finance, and the privatization of space is dependent upon externalised 'others', often identified with the 'street'.[5]

What I particularly want to draw out of Davis' analysis and expand upon in my study of film is his concept of 'paranoid spatiality'. While Davis uses this concept to highlight elements of fear and prejudice in spatial policing and planning he pays relatively little attention to the subjectivity of desires, anxieties and repressions that paranoid spatiality can signify. While there is considerable psychoanalytical debate over the sources and pathogenesis of paranoia as a subjective condition, common elements of Freudian and post-Freudian thought draw attention to the breakdown of subject–object boundaries, the fragmentation or decentring of the self, the concomitant loss of an illusory sense of transcendence, and the projection of aggression and subsequent regarding of that projection as an external threat. In such views normative imaginary relations – of self and other, of the familiar and the unfamiliar – break down, threatening the unity and integrity of the subject.[6] Though imaginary, these distinctly spatialised relations are also manifested in the positioning of the human body. Elizabeth Grosz observes:

> It is our positioning within space, both as the point of perspectival access to space, and also as an object for others in space, that gives the subject a coherent identity ... [T]he subject's relation to its own body provides it with basic spatial concepts by which it can reflect on its own position. Form and size, direction, centredness (centricity), location, dimension and orientation are derived from perceptual relations. These are not conceptual impositions on space, but our ways of living as bodies in space.[7]

The paranoid dilemma of dislocation (mental and corporeal) within space offers a suggestive supplement to what Mike Davis terms the 'underlying relations of repression, surveillance and exclusion' in Los Angeles.

In this paper I construe paranoid spatiality as a key component of the postmodern urbanism represented in American films of recent years. It may be that film is a peculiarly well-suited medium for the expression of urban paranoia. Consider, first, how cinematic representation is commonly associated with modern perception of the city. The cinematic 'spectacle of the city', David Clarke notes, 'both drew upon and contributed to the increased pace of modern city life, whilst also helping to normalise and cathect the frantic disadjusted rhythms of the city ... [it] both documented and helped to transform the social and physical space that the modern city represented'.[8] As well as normalising and documenting urban time and space, though, cinematic representation may also be said to have accentuated growing fears and anxieties about restructurings of modern urban life. In Hollywood film the city has long functioned to focus psychic processes of paranoia, hysteria and repression. I am thinking, for example, of the unease provoked by urban space in film noir, where paranoia is invariably the predominant structure of feeling (though it may have varied sources – sexuality, communism and race are recurrent examples).[9] In the classic noir of the 1940s and 1950s dislocation in space is the common fate of characters whose paranoia suffuses the *mise-en-scène* of deracinated city environments. The visual legacy of such filmmaking is apparent in the filming of postmodern cities today, though the formal techniques are now responding to different ideological and social conditions.

For postmodern subjects in Hollywood film, for whom spatial awareness is heightened in relation to an overdetermined semiology of urban signs and scenes, the city is commonly represented as an uncanny simulacrum of self, an always already interiorised space. Among many examples: there are what have been dubbed 'yuppie nightmare films', such as *After Hours* (1985) and *Single White Female* (1992), wherein, respectively, male and female protagonists struggle for their lives and identities amidst the suggestively gothic interiors and exteriors of the city; there are the 'suburban nightmare' films, such as *Pacific Heights* (1990) and *Unlawful Entry* (1992), wherein dangerous strangers violently threaten marital and familial relationships; and of course, condensing these fears and more, there is *Seven* (1997), which, as much through formal techniques as narrative plotting, provides a stunning exploration and reproduction of our myriad fears of dark urban spaces. In a different generic register, other films have brought ever-greater degrees of reflexivity to the spectacular pleasures of visualising the postmodern urbanscape. Films such as *Die Hard* (1988), *Speed* (1994) and *Heat* (1995) have produced a peculiarly condensed urban aesthetic which subsumes glass office towers, abandoned industrial landscapes, freeway systems and anonymous streets into spectacular tableaux of speed and violence. The postmodern city appears as a spectacle of special effects, of intensified moments of visceral pleasure and voyeurism. All of these films would seem to suggest that in the optics of postmodernism the urban scene continues to compel viewer fascination in the panoramas, visual grids and darkened spaces of the city even as the city dissolves as an object of analysis.[10] At any rate, what I want to emphasise here is that while uncertainty about the meanings and boundaries of the city is hardly new in Hollywood film, it has been much exacerbated by the postmodern transformations of the spatial registers of representation.

I now want to look more closely at features of paranoid spatiality which so often subtend filmic representations of postmodern urbanism. I am particularly concerned here with films that have tended to interpret the contemporary crisis of urbanity as a crisis of white male authority and selfhood. In recent Hollywood films the postmodern urbanscape forms not just the backdrop against which, but also the spatial imaginary within which, white men conduct their highly individualised dramas of masculine authority, existential doubt and moral responsibility. A notable feature of films which have developed these themes in urban contexts is the foregrounding of whiteness as a category of identity formation and more particularly of white male selfhood as an insecure category. I want to provide closer analysis of two such films, *Falling Down* (1992) and *Strange Days* (1995), both of which explicitly address issues of ethno-racial difference and conflict in Los Angeles.

White Noise

I begin with *Falling Down*, an especially intriguing example of Hollywood's response to postmodern urbanism, given the irony and knowingness of the filmmakers in their representation of spatial differences and in their treatment of white male paranoia. *Falling Down* tells the story of the last day in the life of a white middle-class man who, having lost his job and estranged from his wife and child, finally snaps and vents his anger in a violent journey through downtown Los Angeles where he comes into conflict with Koreans, Latinos and a white neo-Nazi amongst others, before he is finally killed by a white policeman. In some areas the film was accused of racist or ethnic stereotyping and drew much publicised protests from Asian American and Latino groups. A Warner Brothers spokesman responded to charges that the film was racist and anti-immigrant: 'We don't believe it condones any of this at all. Quite the contrary, it is holding up a mirror to the things going wrong in our society. We view the film as a wakeup call to the many people who blame their problems on others.'[11] This statement, which acutely defines the film's moralising agenda, also illuminates the difficulties the filmmakers faced in selling their interpretation. Their stated intentions notwithstanding it is by no means clear to whom this 'wakeup call' is addressed or what it says. To be sure, *Falling Down* does set out to dramatise white male prejudices and anxieties and closes on the death of the protagonist who carried these to violently extreme ends. But in its borrowing of established filmic codes of masculinity and in its depiction of ethnic and racial stereotypes the film sends out very mixed, confused messages about the paranoid white male subject it constructs at its centre.

Falling Down is advertised as 'The adventures of an ordinary man at war with the everyday world'. His ordinariness is stressed by director Joel Schumacher, who has stated: 'This is not a bad guy, but he's had it.'[12] The film emphasises the virtual anonymity of his character – throughout he is known simply as D-FENS, the name on his carplate – an everyman whose dilemma is understandable even if his actions are unjustifiable. In the course of the film we discover that the ostensible reasons for his violent rampage are that he has lost his job as a defence worker and his wife has left him, taking their child and placed a restraining order on her husband. While D-FENS' loss of job, wife and child are presented as reasons for his breakdown, we soon recognise that these losses are supplemented by more varied anxieties and prejudices. The opening scene of the film hints at these supplementary pressures at the same time as it establishes his everyman credentials. The film begins with a tight close-up of the sweating face of D-FENS and then pans to the vehicles and people surrounding him in a traffic jam on a Los Angeles freeway. A sense of frustration and growing tension is achieved as rapid intercutting juxtaposes D-FENS' features with the expressions of people within his gaze and of signs adorning neighbouring vehicles and the roadside. Added to this visual mayhem is a growing cacophony of indeterminate sounds. The tension is finally broken when D-FENS scrambles out of his car, gasps for air, and tells an irate motorist, 'I'm going home'. Like the film as a whole this scene is symbolically overdetermined in its representation of the protagonist's dilemma. It sends us a profusion of sounds and signals that function at different levels of connotation and invite different forms of recognition. Manifestly, we have a scene of everyday frustration, a traffic jam, which should elicit a sense of empathy from the viewer and reinforce D-FENS' identity as everyman. But the scene also elicits recognition of a different sort of frustration, for the profusion of sounds and signals work to symbolise this traffic jam as a gridlocked multiracial America populated by different peoples zoned in their own private spaces, isolated in their own concerns, and aggressively warning off others. It is this image of contemporary America as a fractured, disputatious polity that is predominantly reinforced in the film narrative as the *sine qua non* of D-FENS' falling down.

With this scene we are introduced not only to paranoid spatiality as a theme, but as a 'condition of visibility' which will focus representation of the city for the viewing audience.[13] In other words, the enclosing space which surrounds D-FENS in this opening scene – technically signified by circling movement of the craning, panning camera – is the interiorised space of his paranoia from which there is no escape into the public spaces of the city. This is further signified throughout the film by the camera's medium-long shots of D-FENS walking through alien spaces, at once an incongruous figure out of place but also centred by camera viewpoint. In other words, the urban topography through which he moves mirrors components of his disturbed subjectivity; he is at once dislocated in the space of the city and inured in the space of his own psychosis.

The opening scene suitably prefaces the narrative of D-FENS' journey homeward through downtown Los Angeles. His assertion that he is 'going home' would appear to be a last desperate and deluded effort to reunite with his wife and child, but it clearly has a broader symbolic import. His odyssey across Los Angeles to his wife's house in Venice Beach is constructed as a series of 'adventures' in an 'everyday world', which is depicted as a social matrix of territorialised enclaves of power and exclusion based on race, ethnicity, class and gender. The America D-FENS discovers on his journey is not the one he believed he was defending. It is peopled by numerous others – Korean shopkeepers, Latino gang members, homeless people and the retired rich – all making claims, as his estranged wife does, to their own territories and all defining him as an alien presence. Long before he is killed it becomes apparent to the viewer that there is no 'home', no secure place, for D-FENS in this America. What is less apparent, perhaps, is that his growing sense of alienation suffuses the enframing of his experiences as a morality tale of white male paranoia. As he moves through these alien territories (perversely echoing the colonial travels of white male adventurers) the disintegration of his imperial subjectivity is sublimated in the film's projection of his paranoia on to a pathologised urban scene of social disorder and degeneration. What begins as a tale of white male paranoia becomes an encompassing critique of the conditions of both this paranoia and its objects.

The paranoid spatiality Mike Davis refers to as a condition 'LA seems to aspire to' is much in evidence in *Falling Down*, but with the crucial distinction that its beleaguered victim is a white middle-class male. At times the film echoes some of Davis' observations, particularly his view that little or no 'genuinely democratic space' exists in the city – at one point D-FENS complains that a private golf course he enters should be given over to 'children playing ... [and] families having picnics'. But the film elides critique of the hierarchical structures of urban power which construct repressions in space and movement in favour of a levelling critique of all claims to territory – whether from rich white golfers or Latino gang members – which diminish democratic citizenship. This levelling critique, much facilitated by the picaresque movement of D-FENS through disparate social spaces, strains to conceal the ambivalences and contradictions of the film's liberal moralising. A potent example is a scene set in a public park populated by poor and homeless people. The camera surveys these people and foregrounds excessive images of poverty: there is an emaciated white man holding a sign which reads 'We are dying of AIDS please help us!'; there is a black man in a wheelchair holding a sign reading 'Homeless Vet Need Food Need Money'; there are two young black men with a trolley full of empty cans, being arrested by the police – and the background is filled with predominantly African American and Latino people. Whatever the filmmakers' intentions in presenting us with these images, their crude stereotypes compose an obscene depiction of a collective 'underclass' existence, with these people represented as degenerative signifiers of social immiseration and victimisation.[14] This is poverty as spectacle, an aesthetic transfiguration of lived experiences into reified images which detach the viewer from the subjects viewed. As D-FENS moves through the park we share his position as imperial tourist. As with so much of the film, the camera colonises and exoticises scenes of intractable otherness (proffering the viewer voyeuristic pleasures) and ultimately levels distinctions between different social subjects by dissolving difference and conflict into moral equivalence.

Falling Down is a smart film, but it struggles to delimit interpretations of D-FENS' excessively overdetermined paranoia and to convince viewers that he represents an ultimately (mythologically) redundant model of white masculinity. The film is deeply knowing about the codes and conventions of representing white male violence and pulls the audience

in different directions, at one moment eliciting our pleasure in the
wisecracks and spectacle accompanying D-FENS' rampage, at another
seeking to distance audiences from him by rendering him absurd or
psychotic. This is a delicate balancing act which points up the
filmmakers' ambivalent responses to their subject matter as well as their
efforts to parade and parody white male paranoia. A telling example of
their efforts to control audience perceptions of D-FENS' violence occurs
in a scene in which he encounters an army surplus store owner who is
(in Carol Clover's words) 'a homophobic, racist, anti-environmental,
misogynist, neo-Nazi'.[15] Refusing the neo-Nazi's overtures of fascist
kinship and in response to his subsequent violence, D-FENS lectures him
on freedom of speech and kills him. The scene is all too obviously intended
to assure us that D-FENS is not a figure of violent prejudices, just an
ordinary guy who's 'had it'. However, the meaning of this scene of
violence is not easily secured by reference to his 'ordinary', if extreme,
breakdown. D-FENS does not kill the neo-Nazi in an act of self-defence but
in response to a threat of sodomy, and the scene of violence is also one of
homoerotic and homophobic impulses and identifications. As such, the
scene registers the confusions of agency and powerlessness represented
in and by the white male paranoic.[16]

Falling Down may parody the imperial individualism of white
American manhood but it does not negate it, rather it retells the story of
the making of this manhood as a morality tale for multiracial, late
imperial America.[17] While the film renders whiteness visible in ironic
and critical ways and works to suggest that the white male is no longer
the secure centre of American identity, it also places this figure at its
centre in order to 'mirror' and moralise about 'the things going wrong'
in American society. The assumption is that Americans may live in a
fractured, balkanised society, but they can only understand the realities
and dangers of this from the perspective of the white male. *Falling Down*
metaphorises the metonymy of socio-spatial contiguities that connect
urban dwellers into a dysfunctional territorialisation of aggressive claims
to place and identity. As an allegory of urban decline it posits the
fractured polity of the postmodern city as a microcosm of contemporary
American society and the paradigmatic site of its (dystopian) future. It
narrates a crisis of urbanity that subsumes social and political issues into
a closed system of symbolic conflicts, a closed circuit of paranoia, centred
on the fears of a white male.

Helter Skelter

Strange Days is another smart film, and also another muddled one; indeed
it all but collapses under the symbolic weight of its social messages, its
mix of genres and intertextual references, and its reflexive concerns with

the acts of filming and spectatorship. The director Kathryn Bigelow, echoing Schumacher, refers to her film as a 'wake-up call', and as with *Falling Down* it is a call that is confused in its enunciation.[18] A major theme of the film is the growing tensions within Los Angeles as the millenium approaches – the film is set in LA on the last two days of the century. The major protagonist, Lenny Nero, is an ex-policeman turned to peddling an illegal device – SQUID (Superconducting Quantum Interference Device) – which records people's realities directly from their brain on to a disc which others may playback and so vicariously enter that reality. As the millenium draws closer, tension in the already unstable city is heightened by the murder – by white policemen – of a black rap star who had promised to focus much of the urban discontent. Lenny and his erstwhile bodyguard, Mace, become caught up in the events surrounding the murder and the search for a SQUID disc on to which the murder was accidentally recorded.

The theme of impending apocalypse is a common one in representations of Los Angeles. Mike Davis is all too happy to invoke it: 'In LA there are too many signs of approaching helter skelter ... a whole generation is being shunted toward some impossible Armageddon'.[19] Like many filmmakers (and urban geographers) Bigelow views LA as the paradigmatic urban scene of America's future:

> [LA]'s the template, isn't it? Perhaps because there is so little history here, there's a fragile balance, an inherent tension. Also it's not a city. There is no center. And in its lack of identity it has a kind of poly-identity: it's whatever you project onto it, a faceless place that harbors a multitude of identities, all blurred into one. That's not to say the city isn't a microcosm for the rest of the country. LA's polyglot society is critical to the flashpoint world of *Strange Days*, but I don't think it's atypical of the rest of the US. It's just in sharper relief here.[20]

This is a curious statement, one that positions LA as both mirror and palimpsest of the American nation, based upon an absence of history and lack of identity. Bigelow infers here and attempts to illustrate through her film that the 'poly-identity' of LA both feeds its paranoid energies and elects it as a potential space of national cohesion and civic democracy.

What Bigelow calls the 'poly-identity' of LA is treated in the film as (thematically) an issue of race and (formally) of visuality: we need to consider the interaction of these elements. *Strange Days* very deliberately invokes the civil disruptions which occurred in Los Angeles in 1992 through the use of imagery and documentary motifs associated with the LA riots. This includes the video-recorded beating of Rodney King by white policemen and the televised urban unrest that followed broadcasting of the video and the trial of the policemen. The death of the black rap star, which threatens catastrophic urban violence, occurs when his car has been stopped by white policemen and the SQUID film of this scene is clearly intended to recall for the viewer George Halliday's video recording of the beating of King. At the end of the film the King video is again redramatised but now as the beating of a black woman, Mace, by LA police. Fortunately, the white LAPD chief spots foul play and intervenes to save Mace and avert the millenial disaster the film appears to be moving toward, also making possible a new beginning for the thwarted love of Lenny and Mace. While this closure on a vision of a new dawn for race relations (figured as redemptive love) is heavy handed in narrative terms, it also fails to resolve contradictions within the film's visualisation of racialised issues.

Noting that 'racialised metaphor' is commonly used to articulate postmodern urbanism, Michael Keith and Malcolm Cross state: 'Race is a privileged metaphor through which the confused text of the city is rendered comprehensible.'[21] We can add that the forms of legibility this racialised metaphor constructs are profoundly visual, for ways of seeing the city (or particular urban spaces) are affected by the ideological 'condition of visiblity' which is already saturated with meanings. This was notably evidenced by the conflicting interpretations that surrounded video footage of Rodney King's beating in 1992 – interpretations which attested both to the unreliability and the reification of the visual as the surest ground of evidence.[22] *Strange Days*, while making viewers aware of the striking fusion of the eye and the camera lens in comprehension of the urban scene, and also disturbing certain securities of our viewing position, barely questions the racial formation of the visual field it appropriates. The film's visual and dramatic reenactments of the original crime – the beating of King – posit it as a phantasmatic scene of collective urban trauma (for Los Angeles-as-nation), suggesting that through repetition this trauma can be overcome. However, the meanings of the original crime are in the film decontextualised and renarrativised in ways which grossly simplify the role of race in visualisation of the urban scene. The filming of the police beating of Mace is a vulgar effort to focus the visual carnival of millenial unrest on the violent disciplining of a black body; it represents her body as a site of physical and visual violence subject not only to the actions of the police, but also to the privileged gaze of an audience consuming the scene of the return of the repressed as spectacle. The scene elicits empathy with a filmic character rather than understanding of the condition of visiblity it activates.

Contradictions within the film's treatment of the black body as a site of urban fears and paranoia are echoed in its broader efforts to visualise the meanings of the 'poly-identity' of Los Angeles. Bigelow comments that in watching *Strange Days* 'your eye wanders outward to this complex environment that the principal characters don't bother to acknowledge' – this is true for much of the film and a reminder that a city is in many ways a product of peripheralised vision, never quite in focus.[23] However, her idea that the city of Los Angeles is 'whatever you project onto it' also invokes the utopian promise of the American city as a place where individuals could assume new identities and perform a multiplicity of roles. Many commentators have argued that this concern with the performativity of urban identity has become an excessively anxious one in the postmodern city.[24] In *Strange Days*, SQUID metaphorically intensifies the fluidity of identities to suggest that it is a result of new ways of seeing and experiencing the urban scene. SQUID collapses normative boundaries between self and other, inside and outside and private and public space. What it reflects (or, perhaps, prefigures) is an extreme dislocation of space whereby the subject is intensely immersed in the urban scene, losing distance, detachment, and perspective amidst an excess of identification – the result is an appalling parody of the 'blurring' of identities Bigelow offers as the meaning of urbanity in LA (and of the more common perception of urbanity as the close proximity of strangers).

The Distributed Panopticon

Strange Days assumes and foregrounds the intensified visuality of the postmodern city, and, its confused ideas notwithstanding, is suggestive of new ways of seeing the city. Cameras are now everywhere in and above contemporary urban environments – video cameras, closed circuit television cameras, skycams – allowing ever-extending forms of surveillance for individual citizens as well as institutions. The result, Kevin Robins proposes, is,

> the distributed panopticon, the dispersed panorama of the city ... With the camcordering of the city we have the fragmentation and devolution of vision as control to the individual level ... Visual detachment and perspective are difficult to achieve: these cameras also draw the observer into the urban scene, providing a new directness, intimacy and intensity of vision ... These kinds of images – camcorder shots, vigilante documentation, shock reportage, reality voyeurism – have become the basis of a new form of public entertainment ... reality television.[25]

These kinds of video images, more often than not recording urban dysfunction and discord, may be what offer to connect us most intimately to the postmodern urban scene. Certainly this reality television offers a fitting analogue for the paranoid spatiality which attends the postmodern urban scene. It is a television which projects on to the city the fears and anxieties of its populace, and then plays these back to them as externalised threat. Such television completes the circuit of paranoia as a virtual experience of the urban real.

Strange Days and reality television propose that a significant transformation is taking place in our visual relation and connection to the urban world, one that projects feelings of dislocation in space as a collective urban experience, not as an individual psychosis (as *Falling Down* would suggest). Paranoid spatiality has become a prominent condition of visibility, not just in Hollywood cinema representations of postmodern urbanism, but also in those of the newer technologies of representation that promise a more satisfying connection of postmodern optics and the urban scene.

Notes

1   Robert Beauregard has noted that the pervasive 'discourse of urban decline' in the United States 'provides a spatial fix for our more generalised insecurities and complaints'. Robert Beauregard, *Voices of Decline: The Postwar Fate of U.S. Cities* (Oxford: Blackwell, 1993) p. 6.

2   On the history and continued potential of urbanity as a social ideal, see Richard Sennett, *The Uses of Disorder: Personal Identity and City Life* (Harmondsworth: Penguin, 1971) and *Flesh and Stone* (London: Faber and Faber, 1994). The last question quoted was famously posed by Rodney King in the face of violent urban disorder in Los Angeles in 1992.

3   Lewis Mumford, *The City in History: Its Origins, Its Transformations, and Its Prospects* (New York: Harcourt, Brace and World, 1961) pp. 51–3.

4   Mike Davis, *City of Quartz: Excavating the Future in Los Angeles* (London: Verso, 1990) pp. 221–63.

5   For a reading of how 'form follows fear' in urban planning and building, see Nan Ellin, *Postmodern Urbanism* (Oxford: Blackwell, 1995). Martha Rosler has argued that 'increasingly, the street is a waste space left to the socially fugitive and the unhoused – those unable to buy or serve ... The waste space resides where society used to stand'. Martha Rosler, 'Fragments of a metropolitan viewpoint' in Brian Wallis (ed.), *If You Lived Here: The City in Art, Theory, and Social Activism: A Project by Martha Rosler* (Seattle: Bay Press, 1991) p. 19.

6   See Victor Burgin, *In/Different Spaces: Place and Memory in Visual Culture* (Berkeley: University of California Press, 1996) pp. 117–37.

7   Elizabeth Grosz, *Space, Time, and Perversion: Essays on the Politics of Bodies* (London: Routledge, 1995) pp. 92–3.

8   David B. Clarke (ed.), *The Cinematic City* (London: Routledge, 1997) p. 8.

9   See Joan Copjec (ed.), *Shades of Noir: A Reader* (London: Verso, 1993), and James Naremore, *More Than Night: Film Noir In Its Contexts* (Berkeley: University of California Press, 1998).

10 James Donald, considering visual and psychic connections in modern cinema, usefully reminds us of Walter Benjamin's observation, 'the camera introduces us to unconscious optics as does psychoanalysis to unconscious impulses'. James Donald, 'The city, the cinema: modern spaces' in Chris Jencks (ed.), *Visual Culture* (London: Routledge, 1995) p. 84.

11 Robert Friedman, Warner Bros spokesman in Los Angeles, quoted in *New York Daily News*, 3 April 1993, p. 7.

12 Quoted in Carol Clover, 'White noise', *Sight and Sound*, May 1993, p. 6.

13   Rob Shields refers to the 'condition of visibility' as the 'logical and connotative system in which representations are formed'. Rob Shields, 'A guide to urban representations and what to do about it: alternative traditions of urban theory' in Anthony D. King (ed.), *Re-Presenting the City: Ethnicity, Capital and Culture in the Twenty-First Century Metropolis* (Basingstoke: Macmillan, 1996) p. 235.

14   The idea of the 'underclass' was widely disseminated through American media in the 1980s and early 1990s, though never clearly defined. On the one hand it became a metaphor for the socio-spatial structuring of American cities; on the other hand it became a compelling myth of behavioural deficiencies and combined common assumptions about poverty and race. Literature on the topic is voluminous, but for a particularly astute analysis, see Adolph Reed Jr, 'The underclass as myth and symbol: the poverty of discourse about poverty', *Radical America* 24:1 (1990) pp. 21–40.

15   Clover, 'White noise', p. 8.

16   For a complimentary and more detailed reading of this scene, see Fred Pfeil, *White Guys: Studies in Postmodern Domination and Difference* (London: Verso, 1995) pp. 240–1.

17   Ultimately, this manhood is *remade* in the film, through its symbolic transference to the white police detective Prendergast, D-FENS' double and executioner. What is symbolically transferred is not only an imperial masculinity but also the control of a white male protagonist over the film's narrative space. For a more detailed reading of this transference, see Liam Kennedy, 'Alien nation: white male paranoia and imperial culture in the United States', *Journal of American Studies* 30 (1996) pp. 98–9.

18   Jim Shelley, 'LA is Burning. Happy New Year', *The Guardian*, 2 December 1995, p. 12. Thanks to Kathryn Boney for this reference in particular and for stimulating my thinking on *Strange Days*.

19   Davis, *City of Quartz*, p. 316.

20   Andrew Hultkrans, 'Interview with Kathryn Bigelow', *Artforum*, November 1995, p. 80.

21   Michael Keith and Malcolm Cross, 'Racism and the postmodern city' in Cross and Keith (eds), *Racism, the City and the State* (London: Routledge, 1993) pp. 9–10.

22   For an incisive commentary, see Judith Butler, 'Endangered/endangering: schematic racism and white paranoia' in Robert Gooding-Williams (ed.), *Reading Rodney King, Reading Urban Uprising* (London: Routledge, 1993) pp. 15–22.

23   Hultkrans, 'Interview with Kathryn Bigelow', p. 80.

24   This is a theme of many essays in Sophie Watson and Katherine Gibson (eds), *Postmodern Cities and Spaces* (Oxford: Blackwell, 1995).

25   Kevin Robins, *Into the Image* (London: Routledge, 1996) pp. 138–40.

(Post) National Spaces

9

Myrto Konstantarakos, Middlesex University

The *film de banlieue*: Renegotiating the Representation of Urban Space

The numerous Hollywood remakes of French films in the 1980s and 1990s are proof of the Gallic influence on American cinema. Rarely, however, is the *quid pro quo* mentioned, for French cinema flatters itself on being the opposite of Hollywood: elitist, inspired by art (mainly painting, scuplture, music and literature), created by an author and financed by government aids to culture; all this in contrast to the American popular movie produced by a studio with only commercial criteria in mind. The actress Jodie Foster makes the point that in the last two decades the French films most exported to the USA have been historical sagas, serious and classical films, whose background is philosophy or classical music.[1] That was until Mathieu Kassovitz's *La Haine*. This much-acclaimed film came out in the United States at the end of December 1996, and Ms Foster was in charge of its promotion. She welcomed a film that introduced a change in the traditional French cinema to which America was accustomed. Indeed, *La Haine* was the most successful and the most exported film of a new genre in French cinema, the *film de banlieue*, characterised by settings in the projects on the outskirts of the big French cities of Paris, Lyon and Marseille.

The *Banlieue* and the Ghetto

In his review of the year 1995 in French cinema, Keith Reader sees in the *film de banlieue* the direct expression of the Mitterrand years, but at the same time he believes *La Haine* to be inspired by the films of Spike Lee and John Singleton.[2] He reiterates his statement made in *Sight and Sound* when the film was released in Britain, that this is the greatest impact

American cinema has had on France since the *Nouvelle Vague*.[3] The Anglo Saxon tendency is to compare these films with American ghetto films or 'hood movies, such as Spike Lee's *Do the Right Thing* (1989), *Jungle Fever* (1991) and *Clockers* (1995) or John Singleton's *Boyz N the Hood* (1991) and its feminine version, F. Gary Gray's *Set it Off* (1996). The titles of the articles and essays about the *film de banlieue* also emphasise the importance of the comparisions with the 'hood movies in America, to quote just a few: "burbs of Paris'; 'Boys in the banlieue'; 'garçons in the 'hood'; 'Arabz N the Hood'; 'Beurz N the Hood' (from *Beur*, backslang for Arabs); and 'Boyz N the Arrondissement' (which, incidentally, is inaccurate and misleading, as only Paris's inner city is administratively divided into *arrondissements*).

Some similarities with the American genre are undeniable. First, the subject matter: youngsters, mainly males, often three in number, involved in gang wars, drugs and petty crime.[4] Fighting scenes and shootings are often to be found, the most spectacular being in *Ma 6T va cracker* (1997). Second, the characters are excluded from society for, it seems, racial reasons. Because *banlieues* have an important proportion of immigrant population and some of these films in the mid-1980s were made by first- or second-generation North Africans, the *Beur*, critics and scholars sometimes believe these films to depict ghettos like those in America. In addition, comments about the soundtracks have contributed to the apparent links with the American 'hood movies, for, like the American projects, the outskirts of French cities are the birthplace and subject matter of rap music.

Finally, in the *film de banlieue*, like in the American 'hood movie, salvation implies escape. For many of these films, the solution is to go away, to change space: the title of Karim Dridi's *Bye Bye* (1995) is significant in this respect and Thomas Gilou's *Raï* (1995) ends with the departure of the female protagonists. Personal morality is not enough to improve one's lot, one needs to get out of the *banlieue*, to change space in order to change social predicament. This adds up to a quite traditional negative representation of cities in film and literature: indeed, Rob Lapsley confirms that:

Overwhelmingly, fictional representations of the city have been hostile. From the London of Griffith's *Broken Blossoms* (1919) to the New York of *Seven* (1995) the modern city has been presented as inimical to human happiness. Instead of idealising the city the predominant strategy has been to conjure into existence an elsewhere free of lack and ruinance.[5]

This elsewhere is often a non-urban place: Spike Lee's *Clockers* ends with its protagonist finally redeemed from drug selling, saved from prison and the sickness that was invading him, by escaping from the projects in a train crossing the desert in the sunset. The only space that seems to have a potential for happiness in these urban films is the countryside: in *Jason's Lyric* (1994), the young couple spend their happy times together on an abandoned bridge and in a park.

However, in the *film de banlieue* the contrast between urban and rural settings is not always straightforward. The surrealist cow among the housing estates in *La Haine*, or the hawk in Jean-Claude Brisseau's *De Bruit et de fureur* (1986), witness the unexpected intrusion of the 'natural' world into the urban. Nature can only appear in visions, as if to express the impossibility of representing the inaccessible, the unknown, the total otherness of the countryside, from within the urban environment. For the *banlieue* is still the city, but at the same time it is outside the city, at its edge, halfway between the city and the countryside: still urban, but with some rural elements resurging in it, not wanting to let go, reclaiming their territory. In *La Haine*, nature is the city's unconscious, located on its outer edges but thirsty for revenge. Nature, the origin, lies underneath the urban veneer, as in Ahmed Bouchaala's *Krim* (1995). Under Krim's wallpaint lie his daughter's drawings and under the blonde hair of his sister is her original colour, both again visible at the end of the film. Kassovitz's avowed aim in *La Haine* was to convey the feel of a village in his portrayal of the *banlieue*: the dream and the desire of the village persist and manifest themselves in the city.[6] Whereas the countryside has previously meant being slave to hard work, in a mostly urban society the country takes on a new idealistic value of freedom. It remains valued in our filmic systems of representations, as in the image of the peasant (evoked by the cow in *La Haine*), for instance, who has kept a strong link with earth.[7]

The representation of space in the *film de banlieue* is of paramount importance and the intention of this paper is to investigate further its treatment. Most of these films actually give a spatial indication in their title: Jean-François Richet's *Etat des lieux* (1995) and *Ma 6T va cracker*; Malik Chibane's *Hexagone* (1994), *Douce France* (1995) and *Nés quelque part* (previously called *Nés en France*; 1998); Paul Vecchiali's *Zone franche* (1996); Christophe Ruggia's *Le Gone du Chaâba* (1997); Bertrand and Nils Tavernier's *De l'autre côté du périph'* (1997); the title first given to *La Haine* was *Droit de cité*. Indeed, both the American and French genres take their names from a geographical feature for the first time since the Western.[8]

Banlieues are on the outskirts of large cities, but the term cannot be translated by 'suburb', because it lacks the bourgeois cosiness of the English term. Although *banlieue* only means an area at the periphery of town, in recent years it has come to designate more specifically the working-class part of such an area. There are different types of suburb in France, but the affluent ones are not those that are brought to mind by the term *banlieue*.[9] David C. Thorns describes the phenomenon in the following terms:

> The greater variety of types of accommodation in the Paris suburbs ... are not only acres of the universal semi-detached but also incorporate multi-storey flats. Higher densities and multiple dwellings have been very much more part of the culture of the French cities than they have been in either Britain or the United States, where the ideal has always been very strongly that of the single-family dwelling house. The second difference is that the rich, in particular the rich of Paris do not ... have the same desire to live outside the city. Rather, they live in high-class areas within the city, particularly the west of Paris. Consequently, there are not many suburbs for the rich. The suburbs are predominantly lower-middle and working-class, the latter being the industrial suburbs of the city.[10]

The French name then for suburb, *banlieue*, literally means place of exile. Paradoxically, the name for the *banlieue's* spatial opposite, the inner city – the translation one of these films, *Etat des lieux*, was given in America – would better render the deprivation of some housing estates at the periphery of big French towns such as Paris, Lyon and Marseille. The publisher of Gilles Kepel's *A l'Ouest d'Allah*, a study of French, British and American urban deprived areas, labels them all as *banlieues*. In *La Peur des banlieues*, Henri Rey argues that the fear of the *banlieues* – and of their music – is in a way the fear of the United States, of ghettos ruled by gangs and ethnic conflicts. There is a strong apprehension that America is only anticipating what will eventually happen in France.[11] However, Alec Hargreaves points out that 'In the US it is not uncommon for large neighbourhoods to be almost entirely mono-ethnic', whereas, 'there are very few sizeable estates in France where French nationals are in a minority ... areas containing relatively large concentrations of foreign residents are almost always multi-ethnic'.[12] These *banlieues* are not homogeneous – even if the buildings all look the same, their inhabitants do not.[13] Emmanuel Todd maintains that if there are problems, these are social, not racial, and do not stem from ghettoisation.[14]

My contention is that though the French films are influenced by ghetto films, they are not about racial hatred, nor solely about the racial mapping of the city: hence the choice of ethnically diverse protagonists. In *Raï* and *Douce France* there are friendships between French young men and second-generation North African immigrants; in its Parisian first part, *Souviens-toi de moi* (1996) presents us with the same integration in a feminine version. *La Haine* goes even further by showing black policemen, while the central characters are a trio from different backgrounds – *Black, Blanc, Beur*. *De Bruit et de fureur* and *Ma 6T va cracker* also make sure gangs are racially mixed at all times. Indeed, Todd argues that foreigners socialise and mix with each other in the French *banlieues*, even in gangs when they exist. The circumstances and the situations in which characters find themselves are characteristic of all races. American influences on the music and the characters of the *film de banlieue* should not therefore be mistaken for an imitation of American subject matter: the two urban experiences are radically different in their spatial configuration for a number of reasons which go back to the modern formation of French cities in the nineteenth century.

Space on the Margins

The image of the *banlieues* is a legacy of a devalorisation of the margins, deeply rooted in history. The first sign of the stark distinction between centre and periphery in France happens in the sixteenth century, with the expulsion of the *gueux*, the beggars, from city centres. But it is mainly in the middle of the nineteenth century that workers and paupers are exiled from the city to its outskirts. T. J. Clark relates how,

> in the July Monarchy the outlines of a new Paris emerged [...] Slowly, in the course of twenty years ... on the outskirts, in the *banlieue* beyond the ring of customs-houses, grew up a newer and uglier industrial sprawl: makeshift housing following the factories and warehouses, makeshift communities, poor and violent, sprawling crime and disease, producing a new and ominous *classe dangereuse.*[15]

With Haussmann's major works in Paris, *banlieues* came to be inhabited by factory workers; therefore there was a work-based integration in which companies ensured workers had proper living conditions and recreational facilities. In the late nineteenth century, social problems emerged and these areas became perceived by wider society with contempt as *quartiers chauds* – troubled areas. The myth of the *zone* inhabited by *apaches* – foreshadowing the *blousons noirs* of the 1960s and the contemporary *jeunes des cités* – was born. In the 1960s and 1970s, with urban renewal, there was another population move from Paris to the outskirts. However, because of the mass unemployment which started in the 1970s, government money shifted to building *petits pavillons* – semi-detached or detached houses.

Colette Petonnet bases her ethnology of *banlieues* on the crucial distinction between *bidonvilles* and *cités* and, just as Pier Paolo Pasolini did in Rome, favours the former. Indeed, in the *bidonvilles*, or slums, space was occupied by members of the same family or the same group. If a family moved away, they decided who would replace them; hence there is a strong similarity between *bidonvilles* and the space of origin, the village back home. In the summer, for instance, people lived together oudoors in the collective grounds whereas in the housing projects, the *cité*, people stayed home on their own.[16] The community was responsible for the children as much as the parents were: it reinforced paternal authority, ensured surveillance and punishment. It restricted external interference and made sure customs and language were maintained, thereby preventing assimilation into French society. In the 1970s the *bidonvilles* were razed to the ground and their inhabitants relocated sometimes over several districts according to their *degré d'urbanité*, as defined by a *circulaire ministérielle* of 19 April 1972. Some, it was thought, 'ne sauraient pas habiter' – 'would not know how to inhabit' – and were housed in transitional council housing, *cité de transit*.[17] *Le Gone du Chaâba*, Azouz Begag's novel made into a film by Christophe Ruggia in 1997, depicts this traumatic move from a *bidonville* into a *cité*.

The media has played an important role in the construction of the negative collective image of the *banlieue*. In their work on the depiction of the *banlieues* on French television, Boyer and Lochard show how an optimistic version of them was presented at the beginning of the 1960s, but how, with the phenomenon of joy riding in the early 1980s – after Mitterrand's election – the *banlieues* gained particular prominence in the media.[18] They made their appearance in the headlines with riots between police and youth in 1981 in Les Minguettes, a housing estate of Venissieux, subsequently resulting in the formation of the Association SOS Minguettes.[19] In 1983, 300 youths attacked police in Venissieux. The three Vs of the periphery of Lyon, Villeurbanne, Venissieux and Vaux-en-Velin, became famous. Since these episodes, the *banlieues* as seen on television have come to evoke a number of fashionable themes: youth, immigration and violence.

In a survey in February 1993, it was revealed that three million people were living in more than five hundred *quartiers en difficultés* and that 19.7 per cent of them were unemployed, mostly youngsters.[20] The *cité* of Les Minguettes, built in 1960 and sounding very much like the fictional Les Muguets where *La Haine* is set, had 30 per cent unemployment and 28 per cent immigrant population. Another survey carried out in November 1995 in the *banlieues* north of Marseille revealed that one inhabitant out of two was less than 20 years old, 45 per cent of heads of family were unemployed, the average income per inhabitant was less than 2,000 Francs per month and 72 per cent of households were living with an income below the minimum wage.[21] When riots happened there in 1990, and again later on, a gymnasium (Jean Moulin) was burnt, just like in *La Haine*.[22] In 1991, after further clashes in Vaux-en-Velin, the *Renseignements généraux*, the branch of the French police force dealing with political security, created an observatory of urban violences, *Villes et banlieues*, whose aim was to keep a (confidential) list of the Republic's *zones grises*: grey zones. A sign that the *banlieues* have come to signify a series of societal problems is that a sociological observatory, *Banlieuscopie*, headed by Adil Jazouli, has been set up with the *banlieues* as sole concern.

The *film de banlieue* was born at a time of considerable unrest in the French *banlieues*. Mitterrand appointed the first ministre de la ville in December 1990, Michel Delabarre, followed by Bernard Tapie. It is significant that 1995, which saw a considerable number of *films de banlieue* appear, was an election year in France. *La Haine* opened on 31 May (with *Raï* two weeks later), between the presidential election and the municipal elections – even more concerned with *banlieue* issues – and both these elections have the highest participation rates in France. The campaign was largely dominated by what Jacques Chirac and others called *la fracture sociale*, promising to address it, if elected, with a *Plan Marshall des banlieues*.[23] Indeed, Chirac's government included a *Ministre chargé de l'intégration et de la lutte contre l'exclusion*, which disappeared, however, at the first reshuffle at the beginning of November 1995. The government then changed its vocabulary: there was no longer any mention of *lutte contre l'exclusion* and minister Eric Raoult remained *ministre délégué* of only *la ville et l'intégration*. Françoise de Veyrinas, secretary of state until 7 November in charge specifically of *quartiers en difficulté*, had to leave. The prime minister's plan for the *banlieues*, named the *Pacte de relance pour la ville*, announced in January 1996 and published in August of that year, aimed at creating 100,000 jobs for under-25s in the following four years and at increasing security in 30 sensitive areas; *quartiers en difficulté* became *zones franches*, their new official technocratic name. On 27 March 1997, Prince Charles visited one of the *banlieues* of Paris, Clichy, to see for himself what this *politique pour la ville* had achieved. However, violence in the *banlieues* did not end: December 1997 saw public transport being attacked and drivers refusing to work in the *banlieues* as a consequence, and at the peak of the violence in Strasbourg on New Year's Eve 1998 youngsters burned cars, just as in *Ma 6T va cracker*. As a result, Chirac met with the mayors of the *quartiers sensibles* and, on 13 January, the government, led on this issue by Martine Aubry, spoke of reinstating a *ministre de la ville*.

Some politicians blame the present situation on the *décentralisation*, the reforms initiated by the Socialists in 1982 which devolved political power to local government. As Eleonore Kofman has pointed out: 'Decentralisation brought urbanism under the remit of the commune and sharpened conflicts between administrative levels where political affiliation differed.'[24] Under the new system, the government has given responsibility to local communities, but they do not have the power to bring industry in and they must raise taxes in order to survive. Some, therefore, long for a time when the state was more present.[25] Successive local politicians have responded to the troubles by spending money on buildings (pulling them down and rebuilding them), but the inhabitants would have preferred more attention to be paid to the social structures: local associations for instance, which allow a dialogue between youths and the rest of society, the creation of links between political powers and communities, and the setting up of programmes of leisure activities. Although the Communist Party is often still the first party in *banlieues*, very few people vote, and therefore no longer does it represent the identity of the area; the inhabitants, especially the young ones, fulfil their need of representation and expression with the *associations loi 1901* (local youth associations), which have proved very useful.[26] For instance, the shooting of *La Haine* was free of trouble thanks to a local association, *Les Messagers*.

The *banlieues* are therefore powerful constructs of history and politics, but their depiction in literature, media and film also contributes to the perception of them as dangerous places. Reflecting on the social crisis in France, Dominique Baudis, mayor of Toulouse, spoke of the widening gap between '*l'Etat et la cité, entre les ghettos et la ville*', translating by that a social and political situation into spatial terms.[27]

Inside and Outside

It has been argued that the cause of delinquency might be in fact the RER (*Réseau express régional*, the rapid-transit system in the Paris region), for it puts the poor inhabitants of the *banlieues* just 20 minutes from affluent parts of Paris like Les Halles, in which the central scene in *La Haine* is shot: '*Châtelet-les-Halles: capitale de toutes les banlieues.*'[28] Indeed, the most violent *banlieues* are to be found near big cities such as Paris, Lyon and Marseille. Their inhabitants are confronted by wealth as soon as they step outside the neighbourhood, and it is as if, marginalised at the periphery, they are only permitted access to the city centre in order to contribute to its economic prosperity. So, does fast transport abolish the distance between centre and periphery? Gustave-Nicolas Fischer calls the spaces between city and countryside *zones mixes*, characterised by fast 'rurbanisation'.[29] Now, everywhere is periphery, therefore the periphery does not exist any more. Urban countryside is the new term to designate suburbia, as in Holland for instance, and this exemplifies a developmental model that is the aim of many Third World countries. Daniel Bensaïd argues that 'inside' and 'outside' no longer exist: one does not enter or exit the city, urban space has neither centre nor borders any more. For this he blames globalisation, *mondialisation*, because it implies a loss of national markers, hence a loss of identity, of work and home.[30]

However, the point made by the *banlieue* films is exactly the opposite, for they are constructed entirely around the opposition between Paris and periphery. *La Haine* is divided in two, the first half being shot in the *cité*, the second half in Paris. Kassovitz even wanted to shoot one episode in colour and the other in black and white, one in 35 mm and the other in 16 mm. Instead, he shot the *cité* by day and Paris by night, the *cité* with ample travelling shots and Paris with a small crew (on foot and with a hand-held camera), the *cité* in stereo and Paris in mono. Short focal distance was used for the *cité* scenes in order to integrate the characters into their surroundings, whereas Paris is shot with long focal distance to detach the characters from the background.[31] The result is that, as soon as the protagonists get to Paris, the atmosphere and sound changes and they feel out of place and as strangers. Kassovitz also explains that he constructed carefully the part in the *cité*, whereas the episodes in Paris could be presented in a different order. Similarly, Yolande Zauberman's *Clubbed to Death* (1997) alternates between night rave scenes indoors and outdoor day scenes supposedly set in the *banlieues* of Paris, but the credits reveal these to have been shot in Portugal. This was probably done in order to achieve bright light and scattered debris reminiscent of Italian *borgate* or *Germania anno zero* ruins, with the aim of creating a place radically other and exotic. No other place is represented in the film: there are no street scenes in central Paris for instance. The protagonist Lola is seen in her flat and once on her balcony, but the hand-held camera stays so close to her face we can never distinguish any feature of the space surrounding her. Does she live in the city centre or in a suburb? We only see the long, slow, winding journey of the bus at night going to this far-off space.

The vocabulary surrounding the term *banlieue* is highly significant. Until the 1970s, the *quartier* was a place to live, but also a place for work, leisure, cultural and sporting activities; a place of professional, friendly and family socialising. Work was the first to leave the *quartier*; consuming, leisure and socialising followed and in the end only homes remained. The fixed point has therefore moved from the *quartier* to the home. The opposition between fixity and mobility, which structures the art of living, was first reflected in the *quartier* versus the city. The *quartier* was tantamount to intimacy, home, interiority, haven, and the city was perceived as the outside, the space of wandering and of confrontation with alterity. Nowadays this contrast has changed into home versus city as a whole, and the mobility stretches on to a vast territory, encompassing everything. Thanks to transport allowing fast movement across greater distances than before, the places of living can be further from those of work, of consuming, of leisure (sporting facilities, cinemas) and from the city centre. Socialising with friends and family happens on a much bigger scale and there is now a sense of restrictiveness associated with the idea of *quartier*, for territorial belonging is no longer unique, but varied.[32] The old *quartier* gives way to the *quartier à problèmes* or *en difficulté*, which has lost all the usual qualities of the *quartier* (social, cultural, urbanistic). In the collective consciousness, the suburbs became a cul-de-sac, as much social as spatial. Their specificities have become the unemployment and the divorce rates, the low percentage of children in full-time education and the number of immigrants.[33] Whereas before *quartier* referred to a district *in* the city, it now ironically indicates the rundown projects on the outskirts of the city, and the word *cité*, which used to designate the Greek *polis*, the heart of the city, is now paradoxically attributed to the big housing estates of the very parts of the city the centre rejects.[34] The *cité* is now the negative of the city.

Studies have shown that, to inhabitants of the periphery, the centre of activity is no longer the local market and the local bars but the city centre, and this contributes to the loss of identity of the *banlieues*.[35] This is reflected in the *banlieue* films: characters have to go to the city centre. *Hexagone* is the only film in which there is an intentional inverse movement: a Parisian comes to the *banlieues* to visit a friend and go to a party. Conversely, in *Nés quelque part* and *Clubbed To Death*, the trip of the outsiders into the *banlieues* is the result of an accident: a TGV (the high-speed French train) breaks down in the former and the protagonist Lola falls asleep in a suburban bus in the latter. Usually, it is the other way round: the protagonists embark on a journey to the city centre in search of money or sex. This trip is never easy, as if the distance between the two places were immense: in *Hexagone*, the protagonists cannot find a ride to Paris because their friends' cars are all broken down or out of petrol. Furthermore, characters often have trouble returning from the city centre: in *La Haine*, the police keep them in custody until the trains have stopped for the night, and in *Raï* they do not have enough money for petrol. The mobility of the male characters and their ability to use transport seem therefore to be constrained and prohibited. As movement between centre and margins is made so difficult in *banlieue* films, so the perceived distance between the two increases and appears much greater than it is in reality.

As Keith Reader has pointed out: 'The left-wing writer and former publisher François Maspéro's 1989 odyssey through the suburbs of Paris, *Les Passagers du Roissy-Express*, strikingly foreshadows the themes that pervade *La Haine* and other *banlieue* films.'[36] The writer and the photographer of this book force themselves to travel from *banlieue* to *banlieue* without ever stopping in Paris. Unfortunately, one of their friends breaks this promise made to themselves by taking them to the capital to have a drink. And it actually comes as a surprise that, although the two worlds seem far apart, Paris and the *banlieues* are very close by. As Lisa Nesselson comments in her review of *Hexagone*: 'Though only a short commute from the City of Light, the setting of Goussainville is a world apart from the capital.'[37] Indeed, one might argue that distance is over-estimated each time a subjective barrier is crossed, and that therefore all landmarks are highly subjective.

The space of the *banlieues* themselves is often believed to be the guilty part, leading to the destruction of tower blocks (for instance in Les

Minguettes in 1983). After some violent episodes in 1991, the Archbishop of Lyon, Cardinal Decourtray, intervened to blame 'concrete and inappropriate town planning'.[38] But architecture and urbanism are not the only causes. I would suggest that it is rather the entrapment, not 'inside' but 'outside', which is at fault here: '*on est enfermés dehors*' ('we are locked outside'), shouts Saïd in *La Haine*. If, spatially and culturally, the demarcation between centre and periphery is no longer clear (the culture of the *banlieues* having been appropriated by the mainstream through the popular success of rap and streetwear), the entrapment lies now in geography and technology: the means of transport (RER versus TGV in *Nés quelque part*, for instance). Inhabitants do not travel together: what makes the difference between centre and periphery is the 'non-spaces', as Marc Augé calls them.[39]

Centre and Periphery

Over the last few years, as all the essays in this volume suggest, space has become a key concept in the humanities. Abraham Moles suggests that if space only exists when it is filled, beings only exist because they fill space. In understanding the implications of this one might draw on the concept of vital space, of territoriality, derived from the animal world. Marc Augé argues that territory engenders identity: 'it is the spatial arrangements that express the group's identity (its actual origins are often diverse, but the group is established, assembled and united by the identity of the place).'[40] In his *Psychosociologie de l'espace*, Fischer further explains how each one is attributed a given space in society. Each society is organised by attributing spaces – some bigger than others, some more specific than others – to individuals who have more latitude in choosing these spaces than other individuals. This creates a structure of places and of movement between them. One of the subsequent rules is the creation of frontiers, thereby creating an 'inside' and an 'outside' and an idea of closure. Frontiers materialise places and demarcate space and ensure a hold on to the territory.[41] The representation of urban space is important to determine the distinction, in Pierre Bourdieu's sense, between social realities, for the allocation of space is made to allow power to be exercised.

However, once upon a time space used to be calculated in proportion to time: one would measure time according to how long it took to walk from A to B.[42] Even political space was defined by time: by the time one took to cross the *département* by horse for instance. With the acceleration of means of transport, this is no longer true: yet means of transport reproduce inequalities and domination and where you live becomes the most determinative issue. Poor transportation access is tantamount to segregation and works to preserve purity and to avoid hybridity, for, if every area were of similar living quality, segregation would not be necessary in order to preserve the privileges. As we see in *Ma 6T va cracker* – as in actual riots – violence is mostly directed towards means of transportation. Power can also be challenged by modifying the representation of space. In *Parisian Fields*, Tom Conley emphasises the power of film to remap the city and undermine the official distribution of space: 'As mechanism affecting broader processes of acculturation, like urban planning, it reproduces diagrams that fix in place conflicting ideas about the constitution of social space.'[43] Film has, therefore, the ability to remap the city's topography, 'in the blitz of an illumination, Benjamin would simply imply how cinema acquires a power of control that is not unlike the remapping of Paris that Haussmann had caused ... It displays itself as a series of maps that are read in the light of a propensity to mobilize ideology, in other words to function as blueprints of visible formations that bind subjectivity to a consciousness of space'.[44]

In the light of this one might suggest the *banlieue* films tackle the representation the French have of the opposition between the paradise of the urban centre and the dangerous margins where flare-ups happen all the time between youths and police. The rest of the city creates a collective identity of the 'other', the *banlieue*, which is negative, hence *La Haine* opens with footage of riots, the image the rest of France has of the *banlieues* and the prejudice the film intends to dissipate. Writing about *La Haine*, Elisabeth Mahoney argues that it represents 'the possibility of reclaiming or re-imagining the space of the city' for 'texts which set out to inscribe experiences of the city previously marginalised or marked as "other" do implicitly or explicitly challenge traditional discourses on urban space'.[45] However, I would argue that the subversive power of the *banlieue* films goes even further. Indeed, despite their label, they are not strictly about the *banlieues*, but about the distance between the centre and the margin and the stark division between two worlds that cannot understand each other, nor communicate to reduce their tensions. The *banlieue* films challenge the official representation of space by rethinking the relationship between centre and periphery, which may explain why so few of them took advantage of the *Avance sur recettes*, the state subsidy to film.

The fear of the city reveals the desire for no-risk city living, a city of the law, opposed to the *ban-lieue*, the city of crime. Centre and periphery must therefore stay apart and any movement between the two be strictly prevented. In his study of surveillance, Michel Foucault reviews how prisons first ensure the immobilisation of paupers and vagrants, then of any mobile social category, for transgressive mobility creates maps which undermine the official ones. By transgressing boundaries, those excluded from political and economic power offer viewers another construction of the city: the *film de banlieue* repossesses the disused space through the revival of the transgressive figure of the Baudelairian *flâneur*, who *wanders* against civic community, in total irresponsibility, while the responsible workers only commute between home and work and place of leisure. By challenging the representation of space they challenge the power structure. And by so doing, unlike the ghetto film, the *film de banlieue* exemplifies the tensions at work in French society by renegotiating the relationship between centre and periphery.

Note

All translations from the French (except Augé's) are the author's own.

Filmography

Allouache, Merzak, *Salut cousin!* (1996).
Blier, Bertrand, *Un, deux, trois soleil* (1993).
Bouchaala, Ahmed, *Krim* (1995).
Bouchareb, Rachid, *Bâton rouge* (1985).
Brisseau, Jean-Claude, *De Bruit et de fureur* (1986).
Cabrera, Dominique, *Chronique d'une banlieue ordinaire* (1992), documentary.
Charef, Mehdi, *Le Thé au harem d'Achimède* (1985), from his own novel.
Chibane, Malik, *Hexagone* (1994); *Douce France* (1995); *Nés quelque part* (Arte: 19 January 1998).
Dahan, Olivier, *Frères* (1994), produced by two TV channels, Arte and La Sept. There is one 85 mm version for the silver screen and one 60 mm version for television.
Denis, Claire, *US go home* (1994), produced, as above, by Arte and La Sept for the series 'Tous les garçons et les filles de leur âge'.
Dridi, Karim, *Bye Bye* (1995).
Ghorab Volta, Zaïda, *Souviens-toi de moi* (1996).
Gilou, Thomas, *Raï* (1995).
Kassovitz, Mathieu, *La Haine* (1995). His short *Cauchermar blanc* (1991), also in black and white, tackles the same themes.
Labrosse, Sylvain, *Virage Nord* (1995).
Morel, Gaël, *A toute vitesse* (1996), with Elodie Bouchez, produced by Rachid Bouchareb.
Richet, Jean-François, *Etat des lieux* (1995); *Ma 6T va cracker* (1997).
Ruggia, Christophe, *Le Gone du Chaâba* (1997), with François Morel, from the novel of the same name by Azouz Begag.
Tavernier, Bertrand and Nils, *De l'autre côté de périph'*, television documentary in two parts (France 2: 7 and 14 December 1997).
Vecchiali, Paul, *Zone franche* (1996).
Zauberman, Yolande, *Clubbed to Death (Lola)* (1997), with Elodie Bouchez, Roschdy Zem and Béatrice Dalle.

Notes

1   Jodie Foster, *Film Français* 2584, 10 November 1995, p. 23.
2   Keith Reader, 'Review of French cinema in 1995', *Modern and Contemporary France* 3: 6 (1996) pp. 348–51.

3   Keith Reader, 'After the riot', *Sight and Sound* 5: 11, November 1995, pp. 12–14.

4   Although Carrie Tarr makes the point that this kind of narrative is more significant of the white filmmakers than of the ones of Maghrebi origins. Carrie Tarr, 'Ethnicity and identity in the *cinéma de banlieue*' in P. Powrie (ed.), *French Cinema in the 1990s: Continuity and Difference* (Oxford: Oxford University Press, forthcoming).

5   Robert Lapsley, 'Mainly in cities and at night: some notes on cities and film' in David B. Clarke (ed.), *The Cinematic City* (London: Routledge, 1997) pp. 186–208, p. 195.

6   Matthieu Kassovitz, *Première*, June 1995, p. 113. See also Yves Chalas, 'Le déclin du quartier', *Urbanisme* 297, Novembre/Decembre 1997, pp. 49–51, p. 49.

7   Gustave-Nicolas Fischer, *La Psychosociologie de l'espace* (Paris: Presses Universitaire de France, 1981) p. 39.

8   Yann Tobin, 'Etat des (ban)lieues', *Positif* 415, September 1995, pp. 28–30.

9   In the following scene from the script, but not in the film, at the private viewing in Paris a yuppie tries to befriend the trio by asking where they come from:

    Young yuppie – I too come from the *banlieue*, so I know.
    Saïd and Vinz stop dancing and get closer to him:
    Vinz (mocking): Where do you come from?
    Young yuppie: Bagnolet.
    Saïd: It's not a *banlieue*. You must be joking.

    Gilles Favier and Mathieu Kassovitz, *Jusqu'ici tout va bien* (Paris: Actes Sud, 1995) p. 149.

10   David C. Thorns, *Suburbia* (London: MacGibbon and Kee, 1972) p. 71.

11   Gilles Kepel, *A l'Ouest d'Allah* (Paris: Seuil, 1994); Henri Rey, *La Peur des banlieues* (Paris: Presses de la Fondation Nationale de Sciences Politiques, 1996) p. 11.

12   Alec Hargreaves, *Immigration, 'Race' and Ethnicity in Contemporary France* (London: Routledge, 1995) p. 74.

13   André Bruston, 'A la recherche du quartier', *Urbanisme* 297, November/December 1997, pp. 46–7, p. 47.

14   Emmanuel Todd, 'Le paradoxe français', *L'Histoire* 193, Novembre 1995, pp. 36–7.

15   T. J. Clark, *Image of the People: Gustave Courbet and the 1848 Revolution* (London: Thames and Hudson, 1973) p. 148.

16   Colette Petonnet, *On est tous dans le brouillard: Ethnologie des banlieues* (Paris: Galilée, 1985) p. 53.

17   Ibid., p. 61.

18   Henri Boyer and Guy Lochard, *La Banlieue à la télévision française, Genèse et métamorphoses d'un traitement médiatique* (Paris: L'Harmattan/INA, 1998).

19   Title made to match the pattern of SOS Racisme, the national association created in 1994 to counter the rise of the National Front.

20   *Villes, démocratie, solidarité: le pari d'une politique*, carried out by the group *Villes du XIe Plan*.

21   'Ces quartiers où la police n'entre plus: Les Cités interdites', *Le Nouvel observateur*, November 1995, pp. 4–13.

22   Ibid. See in particular Natacha Tatu, 'Ils attendent qu'on s'entre-tue ...', p. 7.

23   Or *facture* (invoice), as Paul Smaïl mocks it. See Paul Smaïl, *Vivre me tue* (Paris: Balland, 1997) p. 73.

24   Eleonore Kofman, 'Cities: a decade of "politique de la ville"', *Modern and Contemporary France* 4 (1993) pp. 379–83, p. 380.

25   See, for instance, Claude Pernes, 'Défense et illustration de la commune', *Le Monde*, 18/19 April 1993, p. 23.

26   Famous examples of these associations are *Idriss*, founded in 1986; *Exit* in Les
       Minguettes and *Jalb* (*Jeunes Arabes de Lyon et sa Banlieue*), headed by Djida Tazdait,
       MEP.

27   Dominique Baudis and Gilles de Robien, 'Des idées plein la ville', *Le Monde*, 7–8 March
       1993.

28   Jean-Patrick Lebel, 'La zone' in François Niney (ed.), *Visions urbaines: villes d'Europe à
       l'écran* (Paris: Centre Georges Pompidou, 1994) pp. 42–6, p. 44.

29   Fischer, *La Psychosociologie de l'espace*, p. 45.

30   Daniel Bensaïd, *Le Pari mélancolique* (Paris: Gallimard, 1997).

31   Claire Vassé, 'Un regard métisse', *Positif* 415, September 1995, pp. 6–7.

32   Chalas, 'Le déclin du quartier', p. 49.

33   Bruston, 'A la recherche du quartier', p. 47.

34   Lebel, 'La zone', p. 43.

35   Hargreaves, *Immigration, 'Race' and Ethnicity in Contemporary France*, p. 74.

36   Reader, 'After the riot', p. 14.

37   Lisa Nesselson, 'Arabz N the Hood', *Variety*, 21–7 February 1994, p. 46.

38   Cardinal Decourtray interviewed by J. A. Richard, *Le Monde*, 9 October 1991.

39   Marc Augé, *Non-Places: Introduction to an Anthropology of Supermodernity* (New York:
       Verso, 1995) p. 34.

40   Ibid., p. 45.

41   Fischer, *La Psychosociologie de l'espace*, p. 54.

42   Ibid., p. 50.

43   Tom Conley, 'Paris as map in film, 1924–34' in Michael Sheringham (ed.), *Parisian
       Fields* (London: Reaktion, 1996) pp. 71–84, p. 73.

44   Ibid., p. 74.

45   Elizabeth Mahoney, '"The people in parentheses": space under pressure in the post-
       modern city' in David B. Clarke (ed.), *The Cinematic City* (London: Routledge, 1997)
       pp. 168–85, p. 183.

10

Stephen Shapiro, Warwick University

'Whose Fucking Park? Our Fucking Park!': Bohemian Brumaires (Paris 1848/East Village 1988), Gentrification, and the Representation of Aids

ACT I

Schaunard: Are you deaf? Are you blind? This man, who's he? [Holds up to a coin to Marcello]

Rudolfo: Louis Philippe! I bow to my king! ...

ACT II

Crowd: All Splendid! The handsomest man in France! The handsome drum major! There he is, there! How he looks, walks, goes!

Bohemians: Glory and honor, honor and glory of the Latin Quarter![1]

On a hot New York City summer night, a crowd had gathered in the intersection of St Marks Place and Avenue A to protest a newly imposed park curfew, which was meant to restrict public access by the homeless. Mainly composed of East Village squatters, the noisy band of about forty people whistled and chanted slogans like 'Whose fucking park? Our fucking park!', announcing their intention to resist the new lockout rules.[2] A lone police car, parked in the middle of Avenue A between Seventh Street and St Marks Place, faced the crowd and a young male demonstrator went up to the car's hood and then began taunting the officers while walking backward with a raised middle finger. When the man was halfway between the crowd and the car, the police leapt out, grabbed him, and forced him into the car. As the now presumably under-arrest man was jammed into the back seat, tens of previously unseen baton-ready police swept on to Avenue A from around the corner of Seventh Street. From the middle of the protesters, a beer bottle was lobbed into the crowd of police, the 'flying bottle' later iconised by the neigh-bourhood's alternative press. When the time for the curfew came, police rushed after those who had gone into the park and then ignored screams for no violence. More riot police appeared, including mounted police and a helicopter that occasionally went low enough to break the rooftop lines of six-storey high buildings. Thus began the Tompkins Square Police Riot of 5 August 1988. As the evening went on, the police often attacked anyone who happened to be on the streets, and when protesters sat down to form a line the police would sporadically charge them and club whoever was not fast enough in running away.[3]

While city authorities initially denied reports of police brutality, videotapes made by a community activist showed that officers had covered their identifying badge numbers with black duct tape, indicating that the violence was somewhat premeditated. Since many participating officers came from Harlem and Bronx precincts, when protesters later shouted 'From Tiananmen to Tompkins Square', the comparison was of how protests in both public squares had been suppressed through the use of agents from distant territories who were unfamiliar, and thus more easily unsympathetic, to the local *outré* style and behaviour. This police action was heavily reported at the time, and features prominently in many retrospective accounts. However, the riot was merely the first of a series of violent confrontations between police (and parks' officials) and East Village community activists from August 1988 through to the reopening of Tompkins Square Park in August 1992, after its forcible closure in 1991 for renovations. In this phase, the police themselves learned the advantages of video as officials frequently, and illegally, taped anti-gentrification rallies in order to identify leading activists. A certain rhythm emerged in this period as demonstrations were inevitably met with even greater numbers of NYPD in riot gear accompanied by undercover police officers who would often act as *agents provocateurs*. Anti-gentrification speak-outs would typically be followed by demon-strators being encircled by police who would rush the crowd to disperse it. In the ensuing confusion, clusters of officers would swarm around targeted individuals, usually when either standing or walking alone, and then functionally kidnap them by having them arrested, processed for several hours, and then released without any charges or on charges that would not stand basic juridical review.[4] The intention was to create a technology of surveillance and mode of harassment to win a war of attrition and demoralisation against dissident voices. In the notorious words of the Ninth Precinct police captain, the 'battle' over popular presence in Tompkins Square Park as a gesture of defiance against rent speculation was not one city authorities were willing to lose.[5]

On the heels of a local and national recession, reports describe a case of stalled gentrification in the East Village in the early 1990s, but 'submerged' might be a better word to describe the economic situation in this area.[6] By 1998, the time of this essay, there has been a strong return of gentrification, here loosely characterised as the process of rent escalation that displaces lower-income, long-term residency renters alongside a conversion from small basic goods stores to ones based on designer products and leisure consumption (cafes and bars). The revived market for higher rents in the East Village is partly due to the accrued structural benefits of the successful implementation of the Tompkins Square Park curfew and renovation. Other factors include the reelection of fiercely pro-real estate interests councilperson Antonio Pagan; the zoning erosion of the Bowery, which had protectively isolated the East Village; and New York University's transformation into a dormitory college throughout the late 1980s and early 1990s. The university's transformation has included building a number of residences along Third Avenue that have institutionally acted to channel students into the neighbourhood where they act (however unwittingly) as the ever-replenishing shock troops for gentrification as high-turnover renters. Rather than prioritising any one (economic, cultural, or political) element for blame, it might be more useful to say that these factors coalesced to form a mutually supporting spur for gentrification. In any case, the political resistance to gentrification seems to have dissolved in the late 1990s. In the summer of 1997, the city stormed (with a tank!) four nearly decade-long squats on Thirteenth Street between Avenues B and C to little media clamour. A few weeks later, another squat on Fifth Street, between Avenues A and B, was dismantled brick by brick without significant complaint, quite unlike the occasion in 1989 when the destruction of an Eighth Street squat required protection barriers of riot police against contentious protests.

The purpose of this condensed history is to ask the question, what, if any, is the necessary relation of the 1988 police riot to the process of gentrification? As the event becomes ensconced within promotional histories about the 'exceptionality' of the neighbourhood (what makes the East Village so charming? – its more than a century-long history of police brutality against popular demonstrations!) are narrative descriptions of municipal terror ornamental distractions to the question at hand, or are these implosive moments integral elements of gentrification that also provide a signpost to its dynamics?[7] While underscoring Neil Smith's outline of the 'rent gap' as a best description of gentrification, I also want to contextualise gentrification as a problem of global–local scaling that can be read through Marx's account of 'primitive accumulation' as a cyclical aspect of capital accumulation that links state

violence to housing dispossession and market valorisation. If gentrification correlates to shifts in the world market system, it is enunciated at the
local level through cultural juxtapositions that produce expressions of
bohemian life where works like Puccini's *La Bohème* can be read as
generic studies of gentrification. Finally, I will conclude by asking why
was it that, even as housing activism was contained, a series of 1990s
works invoked East Village gentrification in ways that relied on or
worked through representations of lesbian and gay identity and
especially that of Aids. What made same sexuality and Aids so resonant
a language about gentrification in ways that were markedly dissimilar
from prior urbanist criticism? This had so frequently portrayed
homosexual communalisation as damaging to the integrity of ethnic or
labouring neighbourhoods that it often seemed as if its discourse about
gentrification operated as a pained compensatory reflex against the
visible emergence of lesbians and gays as a politically viable group within
the public sphere.

Mind the 'Rent Gap'

In postwar boom America, suburbanisation flourished with massive
investments into the built environment through tract housing, regional
planning and concrete pour traffic flows. As the 'American Century',
with the United States as global hegemon, was going full throttle,
automotive suburbanisation was heavily overdetermined in typifying a
new American imagined community that could service the imperium
through new configurations of commodified desire, product obsolescence
and domestic gender roles. Tremendous cultural energy was devoted to
establishing the 'whiteness' of this subjectivity, and much of its wonder-
bread nature was coded against the city, which was represented as the
cesspool of regressive ethnicity, the location of the black American
underclass or unregenerated hyphenated identities (Italian-American,
Irish-American). In retrospect, the highway and the tower-block
developments of the international style epitomise one strand of
modernism that fought heterogeneous ethnic/racial identity by declaring
war on its geographies of social reproduction. Mixed-use residential zones
marked by architectural hybridity were now suspect for materialising
an Old World ethnicity that could not be entirely relied on in the
Manichean world view promulgated by the Cold War. Given that the
urban core and its subject populations were left as roadkill, it is
unsurprising that the revalorisation of the metropole, with gentrification as the increasingly agreed upon term, caught urban studies by
surprise. Critics looked to explain the city's resurgence through
consumer-driven analyses about the possessive individual prerogatives

of new collective subjects ranging from the postmodern yuppies to the single, working woman or lesbians and gays.

Against this DIY approach, geographer Neil Smith sees gentrification as the result of the loss and regeneration of value through a 'rent gap'. Looking at longitudinal studies of land value as it relates to the central business district, Smith describes how property value initially declines in a relative uniformity as the distance from the core increases. In the course of time, a 'land value valley' emerges as value sharply falls on the periphery of the urban core and then sharply rises at the first suburban periphery (and then subsides with increasing distance from this suburban core). Smith explains the appearance of this trough through the relations between house (or building) value, sale price, capitalised ground rent, and potential ground rent. (House) value is formed by the 'quantity of socially necessary labour power required to produce' a structure, while sale price is the variable quantification of that value when that structure is sold (p. 62). Capitalised ground rent is the functional surplus value of the unit seen in the equation 'sale price = house value + capitalised ground rent'. The fourth aspect, crucial for considering gentrification, is potential ground rent, which is the 'amount that could be capitalised under the land's highest and best use (in planner's parlance) – or at least under a higher and better use' (p. 62). This last element involves the calculation of risk factors about what will produce the most profit, and the balancing of credit liability against future returns of investment. Within housing use cycles, ground rent remains stable, or slightly increases, in the immediate period after construction. But as technological advances make new housing cheaper to build and more profitable to sell at the market-rate, previously un(der)developed regions, which can be built up without the cost of repairing existing structures, become more attractive to speculators. In response to their increasingly uncompetitive property, landlords of already existing structures may try to continue to reap profit by not making repairs in order to squeeze as much capitalised ground rent as possible from the site. A reinforcing cycle of disrepair begins as 'the pattern of decline is likely to be reversed only as it is a shortage of higher-quality accommodation occurs, allowing rents to be raised and making improved maintenance worthwhile' (p. 65). This 'rent gap' is produced primarily through capital devalorisation by widening the difference between a declining price and capitalised ground rent and what, in more ideal situations, would be the potential ground rent. This situation creates the moment for gentrification whereby, as Smith explains,

> developers can purchase structures cheaply, can pay the builder's cost and profit for rehabilitation, can pay interest on mortgage and construction loans, and can then sell the product for a sale price that leaves a satisfactory return to the developer. The entire ground rent,

or a large portion of it, is now capitalised; the neighbourhood is thereby 'recycled' and begins a new cycle of use. (pp. 67–8)

I highlight on Smith's account, out of the sophisticated body of criticism on gentrification, not simply because of its persuasiveness, but also for how its answers position further questions. For example, while the rent gap explains how neighbourhoods can become profitably gentrified, it cannot, as Smith admits, automatically predict which neighbourhoods will actually become devalorised and then gentrified. Why do some urban quarters fall apart while others continue to receive the periodic infusions of labour-value that buttress their capitalised ground rent or sale price? Similarly, the rent gap scenario relies on a split between capitalists in their relative position to the business cycle. Why do some landlords commit to a strategy of disrepair in ways that allow others to buy buildings at bargain price? There does not necessarily have to be a global distinction between the two sides; a landlord may simply shift strategies at a key point. But Smith's predictive empirical model, by arguing that the geography of gentrification can be mapped in advance of its occurrence by looking at tax arrears, suggests a turnover of ownership as it implies that one landlord is bailing out. Furthermore, economic concerns and cultural symbolics intertwine since the relation of value to price is influenced by attractiveness of the structure's cultural capital, such as a location's relation to institutions of status creation, like schools. Without belabouring the point, a neighbourhood does not gentrify solely because there is now a pool of potential reserve value ready for activation. To address this, I want to return to the question of 'marginal gentrifiers', or how seemingly elite, but also minoritised, groups, like single working mothers, lesbians and gays and artists, are enmeshed within the process of gentrification. To do this one needs to consider the ways in which the production of world space impacts local regions.

While Smith argues that 'the internal logic of uneven development is most completely accomplished' in cities, I take issue with the declension that the metropole may 'in the end be the least significant in terms of the overall restructuring of the world economy' (pp. 87–8). The city is a regulating location for shifts that create profit-generating gradients in the world-market system. It remains the locale for managing this alteration, and it is precisely in moments of transformation in the world-market system that gentrification occurs as global transitions play out on the local scene through a dual transhumance, the inflows of labour and personnel needed to manage the new order. Alongside this is the state's alliance in facilitating the urban coming home of capital, not simply through its ability to safeguard investment by directing credit lines that will reduce the risks of speculation, but also in its more brutal role of authorising the terror of civilian eviction to make space for its preferred human agents. When police weighed in on that August 1988 night, the event itself was a crucial aspect of the devalorisation/revalorisation cycle. One sees this in the deployment of two predominant metaphors for the city, those of the frontier and of illness, and how these mediate a value circuit that works through a World Market-State-City-Body spectrum.

Landgrabs and Manhunts

In what Kurt Hollander calls 'slumming realism', frontier mythology is often mapped on to urban space as the metropole becomes bisected into the known, 'civilised', valorised regions, and the noir 'naked city' of orientalist fantasies.[8] This evaluative geography is congruent to North/South (or core/periphery) distinctions so that descriptions of metropolitan experience invoke and reinforce cognitive means of understanding the divisions of global space. The city is also modelled through bodily metaphors in terms of its ability to resist infection. Susan Sontag's *Illness as Metaphor* (1978) stresses the ways in which the sick body is metaphorised through evaluations that often summon militaristic 'solutions', but the essay also functions as a reference guide to the language of a negative urbanism, such as Corbusier's gleeful condemnation of tubercular Paris. Frontier and sickness imagery function as a pair that construct and conflate extramural political difference and personal degeneracy (the foreign and sick body) to bespeak urban transformations. To quote Marx we are left with the fable that society has formed as a result of,

> two sorts of people; one, the diligent, intelligent, and above all frugal elite; the other, lazy rascals, spending their substance, and more, in riotous living ... thus it came to pass that the former sort accumulated wealth, and the latter sort finally had nothing to sell except their own skins.[9]

Against this myth of origins, Marx addresses 'the question of property' as an 'actual history, [in which] it is a notorious fact that conquest, enslavement, robbery, murder, in short force, play the greatest part' (p. 873). Marx calls this violence 'primitive accumulation', as the alienation of natural resources from the peoples who have traditionally looked after them, that acts as the first moment in a never-ending circle of capital's movement. We might also call this process the imperial accumulation of 'primitives' as it classically involves the conquest and plunder of the Americas and India, and 'the conversion of Africa into a preserve for the commercial hunting of blackskins' (p. 873). But when Marx turned to describe primitive accumulation, his case example was not the non-Western world, but the enclosure of the Scottish highlands for sheep pastures that would service the global woollens market and free the Gaelic Scots from their commons to tumble into the manufacturing cities as wage labourers. This clearing of estates then goes one stage further as the new rentiers discover that the commodification of pleasure is even more profitable than basic textiles, and the treeless Highlands are turned into deer parks as a leisure zone for hunting.

While primitive accumulation is often considered as describing the teleological rise of the West over the rest of the world, Marx understood it as not simply a one-off, ur-event, but as a cyclical recurring process that initiates every new circuit of accumulation, which 'assumes different aspects in different countries, and runs through its various phases in different orders of succession, and at different historical epochs' (p. 872). Just as we understand coercion and consensus, or compulsion and persuasion, as aspects that exist in constant potential and appearance with one another, so must primitive accumulation and contractual exchange not be seen as exclusionary opposites, but as mutually engaging strategies where the relative dominance of brute appropriation or genteel contracts is always a matter of sequence, opportunity, risk and negotiation. Moreover, this process differs from atavistic mass violence because it specifically uses the state as 'the concentrated and organised force of society to hasten, as in a hothouse, the process of transformation' (p. 873). As the state's monopoly of the legitimate use of violence consolidates alliances and distinctions, primitive accumulation, or direct force capitalism, involves the creation of new kinds of internal and external socio-cultural borders.

While it may be initially unsettling to see primitive accumulation as characterising urban gentrification, it bears remembering that as *tenants* the Scottish Highlanders are losing both the material environment of their agrarian production and their domestic residence. The turn from Scottish subsistence farming to enclosed pastures that are then flipped to become deer-parks captures the iconic time-flow of gentrification: a neighbourhood of yeoman mom-and-pop stores, which often doubles as the storekeeper's primary residence, becomes the cool scene of higher profit cafes and bars. It also needs little translation to see the English devastation of Scottish villages and dispersion of the Highlanders as versions of neighbourhood blowout and anti-homeless spatial deconcentration policies that use super-policing to suppress the visibility of unemployment and the degradation of the human right to adequate, affordable and sensuously pleasing housing. Framed in this way, gentrification can be defined as the convergence of vocational instability, which removes traditional socio-institutional forms of living and working; brute state force that accelerates a transformation which connects different 'global–local' situations (the Highlands and the woollens market, the Highlands and Glasgow/Edinburgh as receivers of new labour force); and the rise of different coalitions that create new kinds of intra-bourgeois hierarchies.

The Highlander's colonial dispossession impacts the city in two directions. First, the Scots come into the city as wage labourers, and this transportation creates housing and employment supply/demand situations within the industrialising city. Second, this imperial respatialisation creates a need for central managers that can negotiate the media of exchange that now channels hinterland goods through urban nodes to global distribution networks. Recent urban studies have argued that certain global cities act as cotter pins that hold together the global system as nodes of information and decision making (command-communications centres).[10] This means that every substantive change in the shape of the global interstate system, like those caused by war's end, typically relies on, if not requires, new informational technologies to handle redefined global domains. Time-space compression media, be it the telegraph or computerised telebyte, compel urban recentralising since new media's implementation expenses demand economies of scale through proximity and rapidly accessible system technicians. Each shift in global relations results in the expansion of the urban core as professional managers are called back 'home' (from the suburbs) to service new production-distribution networks. Thus, global 'frontier' transformations are recorded at the urban level with a dual influx of labour and managers that creates competition for housing and results in a bifurcated city of Dickensian inequalities. The confrontation between these worlds, which plays out the competition between old and new landlords, pivots on the role of a third element, the bohemian.

Bohemian Brumaires and the Authoritarian State

In addition to primitive accumulation's geographic scaling, its relation to the state appears with Marx's explanation, in *The Eighteenth Brumaire of Louis Napoleon*, of how the authoritarian state consolidates rule by bringing together numerous, often contradictory, social interests under collective projects like imperialism. In this creation of a new external frontier to resolve internal conflicts, the Bonapartist state promotes a new body of mixed, urbane characters,

> the ruined and adventurous offshoots of the bourgeoisie ... vagabonds, discharged soldiers, discharged jailbirds, escaped galley slaves, swindlers, mountebanks, lazzaroni, pickpockets, tricksters, gamblers, pimps, brothel keepers, porters, literati, organ grinders, ragpickers, knife grinders, tinkers, beggars – in short, the whole indefinite, disintegrated mass, thrown hither and thither, which the French call *La Bohème*.[11]

The bohemian as catalysing solution to France's disaggregation is more famously elaborated by Marx's contemporary, Henry Mürger, who wrote a series of autobiographical stories, La Vie de Bohème, between 1845 and 1848. These stories about a new marginal identity were later collected and then staged as a play, which premiered in 1849 with Louis-Napoleon himself in attendance.[12] These texts were later used for Puccini's La Bohème, now a staple of opera repertory.

Although known for its romantic arias, La Bohème also stages the social dynamics leading to Bonaparte's *coup d'etat* in specifically geographical ways. First, the play's movement through its four acts locates the artist's studio within a matrix of spatial and historical relations. The play's first act begins atop Paris in the isolated garret of the four bohemians (Rudolfo, Marcello, Colline and Schaunard) and then descends into the streets of Paris to display a panorama of French society from workers to aristocrats. The third act moves further outward with Marcello decorating one of Paris's toll gates with frescos of a Turk and a Zouave, an Algerian member of a French native infantry unit. The demarcating wall links urban Paris to the French countryside (as food goods are shown being brought to market) and Paris and its global hinterlands, as signified by the cartoons of imperial forces. The set also indicates Louis-Napoleon's revision of history as a strange fusion of revolutionary and reactionary motifs. The wall's illustration outlines fantasies about a second (now non-European) empire even while the gates themselves restore the *ancien régime* toll booths, so hated by the revolutionary Parisian communes for increasing the price of basic food goods. Significantly, it is as she is hiding behind these walls that Mimi's tuberculosis is announced as though to equate her demise with the rise of this new regime. The play's final scene returns to the garret, but by moving its setting outward and back, it indicates how the artist's studio is overdetermined within a global-local matrix that sutures together aspects of the globe, nation, city and body.

If *La Bohème* stages the scaling of geography, it also indicates how the contradictory political affiliations of the bohemian become enrolled in the violent Bonapartist state. While Schaunard enters with food and gold coins stamped with the face of the constitutional king Louis-Philippe, he has received this money after a days-long process of killing a parrot, a murder that can be read as parodic citation of the patricide of Louis XVI. But when Rudolfo provides a newspaper as a tablecloth, it is the republican *Constitutional*, an ironic gesture that none the less shows he has used sparse funds to purchase a copy. The mixed messages of the group's politics consolidate as they descend into the city to be immersed within the turbulence of a demotic street scene. Schaunard asserts he 'hates the vulgar mob' and complains about its frantic 'rushing back and forth jostling and lurching, and delight[ing] in experiencing its crazy, insatiable pleasures'. This aesthetic disapproval of the popular dissolves with the events leading to the preintermission finale that is set up by the arrival of the seller of toy soldiers, Parpignol, who sends the neighbourhood's children into an adulatory frenzy: 'Long Live Parpignol, Parpignol! The drum, the little drum, the brigade of soldiers!' What may at first seem a sardonic comment about the little people's love for military spectacle is made serious with the changing of the guard that draws a more adult crowd. As the hawkers admit 'in that drum roll you hear the nation's majesty', the percussion band announces the majesty of national militarism that celebrates its leader, 'the drum major! Fiercer than an ancient warrior'. The bohemians also discover the attraction surrounding 'the handsomest man in France' as a solution to their own shaky economic predicament as they escape paying the cafe bill by merging with the people's pursuit of the military parade. As if to emphasise how the Bonapartist drum major is able to marshal fantasies of glory to enrol a variety of social elements, the next act begins with Marcello at the toll gate, devoting his skill to the aestheticisation of a military past.

My interest here in comparing the similarities between the *Eighteenth Brumaire* and *La Bohème* is to show how the latter complicates the former's understanding of the manner of political integration under the emerging state by using the language of passion between Mimi and Rudolfo to enunciate the struggle over housing. The play opens with Marcello and Rudolfo enduring the rituals of poverty, which they convey with the hallmark of bohemian style – the theatricalising of the self – as the playboy youths burn one of Rudolfo's scripts. After the entry of Schaunard and Colline, they are then confronted by the landlord Benoit, who wants to have only one word, Rent! The bohemians are able to trick Benoit out of payment as they entrap him into confessing an extramarital cafe rendezvous. As first Benoit and then the other bohemians leave Rudolfo, the first act ends with the introduction of the romantic plot as Rudolfo's neighbour Mimi comes knocking at the door. The contrast between Rudolfo and Mimi is that while he seems new to Paris, he is able to enter the metropole with enough skill to be able to subside on mental labour (as a journalist) and manipulate the petty bourgeois codes that motivate Benoit. But if the bohemian's marginality is a knowledgeable (and seemingly semi-voluntary) one, Mimi represents a different kind of metropolitan arrival. Mimi is no Parisian, and she seems to lack a physical familiarity with the city, its mores, or any familial/friendship network that would protect her. Unlike Rudolfo, her fringe existence is life lived on the Parisian homework economy as she survives by embroidering 'silk or linen at home or outside'. With her Italianate real name (Lucia), Mimi represents the proletarianised (and feminised) immigration of a barely skilled labour force, so recently alienated from its connection to the countryside that she poignantly compensates for this loss of nature through the fake flowers she makes. This is nearly the only thing she can cling to, as she is barely one step away from having to survive through street prostitution.

Emphasising the mutual newness of Rudolfo and Mimi to the city and to their apartment building is to ask why, as their relationship breaks down, it is Mimi, not Rudolfo, who is dispossessed and forced on to the streets? While Rudolfo and Marcello's hold on their tenancy is fragile, they none the less remain on site, while Mimi suffers a deterritorialisation that is, to give it its proper name, the result of gentrification. Furthermore, this exclusion seems predetermined since Mimi first identifies herself not with her name but with the tubercular cough, which indicates that her identity is to be one who is *dead on arrival*. As the play ends with Mimi's corpse on display, the play's eviction of the labouring-class subject from their residence is complete, even as the social violence of this dispossession is displaced through an eroticised language of illness, frontierism and the allure of the militarised state.

For the historical moment of *La Bohème*, as Jarrod Siegel argues, the bohemian pose comes as a result of a generation frustrated in their ability to achieve the social and cultural rewards of their predecessors.[13] While the Restoration had provided state support for the arts, Louis-Philippe's July Monarchy was uninterested in continuing these pensions, and this lack of funds shunted writers and authors on to the competitive marketplace for survival and led to the creation of a realm of dissent, *La Bohème*. The bohemian impulse diminished, however, when Louis-Napoleon resumed state financing of the arts. Siegel suggests that the bohemian was created from the conditions of a group that was marginal only to the degree that it was a fraction that would normally have been included within state authentication but, for a range of contingent and volitional reasons, was displaced from these career entitlements. Given the bohemian's proximity to social inclusion, as both Marx and Mürger/Puccini suggest, then what the mid-nineteenth century writings on residential displacement indicate is that the conditions for gentrification arise at the site of collision between *two recently arrived social fractions*, each within a transition from one kind of identity to another. One, a section currently disaffiliated from the rising coalition but that might otherwise have been included, and the other a labouring group coming from an outside/inside expropriation. The meeting of these cultural and economic margins, however, only results in a gentrifying situation with the appearance of a third party that is more ensconced within state affiliations. This third force ('Louis-Napoleon') separates the two *arriviste* factions from an elective affinity based on shared life-world living conditions, and this division further disenfranchises the 'Mimis' as they get removed once more by mainstream force. The 'Rudolfos', unwillingly or not, are then brought back into the coalition of authority.

In New York's instance, the rise of the SoHo arts district was possible because a generational cohort of artists were able to use their educational background and personal or familial contacts to negotiate with city agencies or enlist advocates.[14] Similarly, in the case of the East Village, gentrification occurred when the previously long-standing ethnic community began to move and be replaced by a Puerto Rican population that came to New York during the 1950s and 1960s as part of the importation of manual labour.[15] But just as they were arriving, the ongoing deindustrialisation of Manhattan removed jobs, and this structural erasure of employment opportunities meant that the experience of the Puerto Rican immigrants was closer to that of black Americans than any other ethnic group, not least with the creation of its own local ghettos, like the East Village. Similarly, a generation of educated whites realising personal downward mobility caused by the functional decline of the American Century in the mid-1970s, began returning to city cores. This reenacts their grandparents' life-narratives of social rise by reinhabiting their ancestors' old neighbourhoods as a lived protest of nostalgic industrial ethnicity. The cohabitation of educated white and recently arrived Puerto Rican communities in the East Village/Loisiada remained non-gentrifying, however, until the Manhattan economy responded to the post-1970s global restructuring around the FIRE industries (finance, insurance and real estate). These fields needed at-hand managers who, by increasing competition for core housing, added the crucial element that catalysed gentrification. Faced with bohemian and managerial arrivals, the new labourers, who had not had the generational time to establish strong institutional networks, were forced out as the 'sickly' members of the new frontiers.

The Representational Work of Aids

Given the above, why was it that a number of cultural productions in the early and mid-1990s that sought mainly to represent codes and characters of lesbian and gay identity, and especially those of (gay) People living With Aids (PWAs), would do so through references to changing global conditions, the influx of ethnic labour, and images of the gentrifying East Village, years after the hot time of anti-gentrification struggles? Tony Kushner's *Angels in America* (*Millennium Approaches*, 1992; *Perestroika*, 1994) composes its meditation on epochal changes through the macabre ballet of its three gay graces: Louis Ironson, Walter Prior and Belize. Each represents an example of ethnic transportation to the New World: Ironson is the product of East European Jewish settlement, Prior's WASP ancestry included a trader in indentured Irish, and Belize's name marks a terminal for the African Middle Passage. As the three circle round a sick Prior, the immigrant experience becomes collapsed on the terrain of Prior's bed as a sexualised frontier marked by the angel of Aids. When Ironson, who is a clerical secretary, abandons an ill Prior, the betrayal is sealed when he introduces his new lover, a yuppie Republican lawyer, to his apartment in the 'the Arctic wastes of Alphabetland' (Alphabet City as nickname for the East Village).[16] Jonathan Larson's *Rent* (1996) consciously revises Puccini's opera into a tale of East Village squatters and Aids, where *La Vie Boheme* on Avenue B is endangered by the appropriation of its spirit and the remapping of its domain by a corporatised cyberculture. Larson's proposed strategy of resistance is to subvert authority from within its own structures. The play ends with the Latina drag queen Angel (named with a seeming nod to Kushner) transubstantiated after his death from Aids into a PIN number that will dispense cash to the bohemians through an ATM machine whose very existence in the neighbourhood indicates the process of gentrification as a spatial node for a fast-cash clientele.

In the filmic realm, Mary Harron's *I Shot Andy Warhol* (1996) cinematises Valerie Solanas' attempted assassination of Andy Warhol solely within the context of lesbian-and gay-defined spaces. Both Warhol's and Solanas' queerness are foregrounded in ways that would have been highly anomalous even as short a period as ten years ago.[17] Yet, rather than presenting the tension between the two as a preface to 1970s separatist lesbian-feminism, the film begins with Solanas sleeping on rooftops, and Harron frames her peripatetic journey as the relentless search for affordable housing. As Solanas' anger at Warhol is sequenced alongside his move from the downtown style of the silvery Factory in favour of an uptown office gallery of blonde wood and white walls, her resentment seems to be at his gentrifying redecoration of the spaces available for cultural production. To look to the novel form, Sarah Schulman's *Rat Bohemia* (1996) uses East Village bohemian codes to depict the psychological tension of the lesbian and gay community distressed equally by Aids and the loss of prerogatives caused through abandonment by their middle-class families.

As a collection, the question these works raise is not why 1990s works with lesbian and gay content should have arisen, but why they should have so centrally relied on a theme of housing displacement. One answer comes in Larson's replacement of Puccini's drum major's promenade in favour of a preintermission chorus line shouting a modified version of the ACT UP (The Aids Coalition to Unleash Power) slogan: 'Actual Reality-ACT UP-Fight AIDS.'[18] Founded in 1987, ACT UP's unique legacy was to be at once heir to the 1970s social movements about identity while renewing the 1960s tradition of civil disobedience against government officials, agencies and policies. What distinguishes ACT UP from other 1980s movements was its directed focus on the state as a mechanism of structured violence for failing to protect persons that might have otherwise been included as citizens but, in this instance, were excluded from the 'general population'.[19] ACT UP's expression of anger, combined with middle-class resentment of removed privileges, is largely responsible for propelling the transformation of a lesbian and gay self-presentation and confidence through the late 1980s and 1990s. It provided a language, dress style and attitude that disrupted the usual affiliations of status, and turned metaphors of exclusion and disability into a language of resistance. As such it provided a means for expressing anti-gentrification sentiments for a movement that had by the 1990s run out of steam. Given that ACT UP's salient membership was associated with an East Village bohemian style that had gestated alongside, and occasionally in explicit collaboration with, neighbour-hood housing activism, ACT UP returned the discursive favour by making the connections between attacks on the urban frontier with medicalised ones on the body.[20] The pertinence of ACT UP's instigation of representations of same sexuality and Aids that speak through a syntax of housing activism suggests how a common ground and language of resistance to gentrification can be created when marginal groups, initially encountering each other as strangers in the same neigh-bourhood (and despite their differences in potential status), fuse to create a political network. The lesson is that the appearance of the culturally emarginated is not necessarily or essentially damaging, or gentrifying, as long as it refuses to answer the call of social prerogatives. This is to say that the event of gentrification is contingent on the play of political allegiances and affiliations, and that certain elective affinities may be able to resist speculation of their shared space by resisting, rather than falling in line with, the reassurances provided by the swing of batons parading through the crowd.

Notes

1   Giacomo Puccini, *La Bohème* (New York: Dover Publications, 1962) pp. 6, 47.
2   I use 'East Village', despite complaints that it is merely a real estate developer's neologism, because the term is now conventional. The alternative term, 'The Lower East Side', conflates the regions above and below the Houston that, at least since the 1960s, have distinct histories.
3   Personal participant observation. A frequently cited eyewitness account is C. Carr, 'Night clubbing', *Village Voice*, 16 August 1988. This is collected in C. Carr, *On Edge: Performance at the End of the Twentieth Century* (Wesleyan: Wesleyan University Press, 1994). Further accounts of the 1988–92 police riots can be found in the period's issues of neighbourhood newspapers like *The Shadow*, *The East Villager*, *Downtown* and Sarah Ferguson's articles in *The Village Voice*.
4   Personal participant observation. For more first-hand accounts, see period issues of previously cited community newspapers.
5   The comment is reported in, amongst other places, Martha Rosler, 'Tompkins Square Park, East Village, Lower East Side, Manhattan, New York' in Brian Wallis (ed.), *If You Lived Here: The City in Art, Theory, and Social Activism* (Seattle: Bay Press, 1991) pp. 208–16, p. 212.
6   Janet L. Abu-Lughod, 'Conclusions and implications' in *From Urban Village to East Village: The Battle for New York's Lower East Side* (Oxford: Blackwell, 1994) pp. 335–53.

7   For histories of East Village confrontations see Marci Reaven and Jeanne Houck, 'A history of Tompkins Square Park' in Abu-Lughod, *From Urban Village to East Village*, pp. 81–98; Rosler, 'Tompkins Square Park, East Village, Lower East side, Manhattan, New York'; Neil Smith, *The New Urban Frontier: Gentrification and the Revanchist City* (New York: Routledge, 1996) pp. 3–29. All further references to this will be incorporated in the text.

8   Kurt Hollander, *Low Rent* (New York: Grove, 1994) p. 1.

9   Karl Marx, *Capital, Volume One* (New York: Vintage, 1977) p. 873. All further references will be incorporated in the text.

10   Saskia Sassen, *The Global City* (Princeton: Princeton University Press, 1991); Manuel Castells, *The Informational City* (Oxford: Blackwell, 1989).

11   Karl Marx, 'The Eighteenth Brumaire of Louis Napoleon', section 5, in Karl Marx and Frederick Engels, *Collected Works*, trans. Richard Dixon and others (New York: International Publishers, 1975).

12   Arthur Moss and Evelyn Marvel, *The Legend of the Latin Quarter* (New York: The Beechhurst Press, 1946) p. 123.

13   Jerrold Siegel, *Bohemian Paris: Culture, Politics, and the Boundaries of Bourgeois Life, 1830–1930* (New York: Viking, 1986) pp. 13, 21.

14   Sharon Zukin, *Loft Living: Culture and Capital in Urban Change* (Baltimore: Johns Hopkins University Press, 1982); Charles Simpson, *Soho: The Artist in the City* (Chicago: University of Chicago Press, 1981).

15   See Zukin, *Loft Living*; Simpson, *Soho*; Christopher Mele, '"Neighbourhood burn-out": Puerto Ricans at the end of the queue' in Abu-Lughod, *From Urban Village to East Village*, pp. 125–40.

16   Tony Kushner, *Perestroika* (London: Theatre Communication Group, 1995) p. 2.

17   For treatments on Warhol as a gay artist see Jennifer Doyle, Jonathan Flatley and Jose Esteban Munoz (eds), *Pop Out: Queer Warhol* (Durham: Duke University Press, 1996), especially Simon Watley's 'Queer Andy'.

18   The actual slogan is 'ACT UP! Fight Back! Fight AIDS!'

19   For an analysis of ACT UP's style as representing a crisis of middle-class privilege see Peter F. Cohen, *Love and Anger: Essays on AIDS and Politics* (Binghampton: Haworth Press, forthcoming).

20   See the comments by Rich Jackman in the discussion on homelessness in Wallis, *If You Lived Here*, p. 198. Additionally, one of the main institutional legacies of ACT UP is its parentage of Housing Works, an organisation that seeks housing for PWAs.

11

Gargi Bhattacharyya, University of Birmingham

Metropolis of the Midlands

The city I live in is not a city of angels or dreams. It does not appear on the film screens of the world or in the worthy tracts about urban living. But it does appear as a spectre in Britain's imagination, a sign of a certain kind of city culture. The kind of city culture which Britain tries to deny and ignore, but which increasingly is the main experience of ordinary people. This is the urban experience in which paid work has become peripheral for many, in which the highly publicised events of subsidised culture happen somewhere else a long way away, in which urban living is largely about aimless hanging about without, ostensibly, anything to do. Although this is the landscape of many British lives (including many of the 'really' metropolitan lives lived in London), Birmingham somehow absorbs all the blame for this mundane flavour of living.

In response to this, Birmingham has been busy remaking itself – mainly imaginatively, but also with some rebuilding. It would be easy to knock these attempts and talk about how this project of remaking the myth of Birmingham has made no impact on the ordinary people of the city, but I want to try and avoid this easy name-calling. It is true that the kind of redevelopment of image and landscape which addresses a phantasmic audience outside Birmingham leaves the everyday hardships of much Birmingham living untouched. But like so many parts of the world, Birmingham is really trying to ride the vagaries of global capital, to find ways of sustaining life in clean and decent ways, while minimising hardship and suffering. So much social policy in this end-of-millennium malaise we are living is a defensive attempt to take the edge off the worst hurts of an unpredictable world order – if some clever PR can lift our spirits, then who am I to throw stones? Instead, I want to devote some energy to unpacking the various stories that are doing the rounds.

Myths of Birmingham

Birmingham is a city with an inferiority complex. The signs of this nervous disorder are glaringly obvious in every symptomatic detail of the city's living landscape, from the local authority publicity which heralds Birmingham as somewhere exciting (despite expectations) to the protective defences of the city's residents against a barrage of slights, real and imagined. It is easy for us to forget that until recently most of the rest of Britain also suffered from this sense of inadequacy – until the relatively recent phenomenon of northern renaissance and mass media appreciation of Scottish urban cultures (*à la Trainspotting*), pretty much everywhere wished it was London. This is the tragedy of small countries (even small countries like England which still pretend to own their near neighbours). The space can sustain only a certain area of amenities, one metropolitan area that stands as political and administrative capital and drags all cultural activity in the wake of these harder kinds of business. The upshot of this capital-centred way of organising is that cities that are just cities, not capitals, lack the pull and the glamour of the resource magnet capital. Provincial cities get left with the bad press of urban living.

Birmingham has suffered from a particularly acute version of this syndrome. Tim Hall has argued that the English Midlands have been accommodated into the wider mythology of north–south, industrial–pastoral, unEnglish–English divide through strategic splitting:

> The English Midlands contains elements as 'English' as the deep England of the Herefordshire, Worcestershire and Warwickshire countryside and elements as 'unEnglish' as Black Country factories and Birmingham workshops. Accommodating the English Midlands within the north-south geography of English culture involved little more than consigning the former elements to the cultural south and the latter to the cultural north. This division of the English Midlands has consequently been legitimised in other representations of the 'divided nation' discourse, including the academic, through an enduring silence.[1]

Although Hall implies that the Midlands fits easily into existing mythologies about pastoral 'English' (bypassing the fact that large parts of Wales and Scotland and even Northern Ireland are routinely presented as part of this idealised pastoral in the interests of tourism and other more nebulous feel-good projects) and industrial 'unEnglish' spaces, Birmingham seems to have fallen between these two stools rather than straddling them both. Clearly Birmingham and the rest of the West Midlands were never going to become part of the more privileged story of British landscapes – despite the large areas of green and rolling countryside in the region. The Midlands has been associated too insistently with the industrial heartlands of another era and has been too ill-represented by Britain's class-privileged arbiters of taste (what Gordon Cherry calls the 'capitalist aristocracy') to become part of the special space of pastoral idyll.[2] What is more strange, but still apparent, is Birmingham's exclusion from Britain's obsessive anti-glamour love affair with (formerly) industrial cities. Northern English cities and, in a related but more complex way, major Scottish cities have gained a certain kudos from not being soft, southern and opera loving; instead owning the various positive qualities of grittiness, real-lifeness, friendly no-nonsenseness and being damn hard and resilient, in ways which signify a certain flavour of scary urban excitement. Birmingham, on the other hand, has remained an empty in-between place in the national imagination. Neither chocolate box nor thriller, Birmingham suffers from the worst of all reputations, that of being boring, insipid, lacking any identity or distinction at all. Birmingham misses out on both the privileges of old-style heritage and on the newer pay-offs of 'cool Britannia'. While it is all too easy to critique the dubious values of either celebrating histories of imperial and class exploitation or of remarketing Britain as urban pop culture home to the Spice Girls and the various bad tempers of new British (white) art, there is a cost to not taking part, a cost which Birmingham has been paying. Some places, it seems, are both too industrial and not industrial enough. While Britain struggles with its uncertainty about whether working for a living is a laudable or a laughable predicament, industrial (and deindustrialising) centres become a cipher for the processes of waged work and waged workers. British ambivalence to the city is an echo of this confusion about the value of work.

Of course, this has been true for some time. Britain has derided its own industrial centres and marked value in terms of aristocratic culture and uncontaminated countryside. Industrial centres gained a certain macho status, but were not part of the British tourist experience. However, through the 1980s and 1990s, as local government was ruthlessly stripped of the power to do anything much about the material conditions of the urban dwellers who had put their hopes in municipal socialism, local authorities began to rely on marketing as the most likely route to local salvation. If local authorities were having their budgets capped and their hands tied, then the only hope of prosperity was through attracting resources by other means. For British provincial cities, all those urban centres that were not London, the answer was to develop themselves as different and exotic brands of urban experience. The arts figured strongly in some of these early attempts to revive local economies through canny advertising – so Glasgow briefly becomes city of culture and Liverpool invests public money in the Liverpool Tate. But less highbrow leisure pounds have played their part in certain forms of very British urban renaissance – most obviously in the famous clublands of Manchester, Leeds and Newcastle. If the various modern myths of young and happening Britain have any basis, it is in this widespread reimagining of what can and will happen outside London. Suddenly, British cities have become glamorous places to be, even if this is an alternative youth culture orientated kind of glamour.

But not Birmingham. Birmingham (and to some extent, the Midlands as a region) has missed out on this rebirthing as cool. Despite its status as Britain's second city, Birmingham remains a joke nowhere in the national imagination, a lump of concrete tangled in motorways with no distinguishing features apart from a funny way of pronouncing vowels.

City of Voices

The voice of Birmingham is an object of ridicule. This is the accent most associated with stupidity (like Benny from *Crossroads*) and criminality. A recent study shows that Brummie accents are twice as likely to get you convicted of a crime: 'The Brummie suspect was regarded as less intelligent, more likely to be poor and working-class and less socially competent.'[3] While other regional accents in our newly caring post-class society allegedly incite feelings of warmth and friendliness, Birmingham gets nothing but negative vibes. This is the voice least heard in national broadcasting, the accent of a thousand bad imitations; a way of talking that no one wants to build a TV show around.

Urban Living as Bad

Until very recently, the city has had a bad press as a place to live. In all the academic fuss about *flâneur*ing and the joys of the crowd, it is easy to forget that this celebration is in response to the pervasive disrespect toward urban living. In particular, Britain distances itself from the city culture of the rest of Europe in favour of a self-image based on a dream of the pastoral. In Britain the city means dirt, disease and overcrowding. The country owns all the feel-good factors of rolling fields, open land, greenery, pleasantry, all things sweet, light and wholesome. A thousand analyses of British heritage industries and dubious nationalist rhetorics have outlined the centrality of this frozen version of the rural in the conservative agenda of what is good about Britain.[4] Despite recent returns to the urban centre as a space of culture and consumption, any tourist guide to Britain will confirm that this country still markets itself as an insistently non-urban space. Visitors are entreated to come to London and then view the rest of the country as a series of market towns, stately homes and green fields peopled only by anachronistic peasants. Britain is not alone in this antipathy to the urban. Even the United Nations Centre for Human Settlements (HABITAT), admits that:

Cities have long been blamed for many human failings. Capital cities are often blamed for the failures or inadequacies of the government institutions located there. The wealthiest cities are often blamed for the inequalities in income that the contrasts between their richest and poorest districts make visible. Cities in general and industrial cities in particular are blamed for environmental degradation. Images such as 'exploding cities' and 'mushrooming cities' are often used to convey a process of population growth and urbanization that is 'out of control'. Cities are often blamed for corroding the social fabric. Within the current concern for 'sustainable development', cities are often cited as the main 'problem'.[5]

Although the HABITAT report goes on to refute these allegations, there is something significant about this view of the city. The city is the cipher we use when we want to voice our fears about population growth, or human waste, or crowds or dirt or excess – the city comes to represent the fear that humanity is out of control, beyond any intervention from state or society. Despite the dreams of nature which fill anti-urban rhetoric, the danger of the city is that in this space people become animal again.

This is the parallel logic of the city – those old stories about concrete jungles, unknown dangers, irrepressible but hidden nature(s) lurking in the shadows of urban experience. On the one hand, the city makes us modern: now we are ordered, rationalised, industrialised, able to live in the made-on-the-spot network of relationships with strangers. The city is a sign that now humanity can organise its survival as a large group project, with the city we really start to live with all the benefits and uncertainties of that collective name, society. In the city, we begin to know how intimately our welfare is tied to that of others, most of whom we will never know, and we hope that this sense of humility and collectivity will make us more human. But on the other hand, the city increases the animality of modernity: now we are private, anonymous, individualised, freed from the inborn, inbred hierarchies of feudalism. In the city, we see the empty swagger of authority and lose our fear in man or god. Instead our destinies become tied to forces beyond the control of any authority, subject only to the vagaries of capital or nature and in response we become more short sighted, self-centred, pulled by our bodies beyond the checks of group interest or reason, more animal altogether.

When Angotti talks of the 'profound anti-urban bias' in Western thought, citing the usual concerns about concentrated populations being the breeding grounds of dangerous diseases and lax morals, he is identifying this fear that in the city people become no more than their flesh.[6] The trouble with the city lies in its concentration of human bodies – Western culture's ongoing anxiety about the place of the body in civilisation extends to an unease with the places in which most bodies live. If the call of the physical threatens reason, then surely a greater concentration of physical calls will lead to an unpleasant and irrational blot on the landscape. If it is the needs of the body which keep us animal and stop us ever becoming wholly human, then cities, as places organised (however badly) to meet a hungry multitude of bodily needs, are an unhappy reminder of how vulnerable we are to biological imperatives. In Western thought, anti-urban bias is closely linked to a wider disdain for material concerns and materiality in general. The rise of a white Western subject to a position of global power has meant the development of a culture that celebrates an abstract idea of reason and spirit at the expense of more everyday bodily concerns. The outcome has been that the human activity required to sustain the body in this and future generations, from eating to excretion to sex to work, has been derided and/or obscured. Instead, all this nasty bodily business has become the terrain of the other(s); all those excluded from the privileged status of the white Western subject. Angotti identifies this when he says clearly what few dare to admit: Anti-urbanism merged with anti-immigrant prejudice as the lifestyle of immigrant workers in the slums of London, Manchester, New York and Chicago was blamed for the terrible living conditions created by industrial capital.[8] The mythologies of anti-urbanism transform the unpleasant consequences of waged labour for profit into unpleasant characteristics of particular ethnic cultures – so that it is no longer clear whether the nasty economic arrangements of cities bring sorrow to urban inhabitants or whether the nasty cultures of migrant urban dwellers make the city the unpleasant place that it is.

Birmingham, city of migrants and not-quite-heavy industry, has suffered particularly from this mixed-up dislike of work and foreigners, combining these worst of worlds in its culture of hard labour and come-from-afar people in the imagination of the rest of Britain. Birmingham builds its industrial heritage as the toyshop of Europe – not pretty playthings for childish amusement, but a variety of lighter manufactured objects. The variety of Birmingham's manufactured output ranged from steel implements such as pokers and tongs to the famous industries in buttons and guns to the still-existing jewellery industry. The redevelopment of the Jewellery Quarter (as an area of upmarket Birmingham bars and restaurants and high-priced housing) and the seemingly now defunct plans to redevelop a section of the city centre as the Gun Quarter are allusions to this very particular industrial past, albeit allusions which obscure their links to particular kinds of work. Even when remade as a place of leisure, Birmingham is scattered with signs of the world of work on which it is built.

City of Dissent

Birmingham is famously a city of dissenters and, even more famously, the place that made certain versions of dissenting practice into good business. Through the industrial growth of the eighteenth and nineteenth centuries, Birmingham developed an entrepreneurial class that was insistently non-Anglican and instead dissenting in its religious affiliations to Methodism and Quakerism, and by implication dissenting in its approach to the accumulation of capital. Birmingham's entrepreneurs have a long history of attempting to plan and provide for the living conditions of their workers, most famously in Cadbury's experimental urban village, Bourneville. Whatever the contradictions and shortcomings of these projects, it is worth remembering that Birmingham is a place which has long dreamed of reconciling the pursuit of profit with the need to provide decent living conditions for all.

Rethinking the Urban

Against this long history of anti-urban thinking, some have fought hard to celebrate the transitory pleasures of urban existence. In academic work on cities this is the version that has tended to take centre stage, in more recent discussions at least. This is the version which takes Benjamin's seductively aimless and multisensual stroller and hopes that every city street will offer this same adventure of display and surprise.[9] This is city living as an endless succession of free fun – all places to go and people to see for those with nothing better to do than walk and look. The democratic promise in the figure of the *flâneur*, the implication that we can all do this if only we have a free minute, is, admittedly, hard to resist. All sorts of optimistic thinking about cities depends upon this founding hope, the hope that we all have an equal and open access to the life-enhancing spectacle of the city and that this access will make us into urban subjects who can rub along together in happy civic harmony.[10]

Of course, the fantasy that we will all *flâneur* ourselves into a new way of being (not Benjamin's, but ours, as children of the age of regeneration) must forget about everything that people in the city have to do. This is a way of inhabiting public spaces without the call of work, family or duty. To enjoy it best, you should be alone, with time to kill and access to some private source of funding, because cities are most fun as places of aimless leisure. I appreciate the very significant pleasures of the city as a spectacle that costs nothing to see, and enjoy the endless show of urban living as much as the next person. There is, though, something rather strange about imagining the convivial city as no more than a place in which to hang about. It seems that dreams of a city which could encompass the range of people's material and everyday needs have been contaminated by their relation to authoritarian modernism and its close sibling, nostalgic urban pastoralism. Both versions imagine ways of urban living which could provide what people need to keep body and soul together, but somehow at the expense of any sense that the urban could be a place of adventure, or of any kind of personal liberty. Instead, we give up these small freedoms and succumb to a planned existence (planned by someone else) in recognition of the instrumental benefits of being told what to do. Dissatisfaction with the promises of postwar planning could be seen as a plea for cities that don't lose their sense of adventure, because adventure is also a human need and aspiration. Yet in these pleas once again adventure seems to be placed in opposition to the dullness of work. It seems that cities can only become fun and convivial places if work happens elsewhere. For Birmingham, and other hungry-for-jobs British cities, the trick is to provide employment that looks like leisure. As if working in the service sector is being paid to be yourself.

Urban Living as Cosmopolitan Living

Leonie Sandercock describes the changing shape of our world as being determined by,

> the three dominant sociocultural forces of our time: the age of migration, the rise of postcolonial and indigenous peoples, and the emergence of a range of so-called minorities (women, gays, etc.), hitherto invisible/suppressed, as political actors. Linked with the destabilizing effects of global economic restructuring and integration, these new forces are literally changing the faces of cities and regions, which are becoming much more culturally diverse.[11]

Sandercock argues convincingly that urban living is necessarily cosmopolitan in our time. Certainly, celebrations of city living propose the diversity of the cosmopolis as one of the major pleasures and resources of urban existence. In large part, this is a response to the racist scare stories against city living which have been implied or shouted in various anti-urban discourses. However, it is also a wider reevaluation of what the resources of the city might be. This rethinking has had a particular currency in Birmingham.

No one is from Birmingham. Like all real cities, everyone comes from somewhere else. Ireland or Kashmir, India or the Caribbean, Bangladesh, Yemen, Hong Kong, Vietnam, Smethwick, Oldbury or, most common and most nebulous of all, the Black Country. Birmingham has long suffered a bad press because of its migrant population. From the ugliness of the Smethwick by-election onwards, Birmingham and the Black Country have held a central role in Britain's racist imagination. This is the place of the blacks and the Irish – the place where Anglo culture begins to erode and disappear. The place where there is no economy, only crime and terrorism. A place disintegrating under the pressure of alien cultures. Certainly no place for new investment, leisure industries, the cash injections of tourism and passing trade. Like most British cities,

Birmingham has spent a lot of energy denying its migrant heritage. The shaping powers of racist mythologies are hard to resist – far easier to dodge the issue and go for a marketing strategy which highlights business meetings and City of Birmingham Symphony Orchestra and hope that no one knows or remembers the other stories of Birmingham as dangerous alien territory. Perhaps for this reason, Birmingham has been more successfully sold to people outside Britain than to those within. Barry Cleverdon, chief executive of the National Exhibition Centre Group, explains: 'They don't have any preconceptions and are generally impressed by what they find.'[12] However, in recent years there have been signs that, to non-British audiences in particular, Birmingham's mixed-bag population may be repackaged as a positive asset. The area around Hurst Street and the Arcadian has been redeveloped as a Chinese quarter, building on a former site of Chinese-run business. The close concentration of restaurants around Ladypool Road and Stoney Lane have been marketed as the balti belt or run (and now the balti experience, in a recognition that this experience can be had in many places across the region), selling the usually undervalued contribution of South Asian food to British cities as a positively unmissable tourist attraction. Plans come and go to redevelop the Digbeth area as an Irish quarter. All round, Birmingham has started to sell itself as a distinctively multiethnic experience, somewhere cosmopolitan in an urbane rather than a threatening way.

Relocation of Economy

It is hard to not surmise that the reemergence of trendy city living depends upon the death of older and less glamorous forms of economy in the city. Regeneration itself, in all its varied and nebulous forms, is a response to the nastiness of deindustrialisation and urban decline. Regeneration is what you do when your industrial base has been eroded, when cities need new strategies for sustaining their populations, when the old world is dying and we all need something new to grow in its place. As so many have noted, that something new has turned out to be the leisure economy. The convivial city which most of Britain, including Birmingham, is dreaming of, implies a certain kind of person enjoying a certain range of leisure activities. The main point of contention for those in the business of planning and regeneration is how to expand these definitions of people and activity to include more of Britain's population. The link between conviviality and leisure in its widest sense is the assumed baseline for discussion. Birmingham, like other places, has had to rethink the role of leisure in local economies:

Theresa Stewart, leader of Birmingham Council, was initially opposed
to the city's investment in its 160 million pound convention centre
and public art projects in 1991. But yesterday she said: 'Originally I
thought we should have spent the money on frontline services. But
the convention centre was planned as a new employer when the manufacturing sector collapsed, and the important thing now is to make
sure they are successful. We want to bring people into the city and
create the jobs in the shops, hotels and the arts.'[13]

To remake itself as both a nice place to be and an area in which people
have enough work to live, Birmingham, like much of Britain, has had to
reevaluate what it has to sell. With the much-proclaimed death of manufacturing, old-style ugly and undervalued versions of work are hardly
available in urban centres or anywhere else. Instead, the newer styles of
work pretend not to be work at all, and gain value from appearing to be
effortless and leisurely for both worker and client. The still-animal flesh
of city inhabitants is on display as part of this spectacle of service. Now
cities have to shift away from an anti-urban bias that hates workers and
foreigners as figures of contamination and decay and start to present
these archetypically urban people as the best products of city space.

City of Roads
For a long time Birmingham has figured in the national imaginary as
nothing more than a huge intersection. The mythic status of Spaghetti
Junction overrides any other Birmingham landmark or monument in
the national imagination. For years, visitors to the city have remembered
nothing more than a web of high-speed roads, criss-crossing a city that
has no centre. Now Birmingham city centre is becoming gradually pedes-
trianised – a place for strollers along canal sides through city squares
back to the covered shopping centres of former ridicule.

Metropolis

Birmingham is trying to reimagine itself as a regional centre, beyond the
long shadow of London's showy international status. To become this
much-desired thing, metropolis of the Midlands, Birmingham has to
initiate a whole new way of thinking about what is central about urban
centres:

> The metropolis is indisputably a global settlement, an international
> phenomenon, a nodal point in the international division of labor. It
> serves multiple social, economic and cultural functions across national
> and international borders. It is the urban expression of a new inter-
> connected and diverse world.[14]

To transform itself into this nodal point, Birmingham must learn to acknowledge both its global population and its complex diasporic connections to a range of economic structures, and proclaim itself as an national and international meeting point. Instead of being stuck in nostalgia for a pastoral which never was, Birmingham has begun to acknowledge its internationalised and industrialised heritage as a strength, a history which can prepare us for the hurdles of our globalised futures. Through this process, Birmingham is beginning to win prizes. In 1998 we were home to both the high diplomacy of the G8 summit of world leaders and the international kitsch of the Eurovision Song Contest. The redevelopment of the canal walkways in the Broad Street area have been nominated as the most ecologically friendly tourist attraction in Britain. Slowly but surely, the hard sell of newly remembered civic pride is starting to take effect.

The *Evening Mail* of 27 February 1998 focused its 'Viewpoint' column on this tourism award, asking Birmingham people 'Would YOU want a holiday in Brum?' Strangely, this vox-pop column echoes many of the refrains of the city's marketing partnership – whether genuine or staged, the responses show the extent to which this version of Birmingham has become the official line. In the piece, Abdellatif Erraoul remarks: 'I am a Frenchman and I know Paris well. I would say that Birmingham has similar attractions, especially the cafes and restaurants by the waterfront. I have friends from France coming to visit and they have heard about Brindley Place. It has become very clean in the city centre and that is also important.' A neat soundbite that picks up on ideas of Birmingham as 'Europe's Meeting Place' and the concern to develop a British cafe culture while maintaining ecological priorities. Peter Groom, on the other hand, stresses Birmingham's ability to compete with London and represent an alternative national centre: 'Living in the Midlands, you tend to take what you have in Birmingham for granted, but the canalside is a great place to visit on a sunny Sunday afternoon – our answer to Canary Wharf or Covent Garden. If I lived in another part of the world, I would holiday in Brum because there's so much to see.' The last opinion is that of Irene Castle: 'What an honour! We shan't have to go abroad now! I'm a Brummie and I'm proud of the way the city has changed. Now we're the ones who are laughing.'

It's hard to imagine a more succinct summing up of Birmingham's new myth of itself. The whole repackaging of Birmingham has been a shift from being a standing joke to having the last laugh, a fairytale transformation for the ugly duckling of British cities. The poster campaign run in the first months of 1998 across Birmingham takes this rebirth as its theme. The campaign was an initiative of Birmingham Marketing Partnership and the National Exhibition Centre Group, with a smaller amount of sponsorship from the city council, and featured nine ordinary Brummies in black-and-white close-up headshots in a series which can be seen across the city. These faces of Birmingham range from two to sixty-seven in age, and include two council-employed roadsweepers, two members of Birmingham's African Caribbean community, two from the Asian community, a butcher from the Bullring, a youthworker, a waiter and a personal assistant. Each poster addresses the people of Birmingham (rather than an outside audience) with the slogan 'So be proud and hold your head up high', because, presumably, we the people are the best representatives of what Birmingham is and what Birmingham can offer:

> After years of suffering ridicule from southerners, Birmingham yesterday urged all downtrodden Brummies to show some civic pride and get a haircut. Under the slogan 'Get your hair done, Marge. Bill Clinton's coming to town', Birmingham Council hopes to spruce up the city's image before hosting an eclectic series of international events this year.[15]

Spruced up and hair-cutted, Birmingham's mythologised population can become the key to a new international reputation, a metropolis of the Midlands. I want to argue that the aspiration to be refigured as metropolis – regional centre, site of diverse amenities and activities – is closely tied to the idea that a mixed population can be refigured as cosmopolis.

When cities like Birmingham succumb reluctantly to a project of economic regeneration which is led by tourism and leisure, an inevitable part of this process is a refiguring of what kind of resource the city's population might be. Now the products we are selling are a variety of face-to-face contacts with the people of Birmingham. Unlike the relatively anonymous labour power consumed through manufactured goods, service industries famously sell you a moment of human contact from the service provider. For this to work, Birmingham has to find a way of repackaging its much-maligned people as a positive asset, and rework racist mythologies into the more positive story of cosmopolitan exuberance. As Theresa Stewart says:

> We promise to do everything we can to make these events [G8, Eurovision] a massive success for our city. But the real recipe for success has a very special ingredient that no other city in the world can offer – the people of Birmingham. We want to give our visitors the warmest of welcomes so that they can leave Birmingham thinking: 'Well, that's a city that really knows how to do things.'[16]

I began this piece with my discomfort at the erasure of work in so many celebrations of contemporary living. How could we ever address the pressing issues of social injustice which continue to plague British cities if we could only imagine cities as pleasant when they were filled with leisure? Everyone in Birmingham knows that the famously successful

Midlands yuppy developments behind the International Convention Centre, close to the canals area which wins tourism prizes, back on to a part of Ladywood that is one of the poorest parts of the city – lifetimes away from the conviviality of business conventions and cappucinos by the canal. Birmingham, like many places, is still struggling with these disparities. But if the public relations exercise of selling Birmingham to a doubting world can reclaim the varied people of Birmingham as the good thing they are, perhaps we are moving slowly towards stories of the city which can encompass our various needs. Stories which rethink work as something which involves real people not just faceless products and which love urban spaces because of, not despite, their all too bodily inhabitants. If economic imperatives can be refigured as the textures of everyday lives, then maybe even the PR comes close to identifying the most pressing of issues. Whatever the reasons, these days the streets of Birmingham seem full of people holding their heads up high – and that, at least, is a start.

Notes

1   Tim Hall, '(Re)placing the city: cultural relocation and the city as centre' in Sallie Westwood and John Williams (eds), *Imagining Cities: Scripts, Signs, Memory* (London: Routledge, 1997) p. 210.
2   Gordon E. Cherry, *Birmingham, A Study in Geography, History and Planning* (Chichester: John Wiley and Sons, 1994).
3   'The way we live: guilty as charged: the price of talking Brummie', *Independent*, 25 September 1997, p. 9.
4   One of the best of these remains Patrick Wright's *On Living in an Old Country* (London: Verso, 1985).
5   United Nations Centre for Human Settlements (HABITAT), *An Urbanizing World: Global Report on Human Settlements, 1996* (Oxford: Oxford University Press, 1996) p. 417.
6   Thomas Angotti, *Metropolis 2000, Planning, Poverty and Politics* (London: Routledge, 1993).
7   For more on this see Richard Dyer, *White* (London and New York: Routledge, 1997).
8   Angotti, *Metropolis*, p. 10.
9   Walter Benjamin, *Charles Baudelaire, A Lyric Poet in the Era of High Capitalism* (London: Verso, 1973).
10   For a practically inclined example, see Ken Worpole, *Towns for People* (Buckingham: Open University Press, 1992).
11   Leonie Sandercock, *Towards Cosmopolis* (Chichester: John Wiley and Sons, 1998) p. 164.
12   'Could this be Birmingham?', *Independent*, 15 August 1997, p. 14.
13   'Campaign urges Brummies to brush up their image', *Financial Times*, 9 January 1998, p. 7.
14   Angotti, *Metropolis*, p. 3.
15   'Campaign urges Brummies to brush up their image', p. 7.
16   'So proud to be Brummies', *Birmingham Voice*, 14 January 1998, p. 4.

John Phillips, National University of Singapore

Singapore Soil: A Completely Different Organisation of Space

> They make, they serve
> They buy, they sell.[1]

Prelude

It is just after 12 midnight on Orchard Road and the taxis queue up outside Centrepoint, one of Singapore's first shopping malls, still relatively new. Around the corner on Cuppage Terrace a few diners, among them many European visitors, finish meals of crayfish or prawns as loud blues rock drifts through the palms from a crowded late-night cafe. Just a little further down a solitary figure walks bright in vivid neon glare. Silvery bouffant, leopard print skirt, net tights and purple chiffon – he wanders off to unknown assignations. In another part of town a hawker centre is open-air host to a group of young men watching World Cup football, drinking large bottles of Singapore's Tiger beer and eating raw fish porridge. All around the dim shapes of still new high-rise apartments look down in benevolent indifference.

Singapore Soil: 'Greening Up'

Soils are the products of weathering and other soil forming processes. In Singapore, soils are studied for pedological, engineering or geological purposes. Due to very limited available land area and the intensive nature of development, the decision to select a particular type of land use or development activity is seldom based on soil characteristics. In most cases it is more convenient to modify the soils and ground conditions in order to accommodate the land use.

The fast pace of urban development in Singapore has been responsible for the replacement of the original soils and vegetation cover. Consequently, areas with original soils are continuously decreasing.[2] An equatorial forest has tall, powerful trees, their branches abundant with broad leaves that form vast canopies over the soil, a powerful leaky umbrella through which the rainfall drips. Without these trees the periodic torrential rain would wash away all the topsoil and its essential nutrients, leaving only mudflats and clay, thus making any significant plant growth impossible. Between 1819 and 1965, during the fast urbanisation of the small Malayan island named Singapore, many trees were chopped down to make way for the concrete and steel of a city destined to house over three million people. In 1965 Lee Kuan Yew, leader of the People's Action Party which has ever since been the governing body of Singapore, began a 'greening up' of the city as an integral component of his unique style of urbanism. His methods usefully symbolise his whole approach. He borrowed drainage ideas from Paris, whose tree-lined boulevards he envied, for his new city's streets. He bought in experts from New Zealand, whose green, grassy plains he wanted for the parks and playing fields of Singapore. Buying in plants from countries with comparable climates he produced a garden city using modern botanical science and technology. He says: 'I sent them on missions all along the Equator and the tropical, subtropical zones, looking for new types of trees, plants, creepers and so on. From Africa, the Caribbean, Latin, Middle, Central America, we've come back with new plants. It's a very small sum. But if you get the place greened up, if you get all those creepers up, you take away the heat, you'll have a different city.'[3] In other words he went shopping. The soil itself is now different. Careful use of compost from rubbish dumps, the judicious addition of calcium here, lime there, and super-efficient drainage systems puts Singapore on new soil where trees, grass and shrubs grow up among the concrete high-rise housing and the neon shopping plazas.[4]

This 'greening up' is an example of the kind of technics that has since the start of the 1960s brought about a transformation in the lifestyle of Singaporeans. However, the 'greening up' in this case, which means increasing the number of trees, shrubs and grass in built-up areas, must be measured against an overall increase in the amount of developed land. During the 1980s alone 800 hectares per annum of land was consumed for development of all kinds (industrial, residential, business), which means tree-cutting and deforestation on a scale that amounts to a tree loss of 44,000 per year. The island as a whole has thus suffered further irreparable change in its biophysical condition since the 1960s. It is hotter, has a higher rate of soil erosion, is vulnerable to flooding, has lost much of its once-rich assemblage of vegetation and animal life, is less capable of filtering air pollution and has much lower air regeneration than it had only 30 years ago. Lee's 'greening up' programme, as he himself candidly suggests, is a sophisticated cosmetic touch designed to make an increasingly urbanised society feel a bit more comfortable.

The Points of Singapore (Transitlink Guide): Orchard

The shopping centres are vast, air-conditioned complexes. Along Orchard Road and Scotts Road hundreds of acres are occupied exclusively by large labyrinthine constructions that reach into the low clouds and delve underground to interface with stations on the Mass Rapid Transit. It is possible if you live next to one of the MRT stations, like Commonwealth for instance, to leave home in the morning and catch a train to Orchard or City Hall, where you can spend the morning shopping. You pass from Lacoste to Marks and Spencer, from Next to Timberland, from Levi's to huge department stores like Seiyu and Takashimaya in the Ngee Ann Centre or Tangs in the Marriott Hotel complex. Food of every kind is available in a multitude of restaurants or in food centres, which are a basic development of the hawker stalls that developed indigenously here, once itinerant, now settled into place like the population itself. When Macdonalds appeared on the scene (and they are everywhere) they fitted right in, already more Asian than Western. You buy your food at the counter and take it away and eat it at tables and stools fixed to the floor, any time. You might then go to Borders, the great American bookshop, where you can read, get lunch or just coffee, listen to any CD on the many 'listening points' then go upstairs to The Brauhaus for German beer and cabaret, or through the underpass to Shaw House, and up to the Lido to catch one of the current mainstream cinema releases. Get the last train home at midnight and you will have spent the whole cool day indoors without ever having had to go outside into the permanently tropical heat or possible streaming rain. Against its fetid climate Singapore has built a network of cool interiors housing a fully formed consumer culture.

What Singapore has lost in destructuring its biophysical environment it has gained in terms of urban development and, correlatively, economic growth. At the end of the 1960s large numbers of Singaporeans still lived in urban villages that constituted a kind of suburbia out of which a more vertical Singapore was quickly asserted. Now one or two extremely expensive bungalow areas remain, but more than 85 per cent of the population live in high-rise Housing Development Board apartments. In the 1960s the highest building was 15 storeys high. By the end of 1980s the highest was 70 storeys high on an island dense with vertical blocks.[5] A network of new towns running along the east and west coasts and in a loop to the north was constructed very rapidly. The MRT, which extends to all the new population and employment corridors, ferries well over 600,000 commuters and shoppers every day. Singapore is now a city in which trains and buses run on time. Projected developments are completed by deadlines. A network of bureaucratic ministries, departments and other institutions help to maintain a remarkable level of efficiency.

Space and Place

Geometry as a part of *pure* mathematics throws no more light upon actual space than the multiplication table throws upon the population of an actual town

Anyway it's not easy to remember that countries have nothing to do with dots on charts, or governments, or even pieces of the edge of the world.[6]

Singapore is characterised by the incessant reorganisation of its space. Processes like this rely on subtle and sometimes obscure conditions, like the rules of a complex game, that constrain possibilities even while facilitating them. Reorganisation can only occur within conditions determined by a prior organisation that in some essential ways must not be affected by later adjustments. You can alter the soil, for instance, and replace the biophysical support of a region almost entirely, but the economic and technological conditions that effected the original reorganisation (in this case those following rapid development under a colonial power) remain as conditions and constraints for further change. Facilitations that are at the same time constraints constitute laws that underlie whatever comes into being, whether it is a city or a state, and any understanding of a city depends on the ability to read its laws. But the most fundamental of these laws do not permit themselves to be read. The essential adaptability of a small and vulnerable body, which is what Singapore was at the start of the 1960s, requires a certain autonomy from fixed laws or principles – the single-tier government appears to be an ideal system for adapting quickly to unexpected changes – but is to an extent dependent upon the conditions for that autonomy. This article is an analysis of those conditions in so far as they coincide with what I will call the enigmatic 'point' of Singapore. Point locates the difference between space – geographical and historical coordinates, maps, narratives, plans – and place – the context of housing and dwelling. Strictly one cannot distinguish between space and place in these senses. To the extent that one can make such a distinction, this is a function of the point.

Points

'Then what do you think is the *point* of you?'[7]

'The point of something such as a knife, needle or pin is its sharp end or tip.'[8]

There are points in history, moments that compete for historical priority. The events that mark them can sometimes take on the generative power of myths. Goh Kasan's autobiographical and frustratedly nostalgic 'Sarimboon' is one succinct and typical version amongst others:

In the Sixties, our parents were giddy on independence and Merdeka.
    The first song I was taught on Sarimboon Hill was *Majulah, Singapura.*
    The nation launched whole-heartedly into the experiment of independence.
    Guided by our leaders, who shrank, added, subtracted, dissected, multiplied, and divided the essence of this enthusiasm into a point.
    And this point was called the percentage growth of the nation.[9]

A ruthless shrinking. This distillation of time to single point, a point after which one can always say there was a before and an after – or that at least there will be or may be an after – reduces Singapore to the anxiety of a kind of perpetual adolescence, a permanent awareness of the future's danger, a permanent state of shock at the random finitude of existence.[10] The stories a nation tells about itself play an obviously symbolic function. When the BBC broadcast Princess Diana's funeral to television sets across the globe the mode of representation was fundamentally symbolic/iconic. We Brits know how to bury a princess. Signs in this sense are reducible to the mythic function – tradition, heritage, history, tragedy – the march of pompous mourning through ancient streets with solemn and quietly magnified fanfare. Britain trades on the signs of its past, the solid pavements, the gnarled cobble of ancient streets, the purposeful curve of the dome of St Paul's. Each generation is brought into being according to such signs and this is no less true of the generations born into post-independence Singapore. But if these signs of Britain are the symbols of its past, the typical signs of Singapore are the symbols of its future, adding up to a different kind of iconic narrative. Newness is no less deeply inscribed, internalised, authentic an experience than oldness. The having-only-just-begun story is part of Singapore's mode of being, manifested by constant reminders of changes, crisis, hard-won comfort and survival. So the symbolising stories also play an indexical function, where they intersect both with the material volume of the built environment and, in the case of urban space, with the grids of city planning. What interests me is what I shall refer to as the place that lies both between and beneath the mythologised and rationalised spaces of Singapore, the *place* that is presupposed by the distinction between myth and theory, between signs and meaning – whether those signs are regarded as representations of Singapore or as the representation that Singapore itself is. Beneath representation lies the evanescent place.

Beneath the post-independence narratives like Goh Kasan's there remain residual alternative versions. A few material remains of the British colony still figure for the new Singapore and its pointedly singular postcolonial story. The statue of its founder Sir Stamford Raffles remains in the heart of the city. Raffles Hotel, now restored to a pristine sheen that is possibly more sumptuous than it was in its colonial past, remains an expensive tourist attraction, the doorman still dressed in traditional uniform – a colonial archetype. The story of Singapore's postcoloniality is not of a once-colonised country *per se*. Its historians tell of a colonial project in which Raffles representing the British East India Company and employing forces from many nations – Indians, Chinese and Malays primarily – produces a city from scratch, his 'Manchester of the East'. From that point, the production of space in Singapore is inextricable from a certain spatialised historicity of cultural (racial, religious, customary, aesthetic) difference, an assembling of different cultural hierarchies in productive tension with each other and with the colonists whom in various ways they serve.[11]

Raffles is Singapore's heroic and loved founder. His starting from scratch suits the whole Singapore narrative of the point and its development. It also confers a belatedness on contemporary Singapore, a story of postcoloniality that the city reproduces as its evident surface. Lee Kuan Yew, as ever, seems to get right to the point:

> What made Singapore different in the 1960s from most other countries of Southeast Asia was that she had no xenophobic hangover from colonialism. The statue of the founder of Singapore, Sir Stamford Raffles, still stands in the heart of the city to remind Singaporeans of his vision in 1819 of Singapore becoming, on the basis of free competition, the emporium of the East, on the route between India and China. There were then 120 people on the island. They lived by fishing. Within five years of its founding, there were 5,000 traders – British, Arabs, Chinese, Indians, and others drawn in by this principle of free and equal competition, regardless of race, language, or religion.[12]

Singapore is now a developing postcolonial nation without its colonial founder; it is a country of functionaries without a purpose outside or beyond itself. Under colonial rule subjects served the purpose of an imperial government and its empire. In the absence of that purpose subjects continue to serve, but now they serve themselves.

Points 2

So who are 'they'? The colonial narrative is cut up by tangential tales which map the city on different grids. Shirley Chew remembers her Chinese-dialect childhood with the following observation:

> This Singapore, which was mine in my Chinese dialect, had its own focal points and sprawling spaces, its large business firms and congestion of shops, rich suburbs and tenement houses and shacks. It resisted the municipal names that tried to pin it down to some alien notion of order, and favoured instead a digressive mode in speaking of itself.[13]

The focal points and the digressive modes of self-representation provide an important clue to diverse experiences of Singapore's space. The Chinese language renames the Victoria Memorial Hall as 'the building with the big clock' and Raffles Place, already the site of intense shopping, 'the street of department stores'. Other important landmarks in this tangential, digressive version are 'the back of the temple of the ancient mother goddess', and 'the mouth of the gambling houses'.[14] This is one dialect version amongst others in a city whose inhabitants are divided into numerous dialect groups. The imaginary city is several, its iconicity cut up into dividual grids overlapping each other, there are several Chinese dialects in addition to Tamil, Malay, Eurasian and, of course, English, no longer British colonial but fully fledged Singapore English as a first language. English was Lee's answer to the tensions between the Chinese and Malays and it is now the first national language. But Singapore English, as if reflecting the immense paring down of social existence that economic success has required, strikes the foreigner as a curiously economic form of exchange. Its most typical constructions are the shortened form of the acronym and abbreviation, so that Holland Village becomes Holland V and the National University is NUS. You travel on the MRT or along AYE (Ayer Rajah Expressway) and you live in a condo or an HDB. There are tediously numerous examples often lampooned in comedy and song. Singapore English appears to be consistently to the point.

The Empirial

It is possible to read in contemporary Singapore the remnants of multiple histories, like solidities, material remains, some of which are more insistent, more seemingly permanent, than others. The tributary heritages may be somewhat surprising too – surprising just where they are most persistent – as is the case for the remains of what I call here in a provisional shorthand *the empirial*. We need a shorthand because the empirial has no single source but is the upshot of a series of tensions, struggles and formations of compromise. While emerging in a dispersed and often quite discrete way it has a consistency that characterises its many forms. The following is schematic.

1   In part it is derived from imperialism, the form of centralised government common to the great empires of the east, the forbidden cities of the powerful Chinese dynasties, as well as the great Roman empire preceding and inspiring European imperialism and its colonial fulfilment. The imperial in each case serves the interests of a centralised state power, its military supremacy and the maintenance of economic monopoly.
2   A second aspect is derived from empiricism, its focus on the sensible object and, its correlate, the unquestioned 'subject' of experience, the figure *par excellence* of early modern urbanism with its democratic pretensions and its technics. The empirical is a function of a power organised and distributed nodally, an administration linking points in a network of such administrative orders.

The empirial is not the culmination of a historical progress or development, but the result of a specific pattern that manifests a compromise of economies. Different economies in tension, in struggle with each other, 'produce' (for it is certainly productive) a single if rather rigid and inflexible social order – the empirial – which while enforcing control over many distributive potentials remains itself fragile and vulnerable to the forces that it must continually mobilise, facilitate and encourage. The need to operate a fully free-market economy in Singapore (the success of the city depends upon its function as a nodal point facilitating financial exchange, electronic media as well as cultural and geographical paths between other cities) cannot be separated from the need to maintain an actually very rigid bureaucratic administration, though both needs run counter to each other. The first opens Singapore as a nodal point in the network of international cities, facilitating, if only blandly, social, cultural, cosmopolitan, religious and financial exchange – a fully translatable currency. The second imposes the need for rigid rules, regulations, laws, as the manifestation of a quasi-legalist, neo-Confucian (already a very interesting contradiction) control in the hands of a decision-making governmental elite. A democracy without democracy, there is proof here of the possibility of abstracting aspects of both egalitarianism and imperialism as functions of a greater capital – the empirial.

The supple combination of commodity capitalism and state control requires sharply fissured channels of desire. On the one hand there is the circulation of currency, information, commodities and styles, while on the other there is the necessity for tight bureaucratic control, which is presented as a basic moral standard but internalised and perceived as a choice.[15] Cinema, shopping, consumption, and the vast spaces that facilitate and encourage it, may be ideologically set against the manipulation and administration of the efficient clean running of it all. The emphasis that is placed on the seriousness of education and the imperative for hard work serves the meritocratic hierarchisation of a population whose differences of race, gender, religion and class may be equalised through the commodity or neutralised by Singapore English. This combination simply cannot be reduced to the influence of something confined as Western modernity imposed upon an impressionable Southeast Asian prematurity. Rather, the religious, racial, philosophical, social and economic strata – themselves dizzyingly heteroglot – and the modes by which these intersect with those of the West, must be considered in terms of the traces that constitute an infinitely complex historicity. Against the infinite, the empirial serves as a rough schematisation that can be used to indicate something of this historicity.

Growing Up

Another story: Lee Kuan Yew's words, uttered barely a month into independence in 1965, echo as a reminder of his prophetic status:

> We will set the example. This country belongs to all of us. We made this country from nothing, from mud-flats ... Over 100 years ago, this was a mud-flat, swamp. Today this is a modern city. Ten years from now, this will be a metropolis. Never fear![16]

Singapore is now a slightly larger but flatter island owing to land reclamation, a sign of the desire, or the need, to create more space. Most of the additional 'land' is bought from Malaysia, shipped over and added on to make space for more construction, a physical reminder of the ongoing development that is Singapore, but also a material support, a literal or concrete fact, for the more evanescent geometrical sense that Singapore's interior is a space filled by bits of its outside.[17] Approaching by aeroplane the visitor is surprised by a roughly diamond-shaped island adorned by densely vertical blocks like an early computer chip.

Since 1965, when Singapore was thrown into neonatal independence from Malaysia, the stories have coalesced into the singular narrative of a vulnerable new country facing a dangerous future. By careful management the government of Singapore has brought its people the promise of wealth, happiness and health comparable with the richest nations on the globe. The country's most popular English-speaking TV soap opera is called *Growing Up*, and it charts the formative stages of

Singapore's independent urban society – the late 1960s and early 1970s – but, partly because it is soap opera, its historical aspects are subordinated to the suggestiveness of a present in which Singapore is perpetually growing up. The past represented by *Growing Up* is not only authentically naturalistic – sets and clothes imitate those of the recent past – but it is also filled with the mixed iconography of nostalgic Hollywood and post-Second World War Britain. The opening sequence plays a 1950s styled American doo-wop song (emphasising the essential adolescence of the experiences portrayed) and runs a sequence of sepia-toned black-and-white photographs portraying the cast in various family groups. The same sepia tint remains one of the most popular effects of the many photography studios on the island, immediately backdating your moment (wedding, anniversary or whatever family occasion). This backdating effect produces an interesting artifice so that images of the recent past are put into correspondence with those in the archive, which regularly appear in exhibitions displayed in the museums and shopping malls: 'Singapore Waterfront' circa 1900, splendid Victorian buildings rising above a row of rickshaws awaiting some European charge; and, presaging the popular activity whereby you pay for glamour shots of yourself, 'Chinese Men in a Studio in Singapore' surrounded by European props circa 1900.

The storylines of *Growing Up* portray banally global soap opera concerns – school, adolescent beat groups, mixed-race neighbours, a little gang violence, interminable domestic troubles argued out around the familial supper table – and so provide a sense of the contemporary as well as a built-in nostalgia as one and the same experience. As Singapore producer Glen Goei's 1998 film, *Forever Fever*, knowingly emphasises, it is not simply the narrative but the aspects of narrativity – televisual and cinematic effects – that underlie the artifactual Singapore experience.[18] By focusing on the adolescence of its protagonists, who are always battling against their internal id-like desires and external super-ego-like authorities, *Growing Up* seems to want to say that Singapore's ego is that of an adolescent.[19]

Singapore ...

But if *Growing Up* addresses its audience as nostalgic for an adolescence, it is not really adolescence at all. The Singapore narrative seems to need to backdate its past, to represent it as if it is further back than it is, to form the sense of a past that fits those of the Western representations that pervade the popular media – television, music, fashion, cinema, magazines. Singapore shares a pop chart and a restless enthusiasm for contemporary mainstream Western culture yet it cannot share the same narrative. The keywords that mark much of the development of the last

30 years of Western culture, such as transgression, alternative, revolution and counterculture, are just not appropriate here. The kinds of movement that provide a sense of engaged politics, strategic and interested determinism, like civil rights, black power, women's liberation, gay and lesbian movements, various formations of the labour movement, socialism, in short *opposition*, these are all but missing from the post-independence Singapore story. However dated those keywords now sound, it is difficult to consider Western culture – popular culture and diverse intellectual developments as well – without the involvement, engagement and participation in events implied by them. Nevertheless, the only way to understand the role of this kind of culture in Singapore is to detach those keywords and the sense of involvement implied by them completely. If, as it is possible to argue, they represent nothing less than the mythic mode of adolescence *per se*, then Singapore is a city with no adolescence. While the Western world rebelled and reacted Singapore was growing up. When asked by Ludovic Kennedy in 1977 for the BBC whether he felt the lack of 'a good opposition' (as essential to 'a good democracy') Lee Kuan Yew responded by saying:

> I often wonder whether the foreign journalists, or the casual visitor like you, has fathomed, or can fathom, the mind of an Oriental. And I am having to look after Orientals whether they are of Chinese descent or Malay or Indian or Eurasian or Ceylonese and so on. What's inside is completely different: Is this a good government that I can trust to look after me and my family, and will see that my children are educated and will have a job better than mine?[20]

What's inside is completely different. This polemical sentence disguises a very interesting and complex problem. For Lee Kuan Yew the addressee of Singapore's space is itself considered in terms of the organisation of space. What's inside is completely different. A kind of anti-Orientalism (itself an Orientalist response) governs his own thoughts about this but reveals an aspect of his manifestly insightful approach to the special problems of urbanism in Southeast Asia. Note that the construction of the Asian mind that Lee presents here is of a dependent, a being who looks for guidance. In this sense the construction of Singapore subjectivity would avoid the interests of Western Enlightenment. The Singaporean would be perpetually not quite but almost grown.

The Points of Singapore (Transitlink Guide: Clementi Interchange)

Some tent-like structures appear on the stretch of grass outside the Faculty of Building and Architecture. Tent-like only in so far as they are constructed from lengths of bamboo or aluminium with tarpaulin stretched around, these structures neither hold water (as the recent downpour demonstrates) nor cover anything. Tent mutations of irregular, perhaps accidental, skeletal design, haphazardly organise the spaces within and around them. They express an experience of pointless space, apparently created to draw attention to space itself – space for the sake of space alone. Are these tent grotesques part of some elementary course in architecture or building design – the equivalent of musical *études*, abstract examples of spatial manipulation, studies hastily abandoned in the rain? Indeed they are reminiscent of the curving, space-creating, towers that sweepingly and vertiginously occupy the indweller's eye, as in the Pan Pacific hotel where on the fourth floor you emerge from the lift into a breezy Japanese tea garden. From the outside these towers are just towers, but inside the inhabitants are encircled by ingeniously created spaces that are structurally impossible to fill, spaces that inhabit the inhabitants themselves.

Lynn Pan, whose book *Sons of the Yellow Emperor* charts the history of overseas Chinese, finds a dispiriting 'emptiness' at the 'heart' of Singapore.[21] In a metaphorics of space that focuses on language Pan attributes this emptiness to Lee's 'social engineering', a combination of paternalism and paranoia through which a people are 'turned into children the better to follow the leader's instructions'.[22] The bilingual policy of education, in which each pupil knows both English as a first language and another second language – Mandarin, Malay or Tamil – is designed to ward off racial disharmony while simultaneously maintaining cultural specificity. It is a kind of egalitarianism (everybody is equal under the law) combined with racial/cultural differentiation (everyone is distinguished by their race). The effect is unsuccessful in Pan's view: 'Even the most casual visitor will discern a lack of "inwardness" with the language.'[23] The inside as such remains empty, leaving only the externality of inessential fragments: 'Children are growing up without speaking any language properly, their Mandarin adulterated by English, their English by Malay, unable to use their own dialects in anything other than very limited contexts, and failing to achieve first language proficiency in any tongue.'[24] The insistence on cultural difference, then, for Pan leads to adulteration of linguistic property – an emptying out of the insides of a language.

If these fragments of other languages come together in Singapore not quite adding up to a complete and proper single language, then this is the case more generally for the experience of space. Space in Singapore cannot be filled; it is always in its developmental, formative stage. There is a twist – a kind of temporal delay – built into the environment as such so that it stands out as being neither *under*developed nor *un*developed but *in* development. HDB estates are in a perpetual cycle of upgrading. Unlike those who live in the high-rise decay of an East London estate, for instance, the Singaporean knows that his or her block is close to being next in line for new colour awning, landscaped gardens, a covered walkway, even an extra room (so long as she continues to vote for the PAP). Gardens are treated to a perpetual rotation of placed flora in beds where often nothing can exactly grow in the thick clay, so nothing is planted as such. Placing is the rule. There are miles of immense housing projects, much of it under conspicuous construction, where the majority of Singapore's residents live. And, where the British colonial division of Singapore once emphasised profound cultural differences through strict spatial boundaries (Chinatown for Chinese, Serangoon for Indians) now the population, made up of 76.4 per cent Chinese with 14.9 per cent Malays and 6.4 per cent Indians, is represented by statistically equivalent segments in each HDB block, with 90 per cent ownership, ubiquitous air-con, widely available multimedia and innumerable other modern conveniences – a magical 'equalisation' of unequal quantities.

... And Its Discontents

So where there are complaints, or at least a sense of deficiency, these refer to the fields of 'culture' and 'politics' revealing both a diminution as well as a huge inflation of the importance of the former for the latter.[25] There are two myths involved here. The first suggests that a nation's culture (this is a concept that still retains much of the force and the sense that it had in colonial Singapore – that is, the great artistic achievements of a nation, particularly Shakespeare, particularly England) is intimately related to the value and identity of the nation itself. Great artists are in this sense a great credit to their nation, representing, reflecting and reinforcing the proud sense of national identity a nation needs in order to be strong. The second myth is that culture has nothing at all to do with politics. People who read, write and study literature do so either for leisure, entertainment, self-discovery or as a necessary part of training to be a school teacher. It is not simply that once again any sense of *opposition* is missing from both these conceptions. It is rather a question of what in literature remains necessarily and interminably enigmatic, of that aspect of the literary that approaches as near as possible to an absolute idiosyncrasy that is strictly impossible, and which is in all kinds of demonstrable ways a condition also of what is sometimes too easily just called the 'political'. The history of literature no doubt presents an extremely complex nexus of relations between nation, nationality, poet and poetry. But any attempt to identify culture definitively with national concerns will need either to confront or to bypass the enigma of *place*, that is, to confront or to bypass the fact that *place* is an enigma, once *place* is considered as beyond both political theory and the narratology of myth, as that which receives, holds, 'contains' the nation – the space of the nation's space – but which hides itself from all comers.

The stories of cultural impoverishment suggest that unprecedented economic growth overshadows, represses, stunts the growth of potential cultural riches, which indicates either the rather traditional Western notion of rich artistic national heritage or the nostalgic invocation of a past indigenous heritage impoverished by colonialism and subordinated under postcolonial economic interests. It is often as if culture is some thing, a commodity probably, that has to be added, grafted on to the calculating machine.

One, Two, Three

There are two hypotheses available, as follows.

1   The essence of Singapore lies behind, is hidden by, or at least marginalised by, its brash postmodern exterior. According to this hypothesis the trappings of Western high modern capitalism, a global culture that restlessly conquers all in its path, are the inevitable heritage of modernisation, urbanisation and its technology. Some indigenous, local, particular cultural identity retains an autonomy beneath or beyond, or at least in potential against the onslaught of global capitalism.

2   The lack of original culture just is Singapore culture. The second hypothesis states that Singapore is *essentially* empty of all but the fragments of *other* cultures. Streets, coffee houses, shopping malls, Indianicity, Chinicity, Americana, Germanessence, Britainiana: the mixed cultural iconicity of anything that stylistically Singapore is not comes together to fill insufficiently a space that is being incessantly produced.

Out of these two, either of which could be worked into a demonstrable argument, a third less obvious hypothesis emerges, which suggests that we must manage to think the first two, mutually exclusive as they are, both at once. If there is an essential Singaporean identity apart and distinct from any other (this is the point), it is that there is manifestly no essential Singapore identity apart and distinct from any other. But this is not to be found expressed, at least not in any direct way, in the writings, the fiction and poetry, the plays or the cinema, the music and dance of Singaporeans. Singapore is rather its own performance. No 'text' from Singapore should be regarded as simply representing Singapore's urban space, for urban space itself is Singapore's chief mode of representation. My approach in this article is to read Singapore's text not as a representation of Singapore itself – the text of Singapore – but rather it is to read the text that Singapore is. Singapore is already a response, an interpretation and reconstruction of a set of conditions that are readable and can thus be reconstituted, though never exhaustively; rather the reconstitution is always another step in the interminable recreation. For this reason Singapore especially shows that the distinction between material and text is not pertinent. The most totalitarian version of this distinction is found in the analytic philosophies of Frege and Russell, for whom a distinction between language and actuality was utterly essential.[26] This extended to that between numbers and things as well as geometry and space. On these grounds they were able repeatedly to exclude all forms of literary, poetic and fictional language from any discourse on actuality whatsoever. However, the famous distinction between the 'sense' and the 'reference' of a sign (later repeated in different terms by de Saussure, who in a similar theoretical gesture excludes the referent from any function at all in language) breaks down when one acknowledges that the actual referent itself has a generalisable sense and a number of possible references too. On this point I have taken seriously the possibility of reading a poetic function of the city itself, in a city which persistently domesticates or excludes the poetic as marginal.

Two senses, building space by rearrangement and constructing the inside by building in parts of the outside, together capture something of the experience of space in Singapore. To begin with, there is hardly any. The implications can hardly be overestimated. If a country has only enough space to house its capital city then that country can only be its capital city. The city is the state, the town is the country, the capital is what it is the capital of. Second, as an inevitable consequence of its size, a permanent replaceable expatriate population 'bought in' (to echo Lee Kuan Yew) as an always temporary supplementary workforce is an unavoidable resource for maintaining international status.[27] For private enterprise, education and cultural development temporary assistance from outside is a permanent necessity. Lee's greatest achievement is to have worked creatively with certain powerful constraints like these. But they emerge from wide-ranging historical undercurrents that concern all thinking about urbanism generally.

Urbanism

Urbanism emerges both as a network that can be considered as a series of points related synchronically (the network of cities considered independently of the states to which they each belong) and as a development that can be considered diachronically (in terms of the irreversible historical processes that constitute, at any given moment, the conditions and possibilities of any urbanism whatsoever). Fundamental distinctions can thus be made between preindustrial urbanism and industrial or postindustrial urbanism. Further distinctions concern the apparent belatedness of urban development in some parts of the world – Asia, South America, Eastern Europe – though the term 'belatedness' is misleading. The 'pattern' of urbanisation is always subverted by its historical and economic conditions so one could not talk of urbanisation in India, say, as simply repeating at a later stage the pattern of urbanisation that occurred in nineteenth- and twentieth-century Europe or the USA.

When this is considered the city of Singapore is a peculiar case. In 1819, when Britain took over the island, the transition between urbanism in its preindustrial form and industrial urbanism proper seems to have been an almost entirely British phenomenon. It is inextricably related to British imperial expansion. A heavily armed supremely powerful force, the British prevailed through trade wherever possible, reserving armed force for whatever local 'crisis' inevitably emerged.[28] The British, once they had literally rented Singapore from the Temenggong in charge of the few Malay Orang Lauts then resident on the island, openly encouraged traders to come in from all parts of the region. In addition to the Malays, Javanese and Bugis from the immediate surroundings, there came Eurasians, Arabs and European traders. The British brought in labourers as well as troops from India. But the majority of newcomers were Chinese coolies, artisans and traders from the Straits settlements already in the region, from Malacca or from mainland China itself, either escaping war and hunger or looking for the opportunity to make big money, which a few did, and most managed at worst a meagre living, working hard for slender rewards from the successful traders. Within five years there were 3,000 Chinese in Singapore and from then their numbers far surpassed even the Malays. The dominance of the Chinese population was from the beginning a controversial factor for Singapore and remains so today.

So, from the beginning really, a city – instituted at just the moment when city life is set to be the globally dominant mode – Singapore has always been an urban phenomenon. It has no history outside or beyond urbanism, nothing in its history that counters or contests urbanism. This at first sight seems fairly remarkable, for whatever distinctions one can make between cities and between types of city, whether you take the Greek *polis* or the modern new town, the city usually emerges in terms of a distinction from what it is not.

City/State?

If the first and most obvious distinction is between rural and urban populations, a second distinction, which is rather less obvious but correspondingly more interesting here, is the one between city and state.

We have learned, for instance, to distinguish between the city itself and the palatial or imperial systems of the Orient, which as Etienne Balazs has shown were antipathetic to civic modes of political organisation.[29] The distinction is not just a question of evolution but rather it indicates a tension between modes of organisation – principles of political strategy that are at odds but which underlie the process that I referred to earlier as the empirial. The developments of both types of centralised power are intricately related. On the one hand, in the case of despotic Oriental empires, there were massive concentrations of power in the hands of king and priest, what Balazs calls the Mandarinate or 'scholar-officials', who were all powerful, owned most of the land and monopolised education. For centuries in China the merchant/artisan class remained subservient to the Mandarinate because there was never any other social group powerful enough to compete with them. On the other hand, we find in cities an important contrast to the despotism of the Asian empires. The most celebrated example is the Greek *polis*, a small, self-governing community of citizens for whom the *polis* and its *nomos* constituted a moral order symbolised in magisterial buildings designed for public assemblies.[30] The emphasis on public government and private life feeds into the enlightenment and postenlightenment development of democratic modes of organisation and the pretence to egalitarianism that characterises Western modernity. It is a powerful paradox that the overwhelming dominance of urbanism in the twentieth century is a function not of the civic organisations but rather of state bureaucracies and their interests in controlling and expanding the mechanisms of multinational exchange. However, there is a reciprocal process where the great states are gradually suburbanised while individual cities become the nodes of a global, weblike megalopolis.[31]

So as a function of the imperial expansion of Britain, Singapore's urbanism was for a long time subordinated to imperial trade and military interests. Not merely Raffles' dream of an Eastern emporium established on 'perfect freedom of trade', Singapore was fundamentally an armed forces barracks, Britain's military bastion in the East. Not until 1945, when Britain surrendered Singapore to the Japanese, would this condition change. But it is a key to understanding the nature of Singapore's urbanism. If urbanism develops in the West because the state both encourages and controls it as the mode of organisation that most efficiently increases wealth through trade, then in the East it fails to develop because the state organises itself against urbanism generally. Balazs has shown that the Chinese town, for instance,

> could not become the centre of attraction because its life remained dominated, as indeed the entire social organism was dominated, by the omnipresent and omnipotent state – that is, the uncontested, absolute and despotic power of a class of scholar-officials who could not tolerate

any form of private enterprise, or who seized any private undertaking that had by chance succeeded in flourishing, in order to stifle it.[32]

It is precisely this unchanging bureaucratic machinery that the Chinese in Singapore have escaped. Yet the historicity of a fundamentally bureaucratic society is also what maintains the efficient running of present-day Singapore, as it did under the British.[33] The ghosts of these two dead empires – and of the forbidden city especially – are everywhere in the city where everything that falls outside legal calculation is forbidden. There are two separate aporias working together in contemporary Singapore. One involves the great Western closure through which the finite empirical world is bounded in order to distinguish it from a transcendental beyond, resulting in a dialectic between subject and object. Technology is thus regarded as a functioning tool for a non-technological subject, 'man', so the subject becomes either increasingly technologised or occult. The other involves the remarkable historical permanence of the Asian imperial bureaucracies, on the one hand, and the economic need to adapt to global changes on the other.

Balazs has remarked that the difference between East and West is the difference between yang and yin. But the two dialectics hardly work together in such a harmonious way. Rather, space in Singapore is the equivalent to that found in the impossible geometric form of the Klein Bottle (two Moebius Strips sewn together), which is possible to illustrate in sections but cannot be embedded in three dimensions. The inside of the Klein Bottle is at the same time its outside. In Singapore, the inside of 'the Asian mind' is the outside of the Western object. The state of Singapore itself is a suburb of the network of cities – each a node or point of a global megalopolis and, like the faded European empires, Singapore too rules only locally, its future built in but determined by its outside.

Notes

1   Edwin Thumboo, 'Ulysses by Merlion', *A Third Map: New and Selected Poems* (Singapore: Unipress, 1993).

2   Ausafur Rahman, 'Soils' in Chia Lin Sien, Ausafur Rahman and Dorothy Tay (eds) *The Biophysical Environment of Singapore* (Singapore: Singapore University Press, 1991) p. 89.

3   Han Fook Kwang, Warren Fernandez and Sumiko Tan (eds), *Lee Kuan Yew: The Man and His Ideas* (Singapore: Times, 1998) p. 12. This book contains many transcripts of Lee Kuan Yew's speeches as well as historical and biographical information about the man. It has been one of the biggest selling titles of 1998 in Singapore.

4   K. F. Olszewski and Chia Lin Sien, 'Development, physical planning and environment' in Sien *et al.*, *The Biophysical Environment of Singapore*, p. 199.

5   Ibid., p. 200.

6   The first citation is from Bertrand Russell, 'Logical positivism' in *Logic and Knowledge* (London: Unwin Hyman, 1956) p. 369. Russell's point stands so long as the empirical

can be considered as unproblematically 'actual', which, of course, it cannot. The second is Goh Kasan, 'Sarimboon' in H_2O: Proselyrics (Singapore: Landmark, 1996) p. 51, who is also nostalgic for an evanescent 'actual'.

7   Martin Amis, Money (Harmondsworth: Penguin, 1988).

8   Elaine Higgleton and Vincent Ooi Beng Yeow (eds), Times-Chambers Essential English Dictionary (Singapore: Times-Chambers, 1997).

9   Goh Kasan, 'Sarimboon', p. 48. So much writing in Singapore is self-consciously – almost out of a sense of duty or obligation – about or on Singapore, as if the Singapore writer was ipso facto a Singapore writer, as if aspiring writers are thus aspiring laureates. Goh's dissatisfaction is one that hints at a sense of national commitment and responsibility, much stronger than anything produced by his mild experimentation with form. Goh's point is actually close to the one Russell makes regarding representation. But poetry has no better chance here than logic in approaching the actual.

10   See Sanjay Krishnan's article, 'Singapore: two stories at the cost of one city' in Sanjay Krishnan and Sharaad Kuttan (eds), Commentary: The City 10 (December 1992), where he argues that because Singapore's identity is constructed from two contradictory stories – one concerning political stability and economic growth, the other dealing with insecurity and the fear of total loss – the resulting sense of isolation is potentially damaging. Krishnan's melancholic symptomatology suggests not so much an adolescence, but rather the hebephrenic implosion of a paranoid-schizoid state in which idealisation of the inside and demonisation of the outside are powerful defence mechanisms.

11   See Brenda Yeoh's admirable study Contesting Space: Power Relations and the Urban Built Environment in Colonial Singapore (Kuala Lumpur: Oxford University Press, 1996) for a detailed account of the tensions and negotiations that characterised the organisation and administration of urban space in Singapore during the colonial period.

12   Kwang et al., Lee Kuan Yew, p. 111.

13   Shirley Chew, 'There's another country I've heard of' in Krishnan and Kuttan (eds), Commentary, p. 116.

14   Ibid., p. 116.

15   See Geoffrey Hawthorn, The Future of Asia and the Pacific (London: Phoenix, 1998) in which he points out that where it is said that East Asians 'are disposed to favour harmony and order, and expect their rulers to secure it'. This 'reconstruction of "Asianness" is the creation of self-serving politicians and their publicists ... deployed in dislike of domestic dissent against the insistence of a divided and decadent West on the importance of liberalism and "human rights"' pp. 4–5.

16   Kwang et al., Lee Kuan Yew, p. 310–11.

17   The most recent example of land reclamation and development is at Punggol, on the northeast coast of Singapore. Land has been built to create a promontory that promises 'a town with three rivers, a place to call home, high quality HDB flats and more private housing to provide better mix' (http://www.ura.gov.sg/dgp_reports/punggl21/main.html). The housing will, it is promised, be built around a new MRT link, to provide convenient access to the town centre.

18   Experience is 'artifactual' because the actual is always produced. I borrow the term from Jacques Derrida, who writes: 'actuality is indeed made: it is important to know what it is made of, but it is even more necessary to recognise that it is made. It is not given, but actively produced; it is sorted, invested and performatively interpreted by a range of hierarchising and selective procedures – factitious or artificial procedures which are always subservient to various powers and interests of which their "subjects" and agents (producers and consumers of actuality, always interpreters, and in some cases "philosophers" too), are never sufficiently aware. The "reality" of "actuality" – however individual, irreducible, stubborn, painful or tragic it may be – only reaches

us through fictional devices', *Radical Philosophy* 68 (1994) pp. 28–41. The city itself is an ensemble of such devices.

19   See Ho Chee Lick's 'Representations of school in Singapore teenage magazines', *Asian Journal of Communication* 8: 1, (1998) pp. 87–110 for a disturbing study of the way Singapore teenage magazines make a sharp distinction between the gleeful pleasure of playtime, holiday and leisure and the dull drudgery of school and work, associating the latter with duty and obligation to parents and teachers. If there are constructions of Singapore identity as adolescence *per se* then it is this specific structure of adolescence that is the pertinent one.

20   Kwang *et al.*, *Lee Kuan Yew*, p. 371.

21   Lynn Pan, *Sons of the Yellow Emperor: The Story of the Overseas Chinese* (London: Secker and Warburg, 1990) p. 263.

22   Ibid., p. 258.

23   Ibid., p. 262.

24   Ibid., p. 262. Note the interesting hierarchy, Mandarin – English – Malay.

25   There are many categories of malcontent regarding Singapore. Some are external, others internal. William Gibson is particularly dismissive in his electronically published article, 'Disneyland with the death penalty', *Wired* (1996) http://www.wired.com/wired/1.4/features/gibson.html. He bemoans the lack in Singapore of dirt, pollution, litter, sex and what he calls 'bad' girls. He hates the squeaky cleanness of the city while disapproving of the harshness of the Singapore penalty system. He must have been an odd sight in Changi Airport, snapping pictures of a lonesome piece of litter. Gibson, despite his indignation, does make some succinct and illuminating observations, though in his haste to get away has failed really to think them through. The indignant tone is also manifest in Stan Sesser's 'Singapore: the prisoner in the theme park', from his study of Southeast Asia, *The Lands of Charm and Cruelty: Travels in Southeast Asia* (New York: Vintage, 1994). Sesser finds very little to charm him in Singapore but makes a brave bid to find evidence of cruelty. It seems important for this ambassador of democracy and human rights to find them lacking here and he triumphs faintly in the end. The most devastating testament to cultural impoverishment is in some consternated responses to urban Singapore made by its poets. This is seldom expressed directly and is devastating partly because it is hardly recognised, nor even recognisable as such (attesting to the failure of poetry here to find an effective form of address – an affected addressee even) and partly because it is readable as such in the poetry for anyone who cares. Edwin Thumboo's 'Ulysses by Merlion' is often discussed. On the surface it expresses the shock of recognition by a Singapore national when faced with his government's attempt to produce a fully formed mythology complete with huge statue – the Merlion – a kind of lion with a fish tail – very tacky. The tone, once again, is barely disguised indignation (and a deliberate identification with an ancient mythic figure of the western classical tradition). For various readings, see Ban Kah Choon, 'Ulysses by Merlion/Oedipus at the waterfront', in Lee Tzn Pheng and Leong Liew Geok (eds), *ACLALS Bulletin*, 7th Series No. 2: *Commonwealth Poetry* (Singapore: Association for Commonwealth Literature and Language Studies, 1997) pp. 39–50; Ee Tiang Hong, *Responsibility and Commitment: The Poetry of Edwin Thumboo* (Singapore: Singapore University Press, 1997); Rajeev Patke, 'Singapore and the Two Ulysses' (forthcoming); Kirpal Singh, 'Towards a Singapore Classic: Edwin Thumboo's Ulysses by Merlion', *The Literary Criterion* 15:2 (1998) pp. 77–86. The most extraordinary of readings is the government's own – finding in it support for their mythologising project, it is set in stone next to the Merlion itself.

26   Gottlob Frege, 'On sense and reference' in Peter Geach and Max Black (eds), *Translations from the Philosophical Writings of Gottlob Frege* (Oxford: Blackwell, 1952) pp. 56–78. Bertrand Russell, 'Descriptions' in *Introduction to Mathematical Philosophy* (London: Allen and Unwin, 1919).

27 Even when, in the 1970s, the government wanted to promote neo-Confucian values against the liberal tendencies of the West they bought in Western Confucian scholars to educate the locals. See Hawthorn, *The Future of Asia and the Pacific*.

28 The presence of the British in Southeast Asia made for a significant contrast with the Dutch, who were well known for transporting captive labour from the Chinese mainland to meet the needs of their colonial projects. See Pan, *Sons of the Yellow Emperor*, p. 26–7.

29 Etienne Balazs, *Chinese Civilization and Bureaucracy: Variations on a Theme* (London: Yale University Press, 1964). The extraordinary scholarship of Etienne Balazs, both passionate and meticulous, stands today as an indispensable resource if read carefully for an understanding of Eastern and Western historicity.

30 See H. D. F. Kitto, 'The polis' in *The Greeks* (Harmondsworth: Penguin, 1991) for the classic account of this mode of organisation. And see my reading of Aristotle's *Politics*, 'Aristotle's abduction: the institution of frontiers', *Oxford Literary Review* 14 (1992) pp. 171–95 for an account of the possibilities of constitutional city government and the weaknesses of democratic idealism.

31 Gilles Deleuze and Felix Guattari make this point in their elaboration of the city/state dichotomy in 'City/state', trans. Brian Massumi, *Zone* 1/2, pp. 195–9: 'if it is the modern state that gives capitalism its models of realisation, what is thus realised is an independent, worldwide axiomatic that is like a single City, megalopolis or "megamachine" of which the states are parts or neighbourhoods.'

32 Balazs, *Chinese Civilization and Bureaucracy*, p. 78.

33 See Brenda Yeoh, 'Introduction', *Contesting Space*.

Contributors

Maria Balshaw is Research Fellow in American Literature at the University of Birmingham. She works as part of the Arts and Humanities Research Board project, *Literary and Visual Representations of Three American Cities*, based at the Universities of Birmingham and Nottingham. She has published a number of articles on African American urban literature and culture and is publishing a monograph with Pluto Press entitled *City of Refuge: Harlem and the Urban Aesthetic in Twentieth Century African American Literature*.

Gargi Bhattacharyya works at the Department of Cultural Studies and Sociology, University of Birmingham and is a co-director of the Birmingham Research Centre for Cultural Studies and Sociology. Her research is in the areas of ëraceí, ethnicity and sexuality. Recent publications include *Tales of Dark-Skinned Women* (UCL Press, 1998). She is working on a book with John Gabriel and Stephen Small which addresses new debates in racialisation and globality.

Peter Brooker is Professor of Modern Literature and Culture and Research Leader for English at University College Northampton. He has written extensively on aspects of modernism, postmodernism and contemporary theory. He is the editor of *Modernism/Postmodernism* (Longman, 1992) and author most recently of *New York Fictions: Modernity, Postmodernism, the New Modern* (Longman, 1996) and *Cultural Theory: A Glossary* (Edward Arnold, 1999). A volume of essays, *Modernity and Metropolis*, is forthcoming.

Al Deakin teaches English and cultural studies at the University of Westminster and is also a director of Semiotic Solutions, a company specialising in the commercial application of cultural theory.

Richard Ings is a freelance researcher and writer currently completing a PhD thesis on Race, Photography and the American City at the University of Nottingham. He has had articles and reviews published in *Over Here*, *History of Photography* and *Textual Practice*, and presented papers on aspects of American photography at a number of academic conferences.

Liam Kennedy is Senior Lecturer in American Studies at the University of Birmingham and the co-director of the Arts and Humanities Research Board project, *Literary and Visual Representations of Three American Cities*. He has published widely in the fields of American literary and cultural studies. He is the author of *Susan Sontag: Mind as Passion* (Manchester University Press, 1995) and *Race and Urban Space in American Culture* (Edinburgh University Press, 2000).

Myrto Konstantarakos is Senior Lecturer in French and Italian and Director of the European Research Centre at Middlesex University, London. Her publications include articles on Italian, French and Argentinian cinema. She is editor of *Spaces in European Cinema* (Intellect, 1999) and author of *On the Edge of Darkness: Suburbs in Film* (Intellect, 2000).

John Phillips is Senior Lecturer in English at the National University of Singapore. With research interests in critical theory and continental philosophy, he has published books and articles on these subjects including *Reading Melanie Klein* (Routledge, 1998), co-edited with Lyndsey Stonebridge, and *A Guide to Critical Theory* (Zed, 1999).

Pascal Pinck earned his MA in Visual Studies at the University of California, Irvine. He currently works as a television news producer in Phoenix, Arizona.

Stephen Shapiro is a lecturer at the University of Warwick in the Department of English and Comparative Literary Studies. Currently working on a monograph about the literature of the early American Republic and co-editing a collection of essays on Charles Brockden Brown, he has published articles on topics ranging from mass African suicide, Gramsci, drag, to the introduction of condoms in eighteenth-century America.

Douglas Tallack is Professor of American Studies at the University of Nottingham and Director of the Arts and Humanities Research Board project, *Literary and Visual Representations of Three American Cities*. His publications include *Critical Theory: A Reader* (Harvester, 1995), *The Nineteenth-Century American Short Story* (Routledge, 1993), *Twentieth-Century America* (1991), and *Literary Theory at Work* (Batsford, 1987), together with many articles on American intellectual and cultural history and critical theory. He is currently writing a book entitled *City Sights: Visuality, Space and Modernity in New York, 1880s–1920s*.

Index